Contemporary Anishinaabe Art

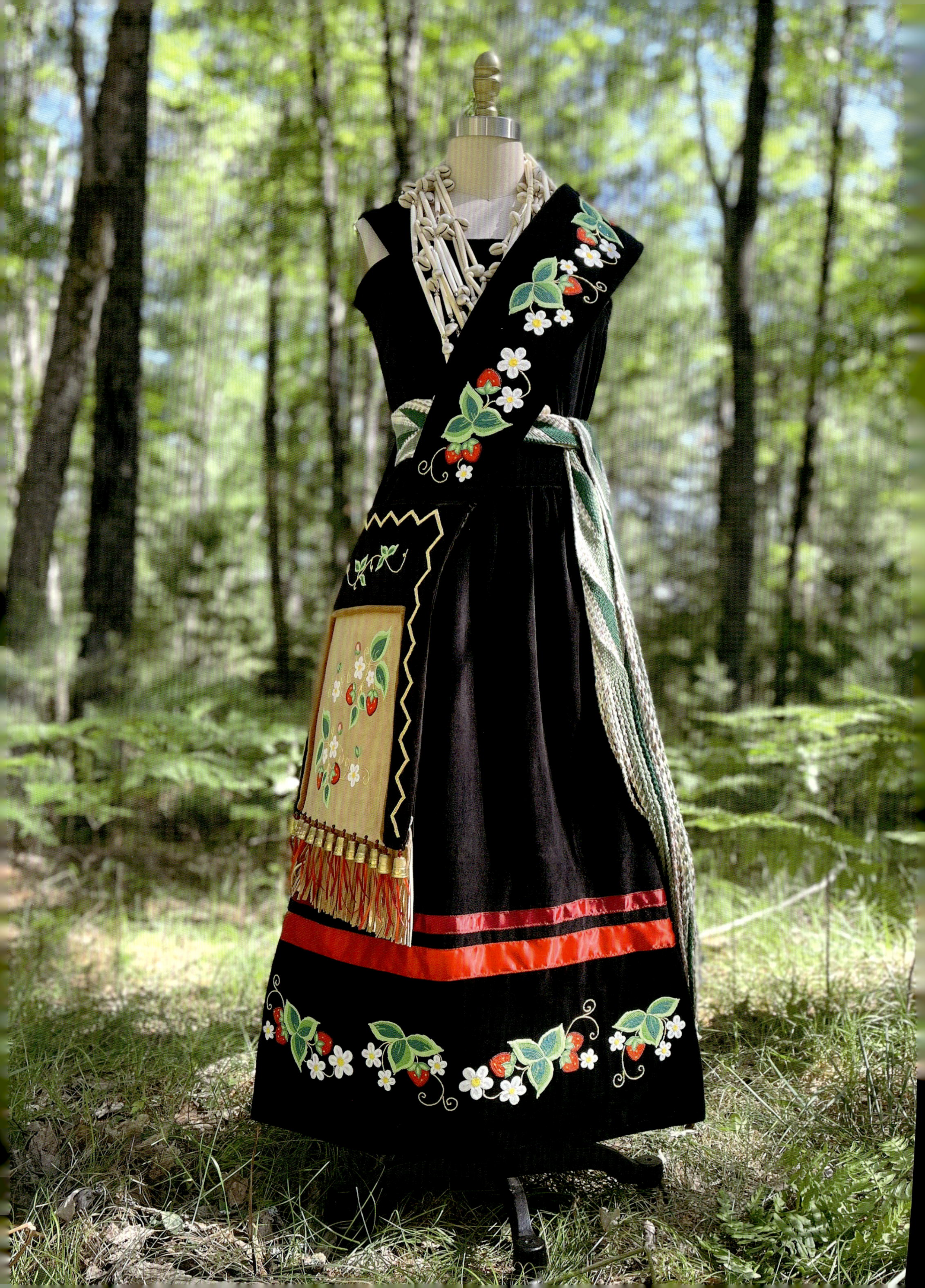

Contemporary Anishinaabe Art: A Continuation

Edited by Denene De Quintal, PhD

Essays by
Matthew L. M. Fletcher, JD
Christopher T. Green, PhD
Kendra Greendeer, PhD
Shawnya Harris, PhD

DETROIT INSTITUTE OF ARTS

Distributed by Yale University Press, New Haven and London

Contents

Sponsors

Contemporary Anishinaabe Art: A Continuation is organized by the Detroit Institute of Arts.

Lead support is generously provided by the Ford Foundation.

Major support is provided by Teiger Foundation, Jennifer Adderley, and the Henry Luce Foundation.

Additional support is provided by the DTE Foundation, Richard Sonenklar and Gregory Haynes, Andra Rush and the Rush Group of Companies, Carlene and Rob Van Voorhies, and Peggy and Dave Meador.

Ford Foundation   **Teiger** **Foundation**   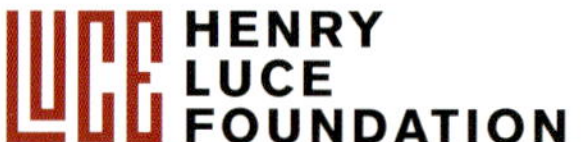

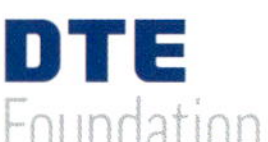   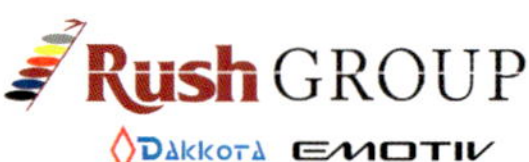

Director's Foreword

The exhibition *Contemporary Anishinaabe Art: A Continuation* is the first major showcase of Native American art at the Detroit Institute of Arts (DIA) in over thirty years, reflecting the museum's commitment to the Native American community and its enduring art. By featuring artists from the Great Lakes region, the DIA aims to raise awareness of the rich cultures and histories of the Anishinaabe people.

The exhibition highlights the artistic achievements of contemporary Anishinaabe artists, showcasing their works that express creativity from the past, present, and future. *Contemporary Anishinaabe Art: A Continuation* features sixty-two artists from across the Great Lakes region, with works including baskets, beadwork, birchbark, clothing, film, graphic art, jewelry, painting, photography, pottery, sculpture, and woodwork. The DIA will select pieces from established and emerging artists to enrich its collection. This exhibition allows the institution to engage with artists and share the stories of the Anishinaabe people for years to come.

In 2019, the DIA hired a curator of Native American art, Denene De Quintal, PhD, after the position had been vacant for over a decade. Her focus has been on building relationships with Native American tribes, compliance with the Native American Graves Protection and Repatriation Act, and enhancing the cultural continuity of Native American art by acquiring contemporary pieces that significantly strengthen both the existing collection and the relevance of the stories that we tell. Furthermore, Dr. De Quintal has helped the DIA ensure that the art installation is respectful of the Native American community and aligns with current best museum practices. We commend Dr. De Quintal for the work she has done and continues to do for the organization and are grateful for it.

For *Contemporary Anishinaabe Art: A Continuation,* Dr. De Quintal collaborated with an Anishinaabe advisory council of Anishinaabe artists, including Kelly Church, Jason Quigno, Monica Rickert-Bolter, Jonathan Thunder, and Jodi Webster, and we at the DIA are grateful for their insights and assistance. We extend our heartfelt gratitude to all of the artists and the private and institutional lenders who generously contributed artworks to the exhibition. To the entire DIA team, thank you for your dedication in helping make this exhibition a success.

Salvador Salort-Pons, PhD
Mary Anne and Eugene A. Gargaro, Jr. Director, President, and CEO

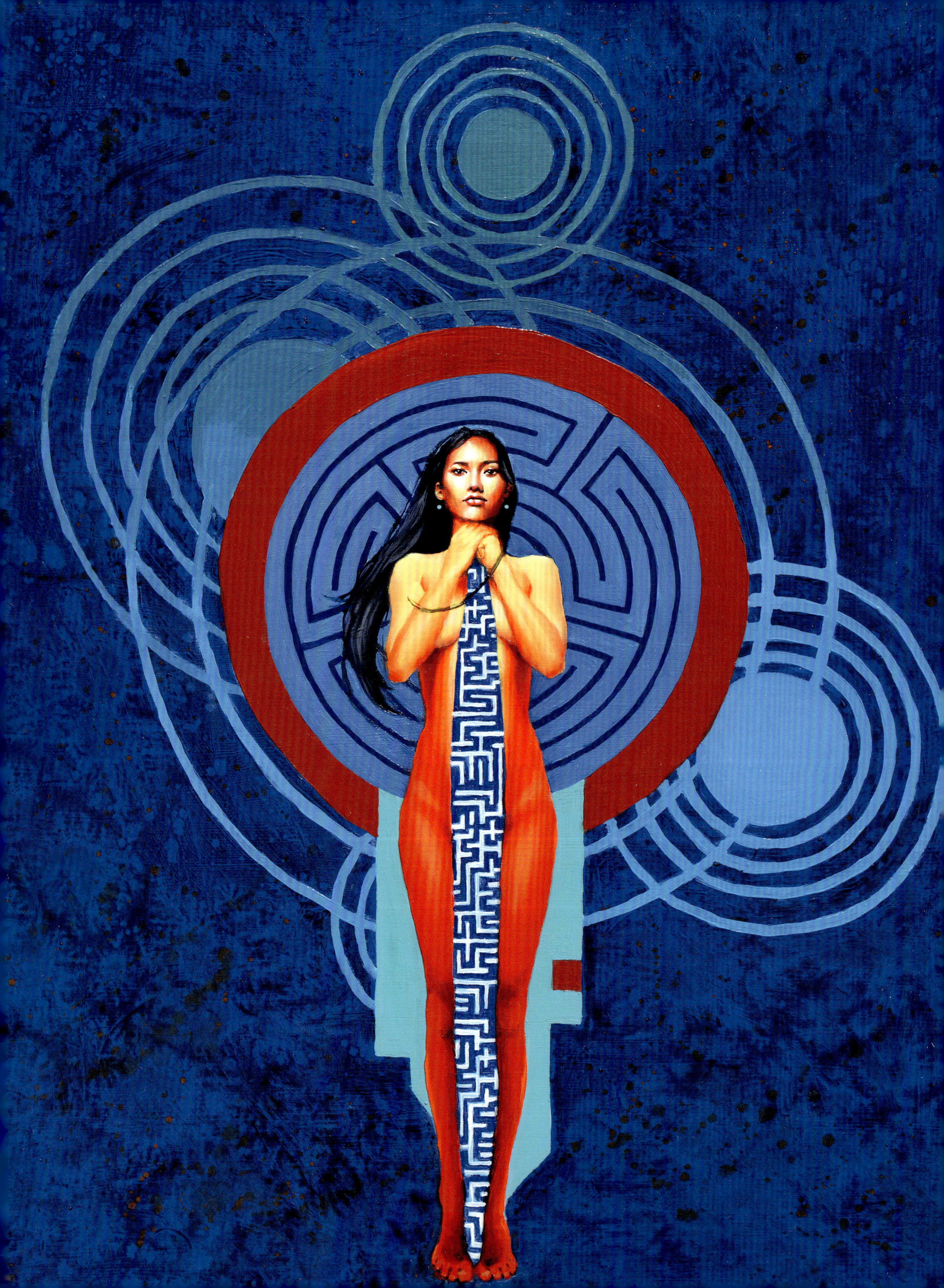

The Moment That We Are In[1]

Denene De Quintal, PhD

As the first curator of Native American art at the Detroit Institute of Arts (DIA) in over a decade, I realized in my tenure's nascency that the first exhibition of such art in over thirty years should focus on the Anishinaabeg.[2] The DIA is world-renowned for its Chandler-Pohrt Collection,[3] part of which contains art from the Eastern Woodlands, Great Lakes area. In addition, the DIA is located in Michigan, the only state whose twelve federally recognized tribes are all Anishinaabe nations, which are the Chippewa, the Odawa/Ottawa, and the Potawatomi. It was thus both important and logical that the first Native American art exhibition at the DIA in many years would feature artworks from the Great Lakes. The original concept of the exhibition was to feature

> Great Lakes Anishinaabe artists (approximately 40) and their selected peers from other Native American nations, this exhibition will focus on the depth, diversity, and majesty of contemporary Native American art created specifically in this region and throughout the continent of North America. —Curatorial Concept Development 2024

The DIA prioritized this exhibition on its calendar to demonstrate how important it was to it as an institution and to its Native American art collection. So, the museum was elated when Michigan Anishinaabe artists approached me and requested that the DIA have an exhibition dedicated to

Opposite: Sarah Wilkinson (Sault Ste. Marie Tribe of Chippewa; b. 1984), *Following the Path Within,* 2024 (detail)

Anishinaabe art as well. This essay discusses the exhibition's development, some of the concerns that arose in its evolution, and selected artworks and artists in *Contemporary Anishinaabe Art: A Continuation.*

Origin Story

As I write this essay, *Contemporary Anishinaabe Art: A Continuation* will feature over sixty mostly US-based artists and approximately one hundred artworks. Originally, the exhibition was to feature forty artworks from Anishinaabe artists and their selected contemporaries from throughout the United States and Canada. However, to address the exhibition's Anishinaabe advisory committee's[4] concerns that previous exhibitions of Anishinaabe art had been dominated by Canada-based artists, there was a shift to feature solely US-based artists. Apart from Norval Morrisseau[5] and perhaps Mary Edmonia Lewis by tribal affiliation, all of the artists' tribes are US-based.

The DIA extended invitations to artists based on recommendations from the Anishinaabe advisory committee and artists I had encountered at regional exhibitions. Each artist was asked to submit two works from which the advisors and I were to select the pieces for the exhibition. However, unbeknownst to the DIA, the call was forwarded and posted on social media, which greatly increased the number of submissions. Due to the number of artworks submitted as well as to their caliber, the process of choosing the works for the show was extensive and led to a large checklist. One of the factors used to determine inclusion in the exhibition was how the artwork fit into the spectrum of contemporary Anishinaabe art.

Contemporary and Historic/Traditional Art

One of the most crucial discussions between the Anishinaabe advisors, the DIA interpretive planner, Megan DiRienzo,[6] and me was how to determine what "contemporary Anishinaabe art" meant for this specific exhibition. As Dyani White Hawk and Joe Horse Capture note: "There is a challenging dichotomy when discussing contemporary Native American art. One wonders if 'contemporary' is a reference to style or when the artwork was created."[7] For *Contemporary Anishinaabe Art: A Continuation,* "contemporary" refers to both a style[8] and the date of creation.[9] The advisors wanted to ensure that what the exhibition's audience viewed were innovative forms and images that would hopefully challenge perceptions and conceptions of Native American art. This sentiment led to thoughtful questions and discussions about contemporary Native American art and how the exhibition would impact Anishinaabe artists today.[10]

A Statement about Contemporary Anishinaabe/Native American Art

The advisors and I recognized that the selection of works displayed in the exhibition would make an important statement not only about contemporary Anishinaabe art but also about contemporary Native American art more generally. There would further be an impact on the livelihoods of both the artists included and those excluded from the exhibition. We thus needed to be sagacious in our decision-making. Some of the artworks were not included in the show based on their need for further development and/or if they reflected more historical forms and

mediums.[11] The decisions made were based on the advisors' concern that the audience might wonder why most of the other artworks would not reflect traditional art forms. This concern was important because many Native American artists are plagued by questions about why their art does not "look Native" or why it does not utilize traditional materials. White Hawk and Horse Capture note, "The prevalent expectations that Native arts should look like or reflect preconceived notions of historic Indian art often leave Native artists continuously struggling for greater recognition of the validity of their contemporary expressions of whatever forms they may take."[12] To discourage such questions of authenticity, the advisors and I decided to limit the works in the exhibition that primarily reflected traditional art forms. The works that were included had to clearly show a contemporary approach.

Enacting the Border

Another element used to determine inclusion was the US border.[13] Previously, shows of contemporary Anishinaabe art, such as the Smithsonian's *Before and after the Horizon: Anishinaabe Artists of the Great Lakes* (2013–14), have featured primarily Canada-based artists. The advisors' desire was to feature as many stellar artworks and art forms from as many talented artists as possible, but from within the United States. However, even with this geographical focus, there were still artists that were missed in the call for participation. Their exclusion does not reflect on them or their work. These artists have been and will be featured in other exhibitions, and some will also be featured in future shows at the DIA—presentations of Anishinaabe artworks will continue, following the theme of "A Continuation."

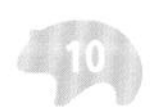

Contemporary Anishinaabe Art: A Continuation

What's in a Name?

The title of the exhibition developed after multiple conversations with various museum departments as well as critical conversations with the exhibition advisors. The original title of the show was *Anishinaabe: The Living Art of the Original People* and was my suggestion, which I based on one of the translations of "Anishinaabe," meaning "the original people." Many Native American people believe that art and cultural items are living entities, so I wanted to highlight this. The advisors approved, but some museum stakeholders considered it too long and potentially confusing.[14] Some colleagues also expressed concerns that not everyone would know what "Anishinaabe" means; the concept of "living art" was also considered something that might confuse audiences. There was an internal brainstorming session, from which three titles were offered to the Anishinaabe advisory committee. One that resonated was *Living Art: Contemporary Anishinaabe Expressions.* One of the advisors, however, informed me that "the Gichigamiin Indigenous Nations Museum, formerly the Mitchell Museum, has an all-Anishinaabe exhibit opening early 2025 entitled: *Living Stories: Contemporary Woodland Native American Art.*"

With that in mind, the advisors, interpreter, and I conceptualized *Continuation: Contemporary Anishinaabe Art.*[15] This was based on the suggestion of advisor Jodi Webster, who shared: "I came up with the title . . . that states our ongoing efforts as artists to preserve who we are, what we represent and how we chose to interpret our culture. . . . I feel when we just state 'contemporary art' it feels like a category and not an action. I feel as Annishinaabe artists we are making our art today which is embedded [in] or informed by the past yet has a true effort behind it to not be seen as historic or forgotten."[16]

The interpretive planner and I were then asked to meet with museum stakeholders again about the title. After a lengthy discussion where more titles were suggested, the title *Contemporary Anishinaabe Art* was proposed. I expressed concern that the title did not distinguish it from other exhibitions of contemporary Anishinaabe art. The final title, *Contemporary Anishinaabe Art: A Continuation,* distinguishes this exhibition from both future and past shows, and allows for the sentiment expressed by the Anishinaabe advisory board members, while acquiescing to the museum stakeholders' desire for an appealing title.

Audience Engagement and Collaboration

I would like to return to one of the concerns that was broached by the multiple teams while developing the exhibition title: the fact that many visitors would not know what "Anishinaabe" means without any explanation of the term.[17] This was never a major concern for the interpretative planner and me, primarily because all exhibitions are opportunities to learn. We hoped that people would learn through public outreach about the themes of the exhibition, and they would learn more about the Anishinaabe(g) through the exhibition labels and catalogue, and hopefully through the artists and artworks. The lack of knowledge about what the word "Anishinaabe" means reinforces the need for an exhibition of this kind. It also provides an opportunity to discuss the importance of the DIA's collaboration with its Anishinaabe advisors and how collaboration led to something unique in the museum's exhibition history.

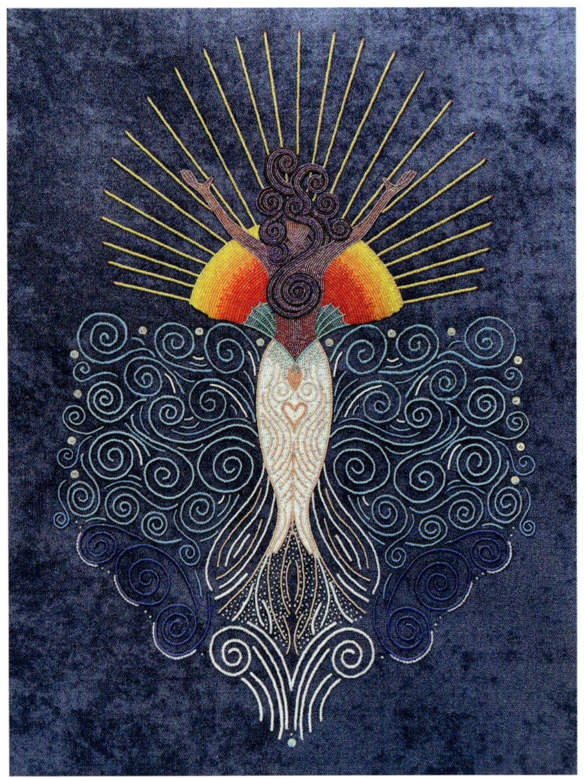

the region the museum is situated in. The original council included a member from the Bay Mills Indian Community, the Diné, the Little Traverse Bay Bands of Odawa Indians, the Pokagon Potawatomi, the Tlingit, and we subsequently added a member of the Pueblo of Acoma/Pueblo of Laguna. The council was created not only to give advice on the stewardship of the Native American art collection but also to be advisors to the institution. It meets quarterly and is available to each DIA department and division to answer questions and address concerns about projects such as this exhibition, but also other non–Native American projects.

Similarly, for *Contemporary Anishinaabe Art: A Continuation,* the museum assembled the Anishinaabe advisory committee mentioned previously. Besides suggesting artists for the exhibition, they have helped select the works in the show, generate the themes for the exhibition, give feedback on the exhibition design, and suggest programming to support the exhibition. One of the learning opportunities to arise in relation to the development of the exhibition was the creation of the Anishinaabe advisory committee: some stakeholders did not understand why there was a need for an advisory committee when the museum had the NAAC. The simple explanation was that the NAAC is a diverse council that can advise on some aspects of the exhibition, but only an Anishinaabe advisory committee could speak directly to the concerns and viewpoints of the Anishinaabe artists.

Community Collaboration

Collaborating with multiple community members or advisors on exhibitions is no longer an exception but is now considered a museum best practice.[18] However, for some team members at the DIA, collaborating with Native American advisors was a novelty and created a few instances of uncertainty about the process, the creation of the title being one. I would like to discuss the ways in which the DIA laid the foundations for a collaborative project, navigating challenges along the way. This discussion demonstrates the development of the DIA's team and process, and it is my hope that it will inform future projects.

In 2022, I spearheaded the creation of a Native American Advisory Council (NAAC) at the DIA. The council members' tribes were reflective of the collection, not of

Another way in which the DIA laid the foundation for this project was through the Museum Partners for Social Justice grant from the Luce Foundation. From 2022–23, the grant partnered the DIA with the Denver Art Museum and allowed staff members from across the museum to visit the other institution and learn from their counterparts about how they worked with or how they were learning to work with their Native American collections and constituents. It was an opportunity to exchange ideas and ask questions. One of the key concepts learned during this time was the benefit of working with advisory committees, and how making this commitment often entails adding additional time to a project's schedule.

Another key idea that developed from the process is that Native American community voices should be centered in relevant projects. This involves decentering the museum and its initiatives and prioritizing the community(-ies) it is collaborating with. It was the hope that the group of individuals who participated in the collaboration would share what they had learned with their DIA colleagues so that navigating Native American exhibitions and work with advisory committees would be easier for all parties involved. However, like many institutions, staff changes and workloads did not allow for all of the important aspects of working with Native American communities to be retained or dispersed throughout the museum. Yet, many team members did benefit from these initiatives and the DIA team came together to bring the exhibition to fruition.

The DIA's Audience(s)

The fact is that many exhibitions are conceptualized with only a general audience in mind—the public—and that having to consider other, more specific audiences can create a challenge to some internal stakeholders.[19] Midway through the exhibition-planning process, based on conversations with the advisors and me, the

DIA interpretive planner helped develop distinct outcomes for different visitors: one focused on the Anishinaabe—the people who have a special interest in the exhibition—and another for the general public.

The key audiences for the exhibition were identified as (1) Anishinaabe people of the Great Lakes region and throughout the United States; the general audience was further defined as: (2) people seeking inspiration from contemporary art; (3) people who want to expand their knowledge; and (4) those with an interest in contemporary art and/or Native American art.

For each group, we hope the outcomes would be:

Outcomes for Anishinaabe People of the Great Lakes Region and throughout the United States

- Experience an opportunity to share and strengthen their own connections to Anishinaabe creativity and community

- Have representation as living, creative people who have always been rooted in the Great Lakes region

- View the DIA as a welcoming place that values Anishinaabe art

General Audience Outcomes

- Consider misperceptions and misunderstandings related to Native American art and be inspired to challenge them

- Realize that these misperceptions and misunderstandings impact working artists now

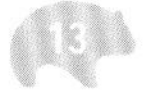

- Change the way they see the Great Lakes region by associating it with Anishinaabe creatives

Outcomes for All Audiences

- Notice the variety of media and techniques Anishinaabe artists use to express their perspectives and experiences

- Appreciate how Anishinaabe artists integrate centuries of creativity and communities into their artistic practices

Centering Anishinaabe experiences was the primary aim in the effort to collaborate with the advisors on the exhibition. It is reflected in the voice and narrative of the exhibition labels and design. It is also reflected in the translation of the labels into Anishinaabemowin, the language of the Anishinaabeg. Prioritizing an Anishinaabe aesthetic allows visitors to experience the exhibition utilizing not what they know or think they know but what they physically and visually experience in the space.

The Moment That We Are In: Contemporary Anishinaabe Art and Artists

Contemporary Anishinaabe Art: A Continuation highlights US-based Anishinaabe artists, bringing their cultures, stories, and artistic achievements to the forefront of American art. Diverging from the belief that Native American art belongs only in certain places and spaces and rejecting the narrative that Native American art is solely craft, not fine art, this exhibition challenges perceptions about what Native American art can be, how it should be seen, and how it can be interpreted. By including works by artists who continue many long-established practices and mediums while engaging

with current themes, as well as artists who work with a variety of other materials, the exhibition presents a more expansive view of Native American art.

Shifting away from a "traditional versus modern" paradigm to the idea of "continuity and connection" was an important element in the development of the exhibition and one that meant forgoing the display of Anishinaabe historic traditional art. The exhibition steps away from this model and allows the works and their artists to draw parallels to historic works only if they choose to do so. However, midway through the project development, the advisors began to have second thoughts about this decision: there was a fear that visitors would need assistance in understanding the origins of what they would be viewing. I asked the advisors to consider the moment that we are in. Contemporary Native American art needs to move past the point of "handholding" and providing a visual context for every exhibition. Other non-Indigenous contemporary art exhibitions do not begin with historical works or highly detailed explanations about cultural influences.

Native American art has been at the periphery of the art world for over 200 years. Although many artists have utilized Native American art as their inspiration,[20] only a few Native American artists have been able to reach world-renowned status, and only recently.

The exhibition begins in "the middle," with artists that have inspired and mentored many of the other artists featured in the exhibition (Denomie, Morrison, Morrisseau) but reaches back to the past (Lewis) and then goes to the future (Brauker, Patton) to discuss and challenge narratives about the mediums employed by Native American artists. The exhibition's introduction begins with art, art forms, and subjects that visitors may or may not expect from Native American artists in general or Anishinaabe artists specifically, but it provides a foundation for the rest of the exhibition, which includes baskets, beadwork, birchbark, clothing, film, graphic art, jewelry, painting, pottery, sculpture, and woodwork.

Featured Artists and Works

Born over seventy years apart, George Morrison (September 30, 1919–April 17, 2000) and Mary Edmonia Lewis[21] (ca. July 4, 1844/45–September 17, 1907) are luminaries in the field of American, Native American, and Anishinaabe art and challenge the narratives about the accepted aesthetics and mediums of Native American art.[22] Their artworks made statements about the periods in which they lived, traversing art worlds that accepted their artworks in both the moment and medium in which they were working. Both artists found success in their own ways while other Native American artists did not.

The exhibition begins with George Morrison's *Totemic Column* (1995–2024), "a stunning example of the rectangular prisms he created throughout the second half of his career, beginning in 1977. Varying in size, from mere inches to over forty feet in height, each wooden sculpture was treated as a three-dimensional collage."[23] Most people are familiar with "totem poles," and they are usually thought to be products of the US and Canadian Northwest Coast. From a statement about the work, "The word 'totem' derives from the Ojibwe *doodem*, meaning clan; and commonly defines tall wooden carvings of relational, narrative, and spiritual significance."[24] While Morrison's totemic forms speak materially and compositionally to lands and waters, he expressed that he was "not telling a story through animal and human images but making an abstract version of structural and organic vertical form."[25] (Bockley Gallery, 2024). This artwork begins the conversation about challenging narratives surrounding Native American art and culture. It is accompanied by Jim Denomie's *Untitled (Totem Painting)* (2016). For Denomie (1955–March 1, 2022), George Morrison was an "art-historical ancestor and mentor . . . [and he was] deeply influenced by his visual and conceptual languages, and how he navigated modernism as a Native artist in connection to their [Denomie's and Morrison's] shared home of Minnesota and the wider Great Lakes region."[26] The exhibition then leads the visitor into works by Norval Morrisseau, the founder of the Woodland School of Canadian art, whose bright colors and use of powerlines and animals continue to influence many Anishinaabe artists today.

Following the pairing of Morrison's and Denomie's works, the first room contains two sculptures by Mary Edmonia Lewis, an artist of both Anishinaabe and African descent. Lewis worked in Europe in the late 1800s, and her story illuminates how Native American artists have had to partner with patrons to sustain their livelihoods and ensure their artworks were brought to wider audiences. Lewis also faced something that many contemporary Anishinaabe artists face today: the desire of many viewers for her to express her Native American identity in her artwork. Her medium, marble, differed from those that most Native American artists used at that time, but her subject matter, Native Americans, connected her to her culture and identity. Lewis is joined in the room by Shirley Brauker's (August 11, 1950–November 22, 2022) ceramic sculpture *Earth Mother (venus féminine power)* (date unknown), which intimates that Anishinaabe and other Native American artists have been and continue to be influenced by multiple sources. Brauker's pottery also inspired the creation of a new category at the Santa Fe

Indian Market, an annual art market for Native American artists' work. Artists featured in the exhibition have made strides in the last century to challenge imposed definitions of Native American art both nationally and internationally. Their artwork illustrates the ways in which they confront these narratives and maintain their agency, their voices, and their connections to their communities.

Counteracting Romanticism—Conclusion

As the curator of *Contemporary Anishinaabe Art: A Continuation,* I have one request for the exhibition's general audience and catalogue readers, which is stated perfectly in the invocation that George C. Longfish and Joan Randall shared for the 1983 exhibition *Contemporary Native American Art*: "In the name of the artists participating in this [exhibition], we ask the viewers to suspend what they 'know' to be Indian art [Native American art] and to make just a few considerations before they pass any judgement on the show. We ask that the feeling of uncertainty which usually accompanies new experiences be allowed to accompany them through the entire [exhibition]. In this way, we expect that more discoveries will be made, that more ideas will be stimulated, and that more pleasure will be derived."[27]

Contemporary Anishinaabe Art: A Continuation opens almost forty-two years after *Contemporary Native American Art,* but today other curators of Native American art and I are still asking for the same thing from audiences: to enter an exhibition with an open mind and allow themselves to develop an understanding of Native American art. What does that mean for the field of Native American art generally? It means that there is still work to do when it comes to engaging audiences with Native American art. That

work is being done with milestone exhibitions like the Minneapolis Institute of Art's *Hearts of Our People: Native Women Artists* (2019–21)[28] and Jeffery Gibson's selection as the United States of America's representative at the Venice Biennale in 2024. But there is still work to be done, so that hopefully, forty-two years from now, no invocations or explanations or justifications will be needed to have an exhibition of contemporary Anishinaabe art. It will be the moment that they are in.

Endnotes

1. The title was inspired by a conversation I had with the Smith Jarislowsky Senior Curator of Canadian Art at the Vancouver Art Gallery, Richard Hill. We discussed having to constantly contextualize Native American art for visitors. I said to him it would be great just to start at the moment that we are in.

2. The Anishinaabeg are a linguistically and culturally related group of Indigenous people from the Great Lakes region of the United States and Canada, and include the Ojibwe, Chippewa, Odawa, Potawatomi, Algonquin, and the Saulteaux, Nipissing, and Mississauga First Nations.

3. This collection was named after its donors, Milford G. Chandler and Richard A. Pohrt.

4. Kelly Church, Match-E-Be-Nash-She-Wish Band of Potawatomi/Grand Traverse Band of Ottawa and Chippewa Indians (Descent); Jason Quigno, Saginaw Chippewa Indian Tribe; Monica Rickert-Bolter, Prairie Band Potawatomi Nation; Jonathan Thunder, Red Lake Band of Ojibwe; Jodi Webster, Ho-Chunk Nation/Prairie Band Potawatomi Nation.

5. Mary Edmonia Lewis's story is compelling as one of the first widely known Anishinaabe artists, and Norval Morrisseau influenced many of the artists in the show as well.

6. Interpretive planners are the educators assigned to special exhibitions and permanent collection installations. They collaborate with curators, designers, and community partners to help shape the visitor experience. This includes developing

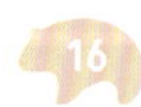

Contemporary Anishinaabe Art: A Continuation

major themes and storylines and the creation of in-gallery interpretation like information labels, videos, interactive elements, and opportunities for visitors to respond to the exhibition.

7. Dyani White Hawk and Joe Horse Capture, "Mni Sota: Reflections of Time and Place," in *Perspectives and Parallels: Expanding Interpretive Foundations with American Indian Curators and Writers,* ed. Kenneth Bloom (Duluth: Tweed Museum of Art, University of Minnesota, 2014), p. 8.

8. Style references new and innovative designs, materials, and techniques.

9. White Hawk and Horse Capture, "Mni Sota: Reflections of Time and Place," p. 8.

10. It also inspired some of the interpretative elements in the exhibition, such as the artists' video interviews.

11. The works that reflect a more historical style were included based on their contemporary themes and/or their contemporary use.

12. White Hawk and Horse Capture, "Mni Sota: Reflections of Time and Place," pp. 8, 10.

13. Anishinaabe homeland encompasses parts of both the United States and Canada.

14. There is often a creative tension between different teams about exhibition titles and their relatability to different audiences.

15. The advisors also emphasized that they did not want titles that romanticized them or their work.

16. Anishinaabe is spelled differently by tribes and nations. The quote is taken from a personal communication.

17. This was confirmed by audience surveys, interviews, and focus groups conducted by the DIA's Evaluation team.

18. Alison Jean and Swarupa Anila, "Whose Museum Is It Anyway? Towards More Authentic Community-Centered Practices in Creating Exhibitions," *Exhibition* (Spring 2019), pp. 43–55.

19. "And not every outcome applied to every audience because the audiences are all coming from very different backgrounds and experiences." Personal communication from DIA interpreter Megan DiRienzo, February 28, 2025.

20. W. Jackson Rushing, *Native American Art and the New York Avant-Garde: A History of Cultural Primitivism* (Austin: University of Texas Press, 1995).

21. She was of Anishinaabe and African American descent.

22. The United States Postal Service issued commemorative stamps featuring Lewis and Morrison in 2022. Little scholarship has been done on the connections between these two artists.

23. From Bockley Gallery pamphlet, 2024.

24. From Bockley Gallery pamphlet, 2024.

25. From Bockley Gallery pamphlet, 2024.

26. From Bockley Gallery pamphlet, 2024.

27. George C. Longfish and Joan Randall, "Contradictions in Indian Territory," in *Contemporary Native American Art* (Oklahoma City, OK: Metro Press, Inc., 1983).

28. The exhibition debut at the Minneapolis Institute of Art June 2–August 18, 2019, then Frist Art Museum in Nashville September 27, 2019–January 12, 2020, the Renwick Gallery of the Smithsonian American Art Museum, Washington, DC, February 21–May 17, 2020, and the Philbrook Museum of Art, Tulsa, October 7, 2020–January 3, 2021.

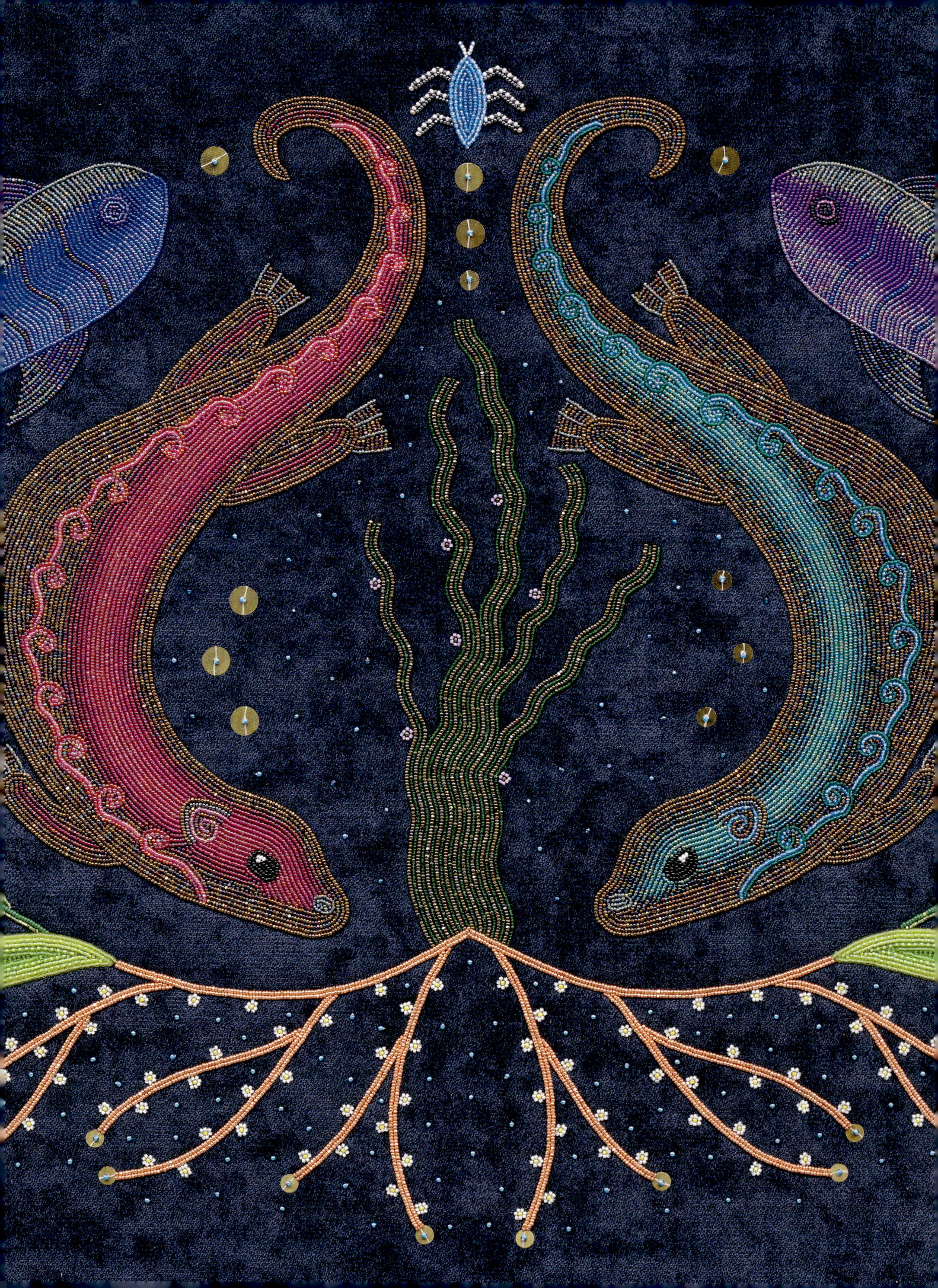

The Michigan Anishinaabeg

Matthew L. M. Fletcher, JD (Grand Traverse Band of Ottawa and Chippewa Indians)

The Anishinaabeg are the inhabitants of Anishinaabewaki, the world of the Anishinaabe. The Bodewadmi (Potawatomi), Odawa (Ottawa), and Ojibwe (Chippewa) tribal nations constitute the tribal nations of the Anishinaabeg, often collectively referred to as Niswi-mishkodewinan, or the Three Fires Confederacy. Altogether, individual bands of these tribal nations are signatories to numerous treaties with the United States. Anishinaabe treaty negotiators usually memorialized their assent to the treaty terms by marking the treaty paper with their *doodem* (clan) symbols, rendering each treaty into a work of art.

Ishkode, or fire, is a powerful metaphor for the Anishinaabeg. In the Anishinaabe oral tradition, Nanabozho is the trickster god who steals fire from the *manidowaag,* or supernatural creatures. Nanabozho is a shapeshifter who snuck into the spirit world disguised as *wabooz,* or the rabbit, represented by early Anishinaabe artists centuries ago in pictograms. The theft of fire, guarded by the *Animiki,* Thunderers, brought warmth and hot food to the Anishinaabe people, and is a significant moment in Anishinaabe history, highlighting the importance of resourcefulness and courage to overcome hardship. Thanks to the artistry of the Anishinaabeg artists going back generations, Nanabozho, the *Animiki,* and the *Mishibizhiw* (Underwater Panther), for example, are easily recognizable to modern-day Anishinaabeg.

Historically, Anishinaabeg tribal nations organized themselves by *doodem.* The *doodem* system was both political and social, where membership was passed from parent to child, usually by gender. The Anishinaabeg recognized their own humble place in Anishinaabewaki, naming their *doodemaag,* or clans, after their animal relatives and supernatural creatures. Each Anishinaabe community recognized seven *doodemaag,* typically from the following list: *mukwa* (bear), *migizi* (eagle), *animiki* (thunderbird), *amik* (beaver), *maang* (loon), *gigoohn* (fish), *ajijaak* (crane), *wawashkeshi* (deer), *wabisheshi* (marten), *mikinaak* or *mishiikehn* (snapping or painted turtle), and others. Each *doodem* had equal status to the others in tribal leadership decisions but would perform different roles. *Doodemaag* based on flying creatures tended to serve as the nominal leaders, but also focused on external or foreign relations, given their ability to fly high and observe long distances. The *mukwa* and *wabisheshi doodemaag* were the martial clans, handling internal and external security, respectively, though these clans also possessed obligations related to the physical and spiritual health of the overall community. Water-based *doodemaag* tended to be more spiritual, medicinal, and philosophical. Every *doodem* had a kind of personality rooted in the characteristics of these animal relatives. Every political representative in tribal decision-making was obligated to present

Opposite: Jessica Leigh Gokey (Lac Courte Oreilles Band of Lake Superior Chippewa; b. 1985), *Companions,* 2022 (detail)

their *doodem's* viewpoint or interest. That the Anishinaabe treaty negotiators choose to mark the treaty paper with an artistic rendering of their *doodemaag* is symbolic of the political roles that each one of them played within their tribal nations.

Anishinaabe leaders, now commonly referred to as *ogema* (singular) and *ogemaag* (plural), governed through persuasion and general consensus rather than divine or sovereign right. An Anishinaabe tribal nation would meet collectively to select individuals with special skills as *ogemaag*, but only for particular purposes. Those purposes could include summer, winter, or sugar bush work. Those purposes could also be for inter-tribal treaty negotiation, treaty negotiation with colonizer nations and their proxies, international trade, or internal or external conflicts, to name a few examples. Once an *ogema*'s job was concluded, that *ogema*'s power and influence would organically fade.

Often, we know these principles because they were preserved and spread through the *aadizookaan*, the sacred stories passed down over generations. Many of these stories are trickster tales featuring Nanabozho, creation stories featuring the *manidowaag* and the original Anishinaabe, and morality tales rooted in Anishinaabe history, often featuring Anishinaabe people interacting with creatures representing the *doodemaag*. The *aadizookaan* form the artistic and literary foundations of the Anishinaabeg, akin to Homer's *Odyssey* and *Iliad*, J. R. R. Tolkien's *Lord of the Rings*, and Marlon James's *Dark Star Trilogy*. Anishinaabe storytellers have managed to maintain their dynamic work in the face of centuries of near-genocidal colonization.

The arrival of the European colonizers to Anishinaabewaki in the seventeenth century began periods of intense, catastrophic disruption. Even before the physical arrival of colonizers, their contagious diseases had already swept through Anishinaabewaki. These waves of disease devastated Anishinaabe communities. The deaths of so many Anishinaabeg undermined their carefully balanced *doodem* structure and lifeways. The survivors then struggled to react to the first wave of colonizers, who were French—referred to by the Anishinaabeg as *wetimigoozh.* The *wetimigoozh* came for the resources found in the area inhabited by the Anishinaabe. Because they learned quickly that *Anishinaabekwewaag* (women) owned and controlled hunting, trapping, gathering, and fishing properties, as well as the trade routes, the most efficient way for the *wetimigoozh* to access those resources was to marry into Anishinaabe families. The *wetimigoozh* used their power and influence to establish a destructive fur trade, pitting tribal nations from the Atlantic coast through Anishinaabewaki and beyond against each other. This disruption contributed to tragic and deadly conflicts between the Anishinaabeg and other tribal nations, notably the Dakota and Haundenosaunee (or Iroquois) nations. This trade led to the near extinction of fur-bearing relatives such as the beaver, the fox, and others. Unfortunately for the Anishinaabeg, the *wetimigoozh* also brought along religious evangelicals intent on coercively converting Indigenous peoples to their religion.

The British, known to the Anishinaabeg as *shaganash,* largely displaced the French after the French and Indian War. The *shaganash* desired even greater control over Anishinaabe lands and resources, including control over the fur trade and Great Lakes waterways and trade routes. After the American Revolution, the British retained control of Canada and much of Anishinaabewaki. The Americans, called the *chmookmon* by the Anishinaabeg, took control of the Michigan Territory after the conclusion of the War of 1812, sometime around 1820. The French and British were awful, but the Americans were much, much worse. The Americans demanded control over Anishinaabe lands and resources, but insisted upon absolute control over Anishinaabe lives as well. By the 1830s, the Americans became obsessed with ethnically cleansing Anishinaabewaki of all Indigenous peoples, either through forced removals or cultural genocide. The continued presence of more than a dozen Anishinaabe tribal nations in Michigan alone attests to the failure of American policy, but the cost of Anishinaabe resistance to colonization was well-nigh apocalyptic.

During the colonizing period, the written historical record generated by colonizers is replete with Anishinaabe *ogemaag* who were mostly warriors and treaty negotiators, nearly all of them Anishinaabe *inniniwaag* (men). Pontiac, for example, an Odawa *ogema* from the Lake Erie shoreline between Detroit and Cleveland, organized a pan-Indigenous uprising against the British Empire involving simultaneous attacks on more than a dozen military installations throughout the Great Lakes and the northern Ohio River Valley. This war pushed the Crown to issue the British Proclamation of 1763, which prohibited American colonists from grabbing Indigenous lands without British consent. The Americans complained about the proclamation in the Declaration of Independence, where they condemned the "merciless Indian savages." Other well-known figures like Assiginack, Aishquagonabe, Augustin Hamlin, Andrew Blackbird, Kewaygoshkum, and Match-E-Be-Nash-She-Wish negotiated important treaty rights on behalf of the Anishinaabeg and/or led war parties as well. While they were certainly important figures, this historical focus on Anishinaabe *inniniwaag* demonstrates the clear misogyny that colonizer cultures used to obtain Anishinaabe land and resources.

Anishinaabekwewaag are underrepresented in the historical record but contributed at least as much leadership as the men. Gender roles mattered, with *Anishinaabekwewaag* managing many of the internal social and familial decisions, but they also played roles in warfare, diplomacy, and especially trade. Recall that colonizer men often married into Anishinaabe families in order to access the trade market. British trader John Johnston married Ozhaguscodaywayquay, an Ojibwekwe from the upper peninsula of what is now Michigan, for that reason. The infamous Michigan Indian agent for the federal government, Henry Schoolcraft, married their daughter, Bamewawagezhikaquay, also known as Jane Johnston, in order to gain influence in the region. Their contemporaries, such as Agatha Biddle and Magdelaine Marcot LaFramboise were *Odawakwewaag* (Odawa women) who owned and operated their own fur trading companies and, in Agatha's case, served as leader of her own tribal nation, the Agatha Biddle Band.

For the first century of the United States, the Anishinaabe tribal nations dealt with the Americans primarily through formal treaties negotiated and ratified under the United States Constitution. In general, these treaties involved large and small land sales, or cessions, from the tribes to the United States, in exchange for permanent Anishinaabe homelands called "reservations," hunting and fishing rights, annuities, and material goods and services. The fact that the federal government utilized the treaty process amounted to recognition by the Americans that Anishinaabe tribal nations were sovereign governments. The American treaty power does not extend to state governments, private individuals, and business interests, only to foreign nations and Indian tribes.

The American treaty negotiators sought power over and ownership of Indigenous lands and resources, while the Anishinaabe *ogemaag* negotiated with the interests of seven generations of Anishinaabeg forward and backward in mind. The fundamental principle of Anishinaabe peoples is *mino-bimaadiziwin,* which translates to "living life in a good way," a kind of continuous rebirth, in English. It encompasses a holistic approach to living that emphasizes balance, health, and well-being in all aspects of life, including physical, mental, emotional, and spiritual dimensions. This concept is integral to the Anishinaabe worldview and is often invoked in discussions about health, education, and community development within Indigenous communities. *Mino-bimaadiziwin* demands relational accountability between humans, our animal and plant relatives, supernatural forces, and Anishinaabewaki.

The Anishinaabeg seek to live life in a good way through the application of the Niizhwaaswi Debwewin, the Seven Sacred Teachings (or Truths): *dbaadendiziwin,* humility; *aakwa'ode'ewin,* bravery; *gwekwaadziwin,* honesty; *nbwaakaawin,* wisdom; *debwewin,* truth; *mnaadendimowin,* respect; and *zaagidwin,* love. The Niizhwaaswi Debwewin guided the *ogemaag* in ethical decision-making during treaty negotiations with the Americans. The teachings emphasize the interests of the natural world of Anishinaabewaki, the responsibility of the *ogemaag* to their communities, and the commitment of the Anishinaabeg to their ancestors and their descendants, which is the reason seven generations of Anishinaabeg were considered. Consistent with these

sacred teachings, in numerous treaties with the United States, the Anishinaabe *ogemaag* negotiated for permanent homelands, educational rights, and a continuing government-to-government relationship originally called the duty of protection and now usually called the trust responsibility.

The Treaty of Greenville in 1795 was the first major treaty signed by the Michigan Anishinaabeg. That treaty arose out the conclusion of Little Turtle's War that ranged throughout in the Ohio River Valley for ten years. Anishinaabe *ogitchidaawaag* (warriors) frequently participated in this war. The treaty set the tone for treaties to follow by recognizing reserved rights to hunt, fish, and gather, and also set boundary lines between the Indigenous tribal nations and the United States.

In the 1807 Treaty of Detroit, the Michigan Anishinaabeg (and Wyandot Indians) ceded millions of acres of land in the southeast portion of what is now the State of Michigan, including Detroit, to the United States— ceding so much land was very often a requirement of the treaties. In exchange, the parties reserved parcels of land for reservations and provided for off-reservation hunting and fishing rights. The 1817 Treaty of Fort Meigs similarly ceded lands in southern Michigan to the United States, but also provided for the funding and establishment of a school (later called the University of Michigan) obligated to educate Anishinaabe students. This was the first treaty negotiated by Lewis Cass, the infamous American Army officer and politician that the Anishinaabeg referred to as Winino Omisad, or "Big Belly."

The 1819 Treaty of Saginaw ceded millions of acres more to the United States in the area north and west of Detroit. Here, the Isabella Reservation would be established for the

Saginaw Chippewa Indian Tribe. The 1818 Treaty of St. Mary's ceded the St. Mary's River falls, where the Soo Locks would eventually be built. The Americans would build a military fort named after General Hugh Brady, who would later lead the Army's forcible arrest and internment of Anishinaabe people in southern Michigan.

The 1821 Treaty of Chicago established the original reservation land bases of the Match-E-Be-Nash-She-Wish Band of Pottawatomi Indians, the Nottawaseppi Huron Band of the Potawatomi, and the Pokagon Band of Potawatomi Indians of Michigan and Indiana. Anishinaabe tribal nations ceded five million acres south of the Grand River in southwest Michigan. Lewis Cass used manipulation and bribery to secure the cession. Grand River Anishinaabe *ogema* Kewaygoshkum signed the treaty over the opposition of his community and suffered banishment from the tribe.

In 1830, President Andrew Jackson and his Secretary of War, Lewis Cass, embarked on a policy of Indian removal, a plan of ethnic cleansing of all Indigenous tribal nations east of the Mississippi River. In 1833, Michigan Bodewadmi tribal nations executed a second Treaty of Chicago. The 1833 treaty was a removal treaty in which the American military led the Bodewadmi tribal nations on the Trail of Death in 1838, a forced march to Kansas causing the death of dozens of Bodewadmi people, mostly children. Only a few Bodewadmi families remained in southern Michigan and northern Indiana. General Brady led multiple sweeps through the area to round up Bodewadmi families, detaining them in prison camps in Battle Creek, Marshall, and Owosso. Many hundreds of Anishinaabeg escaped to Walpole Island, Manitoulin Island, Garden River, and elsewhere in Canada, splitting up

Anishinaabe families.

In 1836, the Odawa and Ojibwe tribal nations of northern lower Michigan and the eastern upper peninsula agreed to the Treaty of Washington, negotiated by Lewis Cass and Henry Schoolcraft. Aishquagonabe from the Grand Traverse Bay Anishinaabe initially led the tribal negotiators based on his experience in fighting the Americans in the War of 1812. The Anishinaabe intended the treaty to involve a relatively small land cession, but the Americans used trickery and manipulation to secure a massive sixteen-million-acre cession. Henry Schoolcraft and his fur trader constituents promised that the treaty would only involve the lower peninsula Odawa tribal nations, but he also invited some of his Ojibwe friends and relatives from the eastern upper peninsula. These invited observers did not have authority from their communities to cede Ojibwe lands, but when the *odawaag* refused to sign the treaty, Schoolcraft and Cass persuaded the Ojibwe observers to sign. In their view, it really did not matter who signed the treaty to the United States Senate, the body that would ratify the treaty, so long as any Indians with even nominal authority did so.

Since the Odawa negotiators were hamstrung by Schoolcraft's deceit, they had no choice. Worse, after they had negotiated for permanent reservations in order to avoid what had happened to the Bodewadmi tribal nations, the Senate unilaterally removed those provisions from the treaty. What remained of the treaty was off-reservation hunting and fishing rights on ceded lands until they were "required for settlement." The 1836 treaty was a debacle for both the Anishinaabeg and the Americans. The Anishinaabeg did not receive the promised permanent homeland, and the United States could not forcibly remove the Indians. Out

of this treaty arose numerous tribal nations: the Bay Mills Indian Community, the Grand Traverse Band of Ottawa and Chippewa Indians, the Little River Band of Ottawa Indians, and the Sault Ste. Marie Tribe of Chippewa Indians. At least two other tribal nations signed the treaty but are not currently federally acknowledged, the Burt Lake Band of Ottawa and Chippewa Indians and the Grand River Band of Ottawa and Chippewa Indians. In 1837, as an additional consequence of the treaty, Congress would grant statehood to Michigan.

In 1842, the western upper peninsula Ojibwe tribal nations executed their own land cession treaty, the Treaty of La Pointe. Out of the treaty arose the Keweenaw Bay Indian Community and the Lac Vieux Desert Band of Lake Superior Chippewa Indians. Eventually, the Hannahville Indian Community, consisting of Bodewadmi communities escaping removal in the west, would settle in the western upper peninsula as well.

Michigan Anishinaabe tribal nations would sign additional treaties in 1855 and 1864. The 1836 treaty tribes would sign the 1855 Treaty of Detroit, a remedial treaty designed to correct the federal government's failures to implement the earlier treaty, but that treaty also failed. The Saginaw Chippewa Indian Tribe would sign a treaty in 1864 that helped to cement the permanence of the Isabella Reservation. Other Michigan tribal nations would not fare so well.

After the land cessions, the federal government largely ignored the Michigan tribal nations, fulfilling virtually none of its promises. The federal government's administration of Anishinaabe property was dominated by violence, fraud, corruption, and incompetence. Eventually, giving up on its own abysmal effort, the Department of the Interior illegally terminated the six lower peninsula Odawa and Bodewadmi tribal nations in the 1870s. For a century, these six tribes received no services from the federal government. Odawa artist Margaret Boyd used her porcupine quill boxes and black ash baskets to fund a trip on behalf of Waganakising (Little Traverse Bay Bands of Odawa Indians) to Washington, DC, in 1876 to advocate for Odawa land rights directly to the President and the Secretary of the Interior.

The United States also distorted and perverted the treaty-guaranteed education rights owed the Michigan Anishinaabeg by establishing several mandatory boarding schools. These boarding schools, paid for out of treaty annuities ostensibly owed to the various tribal nations, operated primarily between the 1860s and the 1930s, though the Holy Childhood boarding school in Harbor Springs operated into the 1980s. These boarding schools were notorious for abuse, poor health care and food, and remedial education. Schoolmasters abused and occasionally killed children who spoke Anishinaabemowin. Children frequently ran away, only to be hunted down by bounty hunters. These schools were genocidal death camps, with hundreds of Anishinaabe children buried in unmarked graves on the grounds of the Mount Pleasant Industrial Indian Boarding School and dozens more at Holy Childhood. Few survivors ever spoke their language or knew their families and traditions, and many never saw their families again. Odawa artists who survived the boarding school era, such as Yvonne M. Walker-Keshick of the Little Traverse Bay Bands of Odawa Indians and Ed and Jennie Pigeon of the Match-E-Be-Nash-She-Wish Band of Pottawatomi Indians (Gun Lake Tribe), became leading quillwork and basket makers, respectively.

During this period, the Americans destroyed Anishinaabewaki. The Americans deforested both peninsulas of the historic white pine, oak, black ash, and other indigenous tree cover. The deforestation nearly ended the Anishinaabeg way of life. Their intense dependence and interrelationship with the land placed them in the most vulnerable situations. Deforestation forced them into exploitative wage labor with terrible conditions and poor pay compared to white laborers. Tribal governance and Anishinaabe religious practices went underground for fear of prosecution. In 1934, when the United States authorized and encouraged hundreds of tribal nations elsewhere to organize into constitutional democracies, John Collier, the Commissioner of Indian Affairs, refused to allow most of the Michigan tribal nations to organize. The federal government underserved the other Michigan tribal nations as well. To say that Michigan Anishinaabeg were in dire straits during this time is a horrific understatement. No other tribal nations in the United States were in worse shape in terms of health, housing, education, employment, and mortality rates.

Anishinaabe activists changed the paradigm in the 1960s and 1970s by exercising treaty fishing rights in the Great Lakes. Anishinaabe fishers like Big Abe LeBlanc, Arthur Duhamel, and George Anthony defied state laws that discriminated against Anishinaabe fishing in blatant violation of the 1836 and 1842 treaties. Eventually, in two cases, *People v. LeBlanc* (1976) and *United States v. Michigan* (1979), the courts recognized the treaty rights. In Art Duhamel's words, fishing was the "push" to seek restoration of tribal status.

In the 1970s, the United States embarked on a policy change toward tribal self-determination. The government established processes by which terminated tribes could receive federal reaffirmation and acknowledgment. Self-determination laws allowed tribes to enter into contracts with the federal government in which the tribes could govern themselves with federal appropriations and revenues generated by tribal economies. In 1983, Fred Dakota of the Keweenaw Bay Indian Community opened the first Indian casino in Michigan. The Bay Mills and Grand Traverse tribal nations quickly followed suit. In 1993, the seven then-federally recognized Anishinaabe tribal nations entered into some of the first gaming compacts with a state government. These compacts authorized Las Vegas–style gaming.

The twelve now-federally recognized Anishinaabe tribal nations are national leaders in tribal self-government. Several Michigan tribal nations raced ahead of tribes nationally in self-governance capabilities. Gaming revenue and federal self-determination money helped to develop the base for broader economies. Anishinaabe tribal justice systems are models for tribal nations and state courts nationwide. Anishinaabe tribal nations now have the resources to fight back against the colonizer's actions against Anishinaabewaki, which has been permanently contaminated with PFAS chemicals, overrun with invasive species like the emerald ash borer and the zebra mussel, and threatened with petroleum pipeline catastrophes from Line 5 and other pipelines. The only real solution to these problems is land back, restoring Anishinaabewaki to the Anishinaabeg.

Contemporary Anishinaabe artists like Jason Quigno, Jason Wesaw, Kelly Church, Cherish Parrish, and many others carry on the traditions of the Anishinaabeg through their artistry. Working with materials common to Anishinaabe artists centuries ago like paints and dyes, plants and trees, beads, shells, and animal parts, these artists create dynamic and powerful works designed to reimagine our culture and philosophy in light of *mino-bimaadiziwin* and the Niizhwaaswi Debwewinaag.

Sources

Blackbird, Andrew J. *History of the Ottawa and Chippewa Indians of Michigan: A Grammar of Their Language, and Personal and Family History of the Author.* Ypsilanti, MI: Ypsilantian Job Printing House, 1887.

Dobson, Pamela J., ed. *The Tree That Never Dies: Oral History of the Michigan Indians.* Grand Rapids, MI: Grand Rapids Public Library, 1978.

Kurath, Gertrude Prokosch. *Michigan Indian Festivals.* Ann Arbor, MI: Ann Arbor Publishers, 1967.

McNally, Michael, ed. *The Art of Tradition: Sacred Music, Dance & Myth of Michigan's Anishinaabe, 1946–1955.* East Lansing: Michigan State University Press, 2009.

Morseau, Blaire, ed. *As Sacred to Us: Simon Pokagon's Birch Bark Stories in Their Contexts.* East Lansing: Michigan State University Press, 2023.

Paquin, Ron, and Robert Doherty. *Not First in Nobody's Heart: The Life Story of a Contemporary Chippewa.* Ames: Iowa State University Press, 1992.

Stark, Heidi Kiiwetinepinesiik. "Marked by Fire: Anishinaabe Articulations of Nationhood in Treaty Making with the United States and Canada." *American Indian Quarterly* 36, no. 2 (2012): 119–49.

Stark, Kekek Jason. "Anishinaabe Inaakonigewin: Principles for the Intergenerational Preservation of *Mino-Bimaadiziwin.*" *Montana Law Review* 82 (2021): 293.

Contemporary Anishinaabe Art: A Continuation

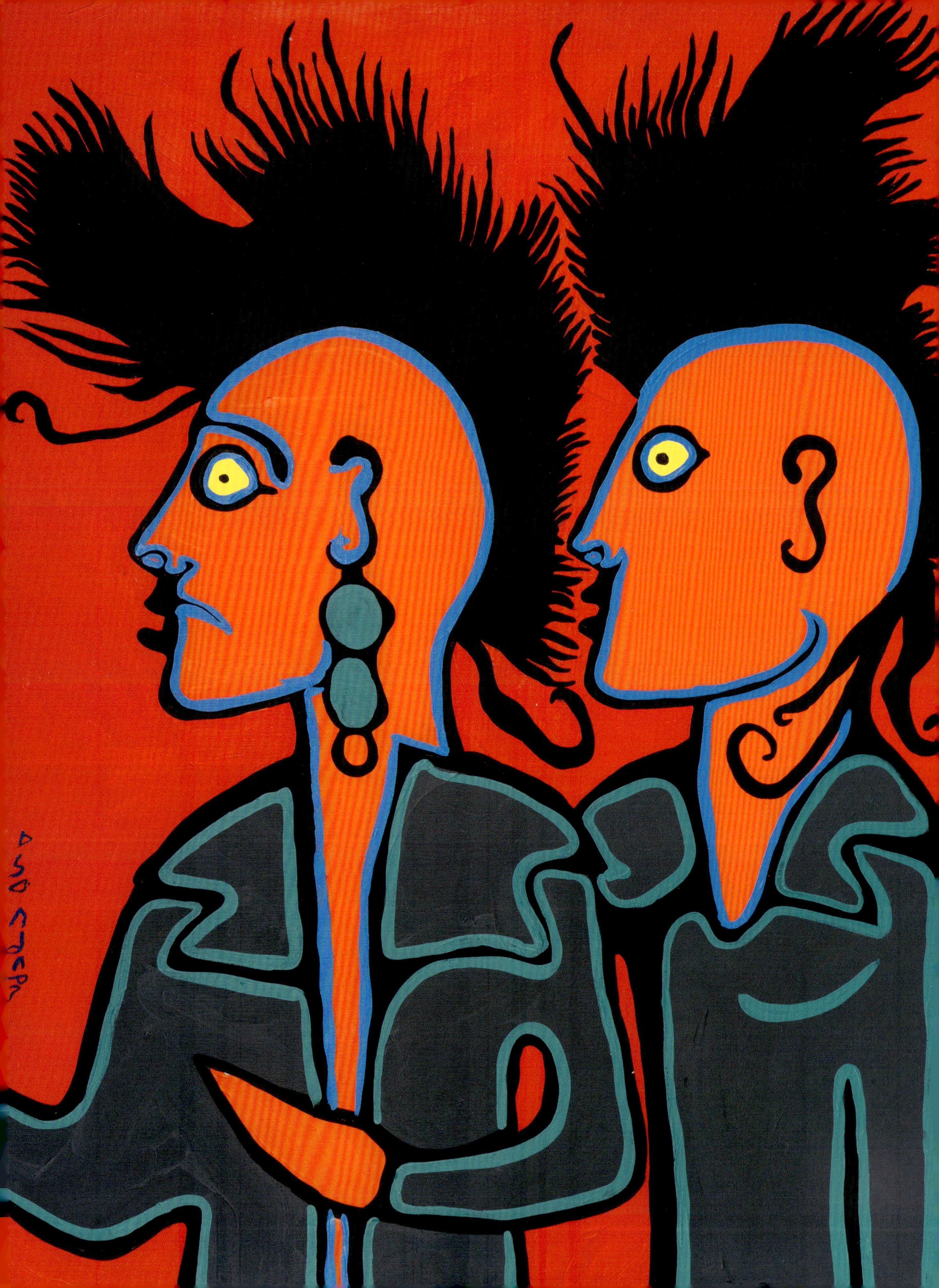

Transnationalism of the Woodland School

Christopher T. Green, PhD

The proper recognition of the Woodland School of art as a transnational stylistic movement is long overdue. I do not just refer to the migration of the style across the US-Canada border and its spread southward and outward beyond the boundaries of the Great Lakes region in which it originated, but also, despite its strong association with Anishinaabe art, its adoption and expansion by artists from across diverse tribal nations.

One illuminating example of this transnationalism came in August 2022, during the annual Sante Fe Indian Market. There, I attended the satellite exhibition *Sovereign Santa Fe*, a contemporary Indigenous art exhibition guest-curated by the Diné artist Tony Abeyta at the hotel La Fonda on the Plaza. Among varied contemporary works I was surprised to find, in this center of Southwestern art, several pieces that emulated the Woodland School. Two works painted on curved, sculptural planks of wood had bright floral, berry, and abstract biomorphic motifs outlined in thick black contours and filled with flat cells of unmodulated color, sometimes internally subdivided. At the bottom of one work was a single head with tendril-like black hair, above which was a bisected circle radiating with color. All the forms were connected by flowing black lines, which in combination with the floral motifs, stylized hair, and floating bisected circles were immediately recognizable as being in the style of

Anishinaabe artist Norval Morrisseau, the father of the Woodland School.[1] The second work made the homage to Morrisseau even more explicit, as it was largely taken up by two figures, a mermaid and an avian form in the midst of a transformation, both direct quotations of some of Morrisseau's best-known paintings, including his six-panel magnum opus *Man Changing into Thunderbird* (1977). A large yellow eye with a red pupil surmounted this design, another of Morrisseau's iconic forms. But quite unlike any Woodland School painting, the artist had mounted glass sculptures into the middle of the works—petaled flowers and human heads, one of which was wearing a Pueblo buffalo dancer's headdress, one of its horns extending outward into the viewer's space.

Despite the clear emulation of Morrisseau's style, this combination of media and tribal traditions was very unlike the preference for two-dimensional media—paintings, drawings, and prints—and visual sources in Woodland oral narratives and cosmologies typical of the movement also known as Legend Painting. Indeed, these works were not by any Woodland artist at all, but by Ira Lujan, an accomplished Taos/Ohkay Owingeh Pueblo glass artist. *Sovereign Santa Fe* sought to showcase "cutting edge indigenous creativity" and the "elusive relationship between traditional and contemporary," but in his emulation of the Woodland School, Lujan revealed the instability of another relationship: that between the Woodland style's origins in place-based narratives and visual traditions, and its plasticity as a visual

Opposite: Norval Morrisseau (Bingwi Neyaashi Anishinaabek First Nation; 1932–2007), *Punk Rockers Nancy and Andy,* 1989 (detail)

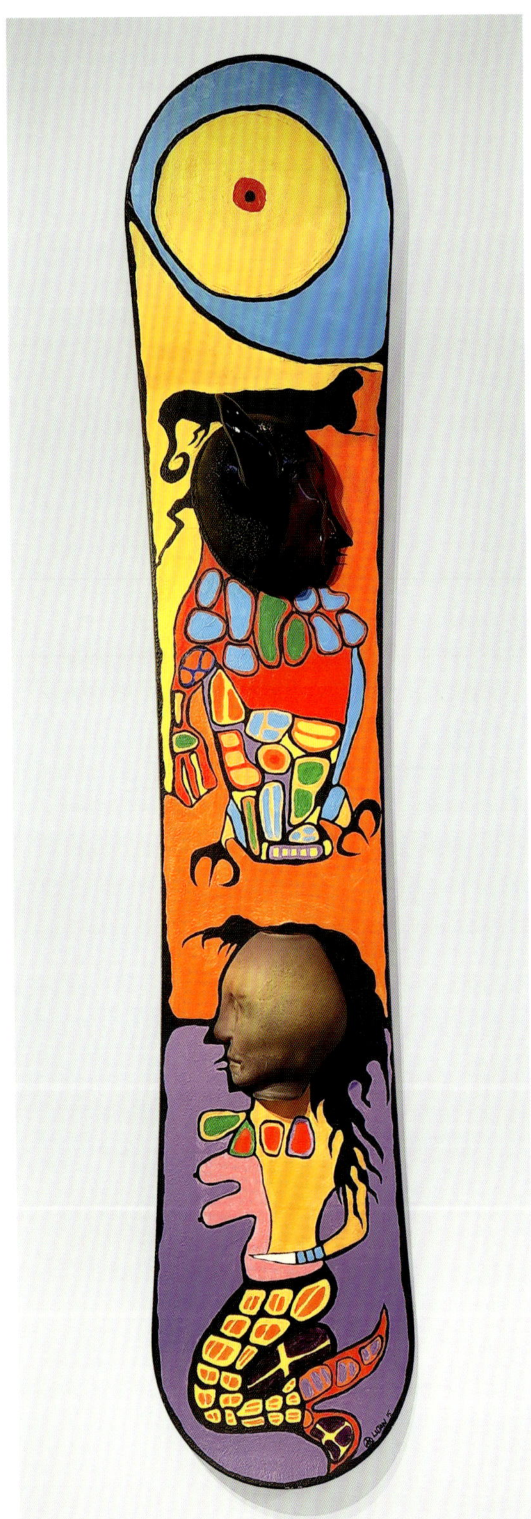 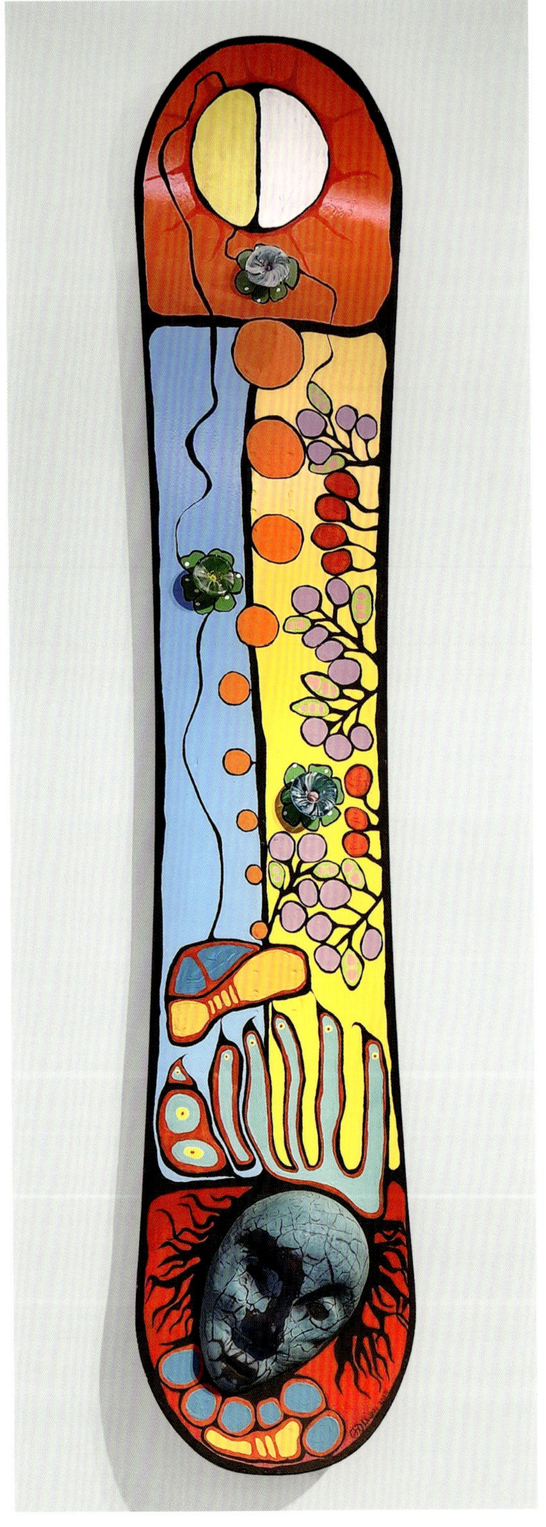

Contemporary Anishinaabe Art: A Continuation

idiom dissociable from its cultural context.

In the twenty-first century, the Woodland School has taken on a life of its own. It is no longer limitable to the work of the Professional Native Indian Artists Inc. (PNIAI), or the "Indian Group of Seven" as they were known, a group of primarily (though not exclusively) Anishinaabe artists who made the style widely recognizable, nor to their immediate successors. Instead, the style has become not only a vital visual adaptation of culturally specific narratives in modernist forms, but also an alienable, migratory style, separable from the Great Lakes–centered stories and spiritual worlds that served as the movement's epistemological foundation. As recent high-profile reports of non-Native artists appropriating the style and forging Morrisseau's work for financial gain demonstrate, the style has also not only exceeded tribal and national boundaries, but also Indigenous authenticity altogether.[2] Thus, despite its strong association with Canadian art history, to the point of being appropriated as a regional and, at times, national style, the Woodland School has become internationalist. This essay attempts to draw out the history of the transnational movements of the Woodland style, particularly its travels across the US-Canada border, and track the ways it has since its beginnings exceeded strict boundaries.

The present exhibition, with its focus on US-based Anishinaabe artists, demonstrates the vitality and continuity of Anishinaabe art across the Great Lakes and the US-Canada divide. It is also an invaluable opportunity to demonstrate how the Woodland School, as an artistic movement centered in Anishinaabe visual heritage, has likewise been a continuous element of Anishinaabe art in the United States, traveling through transnational networks of influence and inspiration despite having been primarily relegated to Canadian histories of Anishinaabe art.

Woodland School Expanded

The Woodland School is best known for its dynamic fusion of Indigenous imagery and stories with expressive color, figures made up of flat planar forms and compartmentalized X-ray-like organic interiors, and bold black interconnected lines of relational power. This energetic expression broke institutional and aesthetic boundaries, providing a language in modernist visual forms that could express Indigenous visual and oral heritage. Morrisseau is often identified as having pioneered the style, but the colorful bodies, wings, limbs, flowers, and celestial bodies that typically fill the works of this style, initially inspired by petroglyphs and imagery from birchbark scrolls, were also quickly adopted, adapted, and refined by many of his peers, most notably several of the group of artists who became known as the PNIAI. First gathering in the early 1970s around the organizing influence of Daphne Odjig, PNIAI was officially founded in 1973 with members Morrisseau, Odjig, Alex Janvier, Jackson Beardy, Eddy Cobiness, Joseph Sánchez, and Carl Ray.

While the majority of the founding artists were Anishinaabe, and its first incorporation application was revised and approved under the name "Anisinabe Professional Native Indian Artists Inc.," the members hailed from a variety of tribal backgrounds and both Canadian and US nationalities.[3] Like the innovations of Morrisseau, these artists combined modernist forms with Indigenous stories, politics, and worldviews in new ways at a moment when Indigenous cultural traditions were under great pressure from colonial institutions. Their example would prove crucial for opening the door to fine art

institutions for Indigenous artists. And while it is a misconception to identify all members of PNIAI with the Woodland School, and none of their work can be defined solely by this style, the prominence of this group helped establish the Woodland style among contemporary Indigenous artists of the Great Lakes, including Joshim Kakegamic, Saul Williams, Roy Thomas, and Blake Debassige.[4]

As Nêhiyaw (Plains Cree) scholar and curator Gerald McMaster further points out, the terms "Woodland School," "Legend Painting," and less commonly "Medicine Painting," are problematic designations, rooted in either the anthropological region-specific and romanticized connotation of the "woodlands," or the temporally rear-facing connotation of legends, both suggesting the style is limited to cultural traditions and lifeways of the past and of a specific place.[5] But artists from across the continent have since taken up the style originated by some of the PNIAI, adapting it into a malleable visual format that stands as one of the most significant Indigenous modernist movements of the twentieth century. The art historian Matthew Ryan Smith has identified contemporary iterations of the style and its expanded field as a "Neo-Woodland movement," noting the visual continuity with the Woodland School, but differentiating the content and context of successive generations.[6] Smith differentiates the Neo-Woodland style as evolving the Woodland style's "themes and subject matter into secular and digital expressions," suggesting that in place of spiritual or ancestral petroglyphic imagery is a transfer of the style to political and vernacular subject matter. Whereas the earlier Woodland School typically is distinguished by flat unmodulated planes of color within figures delineated by thick black lines, a stylistic expansion has included modulated or gradient blocks of color rather than single flat cells, outlines in colors other than black, and the incorporation of text or mixed media such as stencils, photo-collages, silkscreen imagery, and digital effects.

This distinction between phases of Woodland School art is valuable, though perhaps overwrought. The work of Morrisseau and his peers was often political, and to distinguish between "spiritual" and secular imagery by Woodland School artists would be to artificially distinguish between Indigenous worldviews of a universe filled with animate other-than-human beings and Euro-American understandings of spirituality or religion. For contemporary artists, the Woodland School remains an important means of maintaining Anishinaabe and Indigenous cultural identity, just as Morrisseau and his peers used art to revitalize the "ailing Ojibwa culture," as Elizabeth McLuhan once observed.[7] And as in the early days of the PNIAI, artists aligned with the Woodland School have always produced diverse and distinct work. What Smith accurately accounts for is the expansion of the Woodland School to commercial and souvenir design, new media, and to artists and communities outside of a strictly Anishinaabe cultural sphere. Many Haudenosaunee artists, for example, have adopted the style to their own artistic histories of the Six Nations. Alongside the diversity there is as much continuity within the style as breaks, through time as well as across arbitrary geographic borders.

US Borders

When Elizabeth McLuhan and Tom Hill's 1984 exhibition *Norval Morrisseau and the Emergence of the Image Makers* introduced the Woodland School, it not only positioned Morrisseau as a primary progenitor of the movement but also entrenched its history

Contemporary Anishinaabe Art: A Continuation

in a Canadian context. More recently, exhibitions such as the Smithsonian-organized blockbuster *Before and after the Horizon: Anishinaabe Artists of the Great Lakes* (2013–14) and the University of Minnesota's *Dreaming Our Futures: Ojibwe and Očhéthi Šakówiŋ Artists and Knowledge Keepers* (2024) have better recognized US-based Anishinaabe artists, including those working in the Woodland style, on both sides of the border. That the Woodland School originated in Canada is not in question, but a key element of its history has been the migration of its artists and influence southward. Exhibitions of Woodland School art were organized in the United States beginning in the 1970s, including an early exhibition of Woodland artists organized at Northwestern Michigan College, from which a large collection was acquired for what would later become the Dennos Museum Center.[8] The University of Minnesota's Tweed Museum likewise hosted an early exhibition of Carl Ray's work in 1972, and would continue to support the artists of the movement for decades to come.

The early support of the Woodland School by US institutions is unsurprising. Morrisseau's early career, for example, included multiple exhibitions and personal travels in the United States. A 1967 exhibition of Morrisseau's paintings organized by Herbert Schwarz at Galerie Cartier in Montreal traveled to the Art Gallery of Newport in Newport, Rhode Island, in 1968 before traveling to St. Paul de Vence in France. In the 1970s, Morrisseau embraced Eckankar, a new-age spiritual movement that combines Abrahamic and Eastern belief systems. For Morrisseau, the religion provided a visual and spiritual vocabulary for combining his artistic and shamanic practices beyond Anishinaabe protocols, such as sourcing the creative inspiration for his expanding imagery and color palette in what he referred to as

travels to the astral plane and "House of Invention." The spiritual home of Eckankar is headquartered in Minneapolis, Minnesota, likely further encouraging Morrisseau to look southward. Exhibitions in California in 1987, including *A Celebration of Contemporary Canadian Native Art* at the Southwest Museum in Los Angeles and a solo show at La Casa de la Raza in Santa Barbara, ensured his consistent exposure to an American audience alongside his work's prevalence in Minnesota and Michigan institutional collections.[9]

And while PNIAI should not be conflated with the Woodland School and was founded in Canada, its membership was a transnational, intertribal group. Eddy Cobiness, for example, was born in Minnesota and, though raised on Buffalo Point Reserve in Manitoba, served in the United States Army from 1954–57. Joseph Sánchez, likewise, was born in Trinidad, Colorado of Pueblo, Spanish, and German descent and was raised in Whiteriver, Arizona, on the White Mountain Apache Reservation. He served in the US Marine Corps before traveling to Canada, where he met Daphne Odjig in 1971. Several years later, in 1975, Sánchez moved to Arizona and formed several artist groups, including MARS (Movimiento Artistico del Rio Salado) and Ariztlan. The most stylistically distinct of the Indigenous Group of Seven, Sánchez's style veers more heavily toward the surrealistic, though work such as the sculpture *Fertility Totem* (1973), a carved nine-foot column of intermingled forms, demonstrates that his work nonetheless exists on a spectrum with the Woodland School style.

Sánchez would go on to work teaching and curating in Phoenix and Santa Fe, including positions held at the Phoenix Art Museum, Scottsdale Center for the Arts, and the Institute of American Indian Arts Museum of Contemporary Native Art, establishing a connection to the Woodland School in the Southwest.

Woodland Art: From the Southwest to Today

Figures like Joseph Sánchez are important nodes in the spread and surprising efflorescence of the Woodland School in the American Southwest. Similarly, the Institute of American Indian Arts (IAIA) in Santa Fe has from its inception served as a beacon for intertribal aesthetic exchange and experimentation that exposed many artists from Anishinaabe and other diverse backgrounds to the tenets of the Woodland School. Founded in 1962, the IAIA and its faculty such as Lloyd Kiva New, the Institute's founding art director, encouraged its students to draw on their own cultural traditions for innovation and to evolve new contemporary art forms, New famously stating that "the future of Indian art lies in the future, not in the past."[10]

The first decades of the IAIA included numerous American students of Anishinaabe descent, many of whom went on to have significant careers in the arts. Some, such as Joe Dudley (Chippewa) and Doug Hyde (Nez Perce/Assiniboine/Chippewa) found abstraction to offer productive creative possibilities, much as George Morrison had before them.[11] Others, like Alice Loiselle (Chippewa) and Shirley Brauker (Little River Band of Ottawa Indians) experimented with diverse styles, from Pop Art to Southwest-inspired forms. More, including brothers Doug, Barry, and Tom Coffin (Potawatomi/Creek), Anthony Gauthier (Menominee/Winnebago), and John Fox (Potawatomi), found a resonance in the Woodland School, producing abstract murals and figurative work that to different extents emulated the forms pioneered by Morrisseau and

his peers. Still other classmates from diverse tribal backgrounds, buoyed by the collaborative environment of cultural and artistic exchange at the school, emulated and adopted the Woodland style, likely intuiting its congruity with the IAIA's philosophy of utilizing new modernist forms while pursuing "cultural difference as the basis for creative expression."[12] David Montana (Tohono O'odham), for example, regularly incorporated Woodland motifs like the *Mishipeshu,* or Underwater Panther, in paintings such as the aptly titled *Ojibway Spirit* (1967).[13]

Today, a wide variety of US-based artists continue to practice in the Woodland style. Artists such as Michelle Defoe, Awanigiizhik Bruce, Moira Villiard, and Joe Geshick all work in some relation to the Woodland School, incorporating its principles and lessons to varying degrees. The often-psychedelic works of Jim Denomie and Frank Big Bear rest on the foundations of Woodland art, and elements of the style occur amid the pop-laden imagery of Star WallowingBull, Big Bear's son, particularly in the combination of beadwork-inspired floral motifs, abstract planes of geometric forms, and figures reconfigured into facets of color, as seen on the Statue of Liberty in his *Twinkle, Twinkle Little Star Now I Know Who You Really Are* (2003). And in the densely layered prints and paintings of Andrea Carlson, referents to the Woodland School recur amid the varied lexicon of imagery that fills her works. Like Morrisseau, she references petroglyphs such as those from the Agawa rock site (as in *Perpetual Care,* 2024, and *Red Exit,* 2020), as well as other Woodlands sources such as mica hands and talons from Hopewell sites, earthworks like the "Man Mound" of Baraboo, Wisconsin, and birchbark canoes and black ash baskets. Other works, like her painting *New Shroud* (2024), directly quote

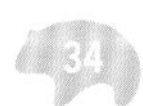

Morrisseau, overlaying moose sourced from one of his early paintings with the designs of l'assomption sashes, worn by Anishinaabeg and Métis in the nineteenth century. In so doing, she seeks to link the fake-Morrisseau forgery rings and false claims of Métis identity playing out in northeastern Canada and the United States as related threats to Indigenous sovereignty through acts of appropriation. Her *VORE* series references such acts of cultural consumption in terms of the Anishinaabe legendary figure of the *Windigo*, a fearsome cannibal and a recurring subject in Morrisseau's oeuvre. Even in postmodern conceptual maneuvers, then, Anishinaabe artists today find value in adapting cultural stories to contemporary visual idioms in order to express and understand pressing concerns of today—perhaps the defining feature of the Woodland School.

For contemporary Anishinaabe artists, the Woodland style, rather than being a "nostalgic or documentary exercise," as curator Carol Podedworny describes, can crystallize a state of being.[14] Frank Big Bear notes the complexity of Indigenous life far beyond the stereotype of living between two worlds: "Many Indians say they live in two worlds, but they actually have to live in more than two worlds. . . . The more worlds you live in, the better it is."[15] Woodland art emerged to visualize this complexity. Cherokee Nation/White Earth Ojibwe curator Lois Taylor Biggs draws on a related idea for the 2024 exhibition *Gagizhibaajiwan*, titled after the Anishinaabemowin word for a continuous swirling motion of water portending the emergence of the *Mishipeshu*.[16] In the churning of water, Biggs sees a concept for paradoxically holding duality, such as the duality of the *Mishipeshu* and its opposite the *Animikii*, or Thunderbird, or the duality of "two worlds," in constant tension. One of the featured artists in that exhibition, Zoey

Wood-Salomon (Odawa Nation, Wikwemikong Unceded Indian Reservation), focuses much of her work on the figure of the *Mishipeshu*, depicted in what Smith would identify as a "Neo-Woodland" style, rich with bright and metallic pigments, expressionistic surface treatments, and the linear silhouettes and subdivided forms indebted to Morrisseau and his peers. The Underwater Panthers frolic, dance, and do battle across Wood-Salomon's oeuvre, fluidly maneuvering in lake-filled landscapes and demonstrating the continued relevance of the forms for present-day Anishinaabe artists. The history of the Woodland School sustains its own paradox in productive tension: despite being a style that is accused of overly restricting and stereotyping Indigenous art within entrenched cultural heritage, it nonetheless remains mobile and relevant for a diversity of artists across space and time, exceeding its relegation to a singular telling of its history.

Endnotes

1. Greg Hill, *Norval Morrisseau: Shaman Artist* (Ottawa, Ontario: National Gallery of Canada, 2006).

2. Shanifa Nasser, "Toronto Gallery Cancels Show after Concerns Artist 'Bastardizes' Indigenous Art," CBC News, April 28, 2017, https://www.cbc.ca/news/canada/toronto/toronto-gallery-indigenous-art-cancels-amandapl-1.4091529. On the Morrisseau forgery ring, see Jordan Michael Smith, "Inside the Biggest Art Fraud in History," *Smithsonian Magazine* (March 2024), https://www.smithsonianmag.com/arts-culture/inside-biggest-art-fraud-history-180983692/; Norimitsu Onishi, "Vast Art Fraud, with Colorful Figures," *The New York Times*, January 28, 2025, A1.

3. Michelle LaVallee, *7: Professional Native Indian Artists Inc.* (Regina, Saskatchewan: MacKenzie Art Gallery, 2014), p. 118, fn. 1.

4. On the overidentification of the PNIAI with the Woodland School, see ibid., pp. 63–64.

5. Gerald McMaster, "The Anishinaabe Artistic

Consciousness," in *Before and after the Horizon: Anishinaabe Artists of the Great Lakes*, ed. David W. Penney and Gerald McMaster (Washington, DC, and New York: Smithsonian Institution's National Museum of the American Indian, 2013), pp. 84–85. On the nostalgia of the Woodland School denomination, see Carol Podedworny, "Revisiting the Woodland School: Art, History, Politics, the Woodland Legacy, and Jackson Beardy," in *Jackson Beardy: Life's Work*, ed. Shirley Madill (Winnipeg: Winnipeg Art Gallery, 1994), p. 116.

6. Matthew Ryan Smith, "The Neo-Woodland Movement," *First American Art Magazine* (Spring 2021), pp. 38–45.

7. Elizabeth McLuhan, "The Emergence of the Image Makers," in Elizabeth McLuhan and Tom Hill, *Norval Morrisseau and the Emergence of the Image Makers* (Toronto: Art Gallery of Ontario, 1984), p. 49.

8. See "A Style All Our Own: Canadian Woodland Artists," Dennos Museum Center, September 27, 2024–September 28, 2025, https://www. dennosmuseum.org/art/now-on-view/canadian-woodland-artists.html.

9. On Morrisseau's US travels, see Carmen Robertson, *Mythologizing Norval Morrisseau: Art and the Colonial Narrative in the Canadian Media* (Winnipeg: University of Manitoba Press, 2016), pp. 123, 130–31.

10. Lloyd Kiva New, "A Proposal for an Exploratory Workshop for Talented Younger Indians," October 15, 1959, University of Arizona, Lloyd H. New Papers, Institute of American Indian Art Archives, Santa Fe, New Mexico, n.p.

11. Doug Hyde's work, such as his sculpture *Sun and Moon Gods* (1967), frequently combines abstract forms with an X-ray internal style reminiscent of the Woodland School. On abstract work by Anishinaabe artists at the IAIA such as Hyde, Dudley, and Alice Loiselle, see *Action/Abstraction Redefined: Modern Native Art, 1940s to 1970s* (Santa Fe: IAIA Museum of Contemporary Native Arts, 2018).

12. Tatiana Lomahaftewa-Singer and Ryan S. Flahive, "Introduction to the IAIA Museum of Contemporary Native Arts Collection and the IAIA Archives," in *Making History: IAIA Museum of Contemporary Native Arts*, ed. Nancy Marie Mithlo (Albuquerque: University of New Mexico Press, 2020), pp. 5–10.

13. Rick Hill, *Creativity Is Our Tradition: Three Decades of Contemporary Indian Art at the Institute of American Indian Arts* (Santa Fe: Institute of American Indian and Alaska Native Culture and Arts Development, 1992).

14. Podedworny, "Revisiting the Woodland School," p. 116.

15. Frank Big Bear, quoted in David W. Penney, "Water, Earth, Sky," in *Before and after the Horizon: Anishinaabe Artists of the Great Lakes*, ed. David W. Penney and Gerald McMaster (Washington, DC, and New York: Smithsonian Institution's National Museum of the American Indian, 2013), pp. 34–35.

16. Lois Taylor Biggs, *Gagizhibaajiwan*, Center for Native Futures, Chicago, Illinois, June 15–December 14, 2024, https://www.centerfornativefutures.org/13035375-gagizhibaajiwan. See also Lois Taylor Biggs, "*Gagizhibaajiwan,* or Living with Paradox," *Forging,* April 30, 2024, https://forgeproject.com/forging/gagizhibaajiwan-or-living-with-paradox.

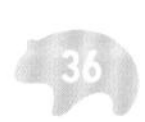

Contemporary Anishinaabe Art: A Continuation

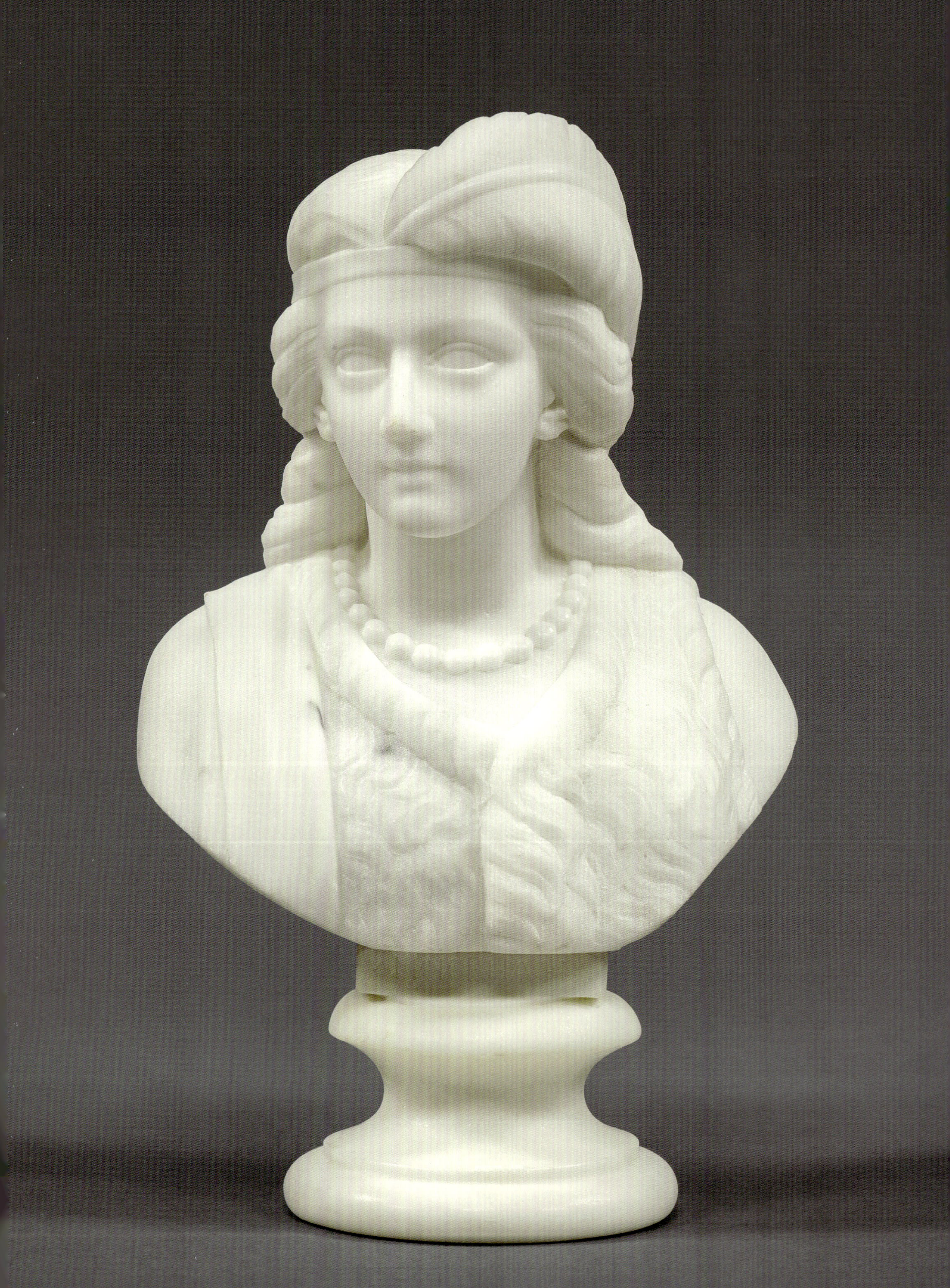

Mary Edmonia Lewis, Longfellow, and the Art of Cultural Negotiation

Shawnya L. Harris, PhD

Mary Edmonia Lewis occupies a singular place in the history of American art, not only as a pioneering sculptor of African American and Anishinaabe descent, but also as an artist whose work represents an early assertion of Indigenous identity within the European neoclassical tradition. Her marble busts of *Hiawatha* and *Minnehaha,* created in 1868, reflect both the limitations and possibilities of Native representation in the nineteenth century, offering an alternative to the romanticized, colonial narratives that often defined Indigenous figures in Western art. By depicting these characters from Henry Wadsworth Longfellow's *The Song of Hiawatha* (1855), Lewis engaged in a form of cultural negotiation, using the visual language of classical sculpture to elevate her subjects at a time when their presence in fine art was largely shaped by outsider perspectives. Her work anticipates the concerns of contemporary Anishinaabe artists, who continue to challenge conventional ideas about their art, identity, and representation. Seeing Lewis's work in exhibitions such as *Contemporary Anishinaabe Art: A Continuation* not only positions Lewis inspirationally but also reasserts the challenges of Native representation today.

Mary Edmonia Lewis's marble busts of *Hiawatha* and *Minnehaha,* housed in the collection of the Detroit Institute of Arts (DIA), are not only skillful examples of nineteenth-century neoclassical sculpture but also profound statements on identity, cultural legacy, and artistic resistance. Created during the height of the United States' post–Civil War period, these works encapsulate the complex negotiations of race, gender, and national identity that marked Lewis's career. They also highlight her ability to navigate the largely European tradition of classical sculpture, while infusing it with the cultural histories, both real and imagined, of her Anishinaabe heritage.

Born in 1844/45 in Greenbush, New York, to a mother of Mississauga Ojibwe descent and a father of Afro-Caribbean descent, Lewis's upbringing was one marked by both tragedy and resilience. Her parents passed away when she was very young, and she was raised by her mother's relatives, learning skills such as moccasin making, which instilled in her a deep connection to her Indigenous roots. By the time she was fifteen, Lewis enrolled at Oberlin College in Ohio, one of the first institutions in the United States to admit African American and female students and known for its progressive stance on education and abolitionism. While there, she studied various subjects including literature and art. The environment at Oberlin introduced her to intellectual and cultural ideas that would influence her work, including the importance of social justice through the chance visits and lectures of notable activists such as Frederick

Opposite: Mary Edmonia Lewis (Mississauga Ojibwe; ca. 1844/45–1907), *Minnehaha*, Detroit Institute of Arts, Museum Purchase, Ernest and Rosemarie Kanzler Foundation Fund

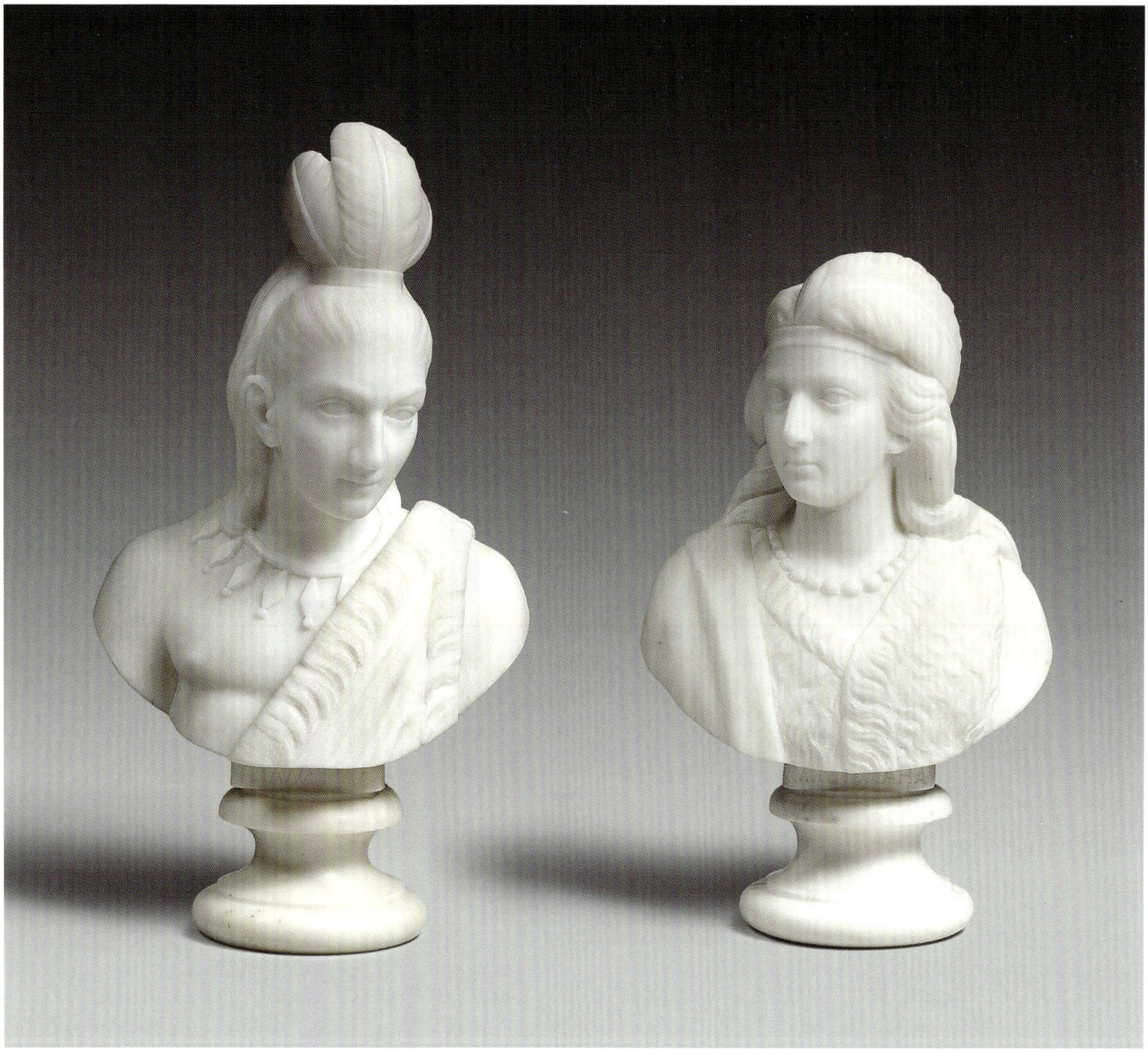

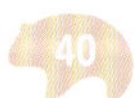

Left: Mary Edmonia Lewis (Mississauga Ojibwe; ca. 1844/45–1907), *Hiawatha*, 1868. Marble, 13 3/4 × 7 3/4 × 5 1/2 in. (34.9 × 19.7 × 14 cm). The Metropolitan Museum of Art, New York, Morris K. Jesup and Friends of the American Wing Funds, 2015 (2015.287.1)

Right: Mary Edmonia Lewis (Mississauga Ojibwe; ca. 1844/45–1907), *Minnehaha,* 1868. Marble, 11 5/8 × 7 1/4 × 4 7/8 in. (29.5 × 18.4 × 12.4 cm). The Metropolitan Museum of Art, New York, Morris K. Jesup and Friends of the American Wing Funds, 2015 (2015.287.2)

Douglass. However, Lewis's time at Oberlin ended in controversy due to racial bias.[1]

Despite the difficulties she faced at Oberlin, her time there was instrumental in her development, and it was likely at Oberlin that Lewis first encountered the works of Henry Wadsworth Longfellow, whose 1855 poem *The Song of Hiawatha* would later inspire some of her most iconic sculptures. After leaving Oberlin, Lewis moved to Boston in 1863, where she began her artistic career in earnest. She worked under the mentorship of sculptor Edward Augustus Brackett, learning the technical skills of sculpture and developing her artistic style. It was also in Boston where Lewis had the patronage of abolitionists, who promoted her talent and eventually funded her passage to Europe. Her early experiences in these diverse environments became the foundation for her later artistic decisions, which consistently

Contemporary Anishinaabe Art: A Continuation

engaged with questions of cultural identity and the broader challenges of racial representation in art.

By the time she arrived in Rome in the mid-1860s, Lewis was quickly establishing herself as an artist, seeking both the freedom and recognition that could not be easily obtained for a woman of color in the United States. In Rome, she was surrounded by other expatriate women sculptors, including Harriet Hosmer and Anne Whitney, whose works were shaped by similar intersections of race, gender, and artistic ambition. Lewis's now iconic Emancipation Proclamation–inspired sculpture, *Forever Free* (1867), began conceptually in Rome with Lewis seeking out subscribers such as writer and abolitionist Lydia Maria Child for its completion. It was in Rome that Lewis began sculpting her busts of *Hiawatha* and *Minnehaha,* characters drawn from Henry Wadsworth Longfellow's *The Song of Hiawatha.* The poem had become a major cultural phenomenon in the United States by the mid- to late 1850s. Lewis was one of several fine artists and illustrators to embrace the story for its visual representation, mimicking various scenes and allusions. In the prior decade, for example, printmakers Currier and Ives published seven lithographs by Louis Maurer, and it is possible that Lewis borrowed from this or similar imagery.[2]

Longfellow's epic poem was based on a blend of oral traditions from Native American peoples, filtered through the lens of Romantic nationalism and ethnocentric bias. The poem's fictional narrative follows the life of the heroic Hiawatha, a leader of the Ojibwe people, and his tragic romance with the Dakota woman Minnehaha. The poem's enormous popularity made its characters well-known symbols of Native American life, though Longfellow's portrayal of these figures was more allegorical than historically

accurate. His vision of the noble, romanticized Native American warrior and the suffering lover was shaped by the broader cultural anxieties of a nation grappling with the consequences of its expansionist policies and the displacement of Native peoples.

While Longfellow's work was applauded by many, it was also critiqued for its "noble savage" portrayal of Indigenous groups. Such stereotypes erased the complex realities of Indigenous life, reducing it to a mythical and distant past. Yet, for Lewis, the figures of Hiawatha and Minnehaha represented an opportunity to reshape the narrative of Native American identity—one that was both intimately personal and publicly resonant.

In addition to Indigenous subjects, Lewis also produced busts of Longfellow himself. Longfellow had been a professor in the modern languages program at Harvard University for several years, retiring a year before *The Song of Hiawatha* was published. Longfellow had visited Rome in 1869, and published accounts suggest that Lewis caught a glance of the author on the streets and published images may have supplemented her portrayal.[3] Additionally, Longfellow sat for Lewis. The Harvard University Art Museum example, done in 1871, was described as "colossal" when various newspapers from Hartford to San Francisco ran ads requesting subscriptions for its commission in marble two years before.[4] The enormity of this bust runs parallel to Longfellow's stature as a popular literary icon, yet its commission would follow that of the characters from the poem.

Lewis's busts of Hiawatha and Minnehaha reflect her careful attention to both technical skill and creative nuance. In *Hiawatha,* the figure's slightly downward gaze and composed features suggest focus and intensity, in her depiction of this popular

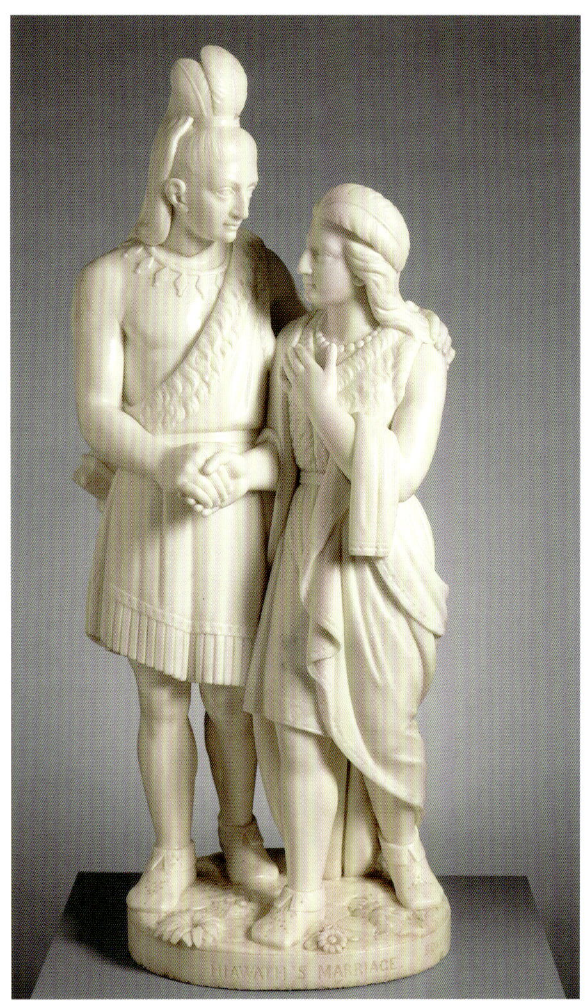

Left: Mary Edmonia Lewis (Mississauga Ojibwe; ca. 1844/45–1907), *Hiawatha's Marriage,* 1871, marble. Cincinnati Art Museum, on loan in loving memory of Drs. George and Sarah Hale, L11.1993

Opposite: Mary Edmonia Lewis (Mississauga Ojibwe; ca. 1844/45–1907), *The Old Arrow Maker,* ca. 1872, marble, 21 1/2 × 13 5/8 × 13 3/8 in. (54.5 × 34.5 × 34.0 cm.), Smithsonian American Art Museum, Gift of Mr. and Mrs. Norman Robbins, 1983.95.179

symbolizes the bridging of cultural divides and the harmonious coexistence of different tribes, echoing Longfellow's romanticized vision of Native American life. Lewis's portrayal emphasizes tenderness and mutual respect, challenging the stereotypes of Indigenous peoples as either noble savages or vanishing figures. It also is suggestive of an adoption of Victorian ideals around chastity and marriage.[5]

In *The Old Arrow Maker,* Lewis explored the relationship between father and daughter, a theme that underscores the generational transmission of wisdom and cultural values. The father, who is depicted as the skilled craftsman making arrowheads, is pictured alongside his daughter seated on a stone as she weaves a mat. They stare toward the impending future, absent to the viewer, in the form of Hiawatha whose presence is evidenced by the roe at the feet of the two, which represents his offering for the hand of the maiden Minnehaha. Lewis's medium of marble was closely associated with the European neoclassical tradition, used for busts of historical figures and mythological subjects. By using a European tradition that had long been dominated by depictions of white male heroes, she reasserted the agency of Indigenous peoples, placing them on equal footing within the visual language of Western art. Lewis's *Song of Hiawatha* busts of Minnehaha and Hiawatha, and indeed all her sculptures, were shaped by her awareness of the political dynamics of racial identity in her time. The popularity of *The Song of*

literary character. Minnehaha, meanwhile, turns her head gently over her right shoulder, her directed gaze and serene expression capturing a moment of wistful tenderness. By highlighting the emotional and intellectual complexity of her subjects, Lewis challenges stereotypes that cast Indigenous people as either noble or vanishing.

Prior to the busts, Lewis created larger group sculptures inspired by Longfellow's poem, including *Hiawatha's Marriage* (1871) and *The Old Arrow Maker* (1866). These works expanded on the themes of unity, love, and cultural transmission central to *The Song of Hiawatha. Hiawatha's Marriage* captures the union of Hiawatha, an Ojibwe warrior, and Minnehaha, a Dakota woman. This sculpture

Contemporary Anishinaabe Art: A Continuation

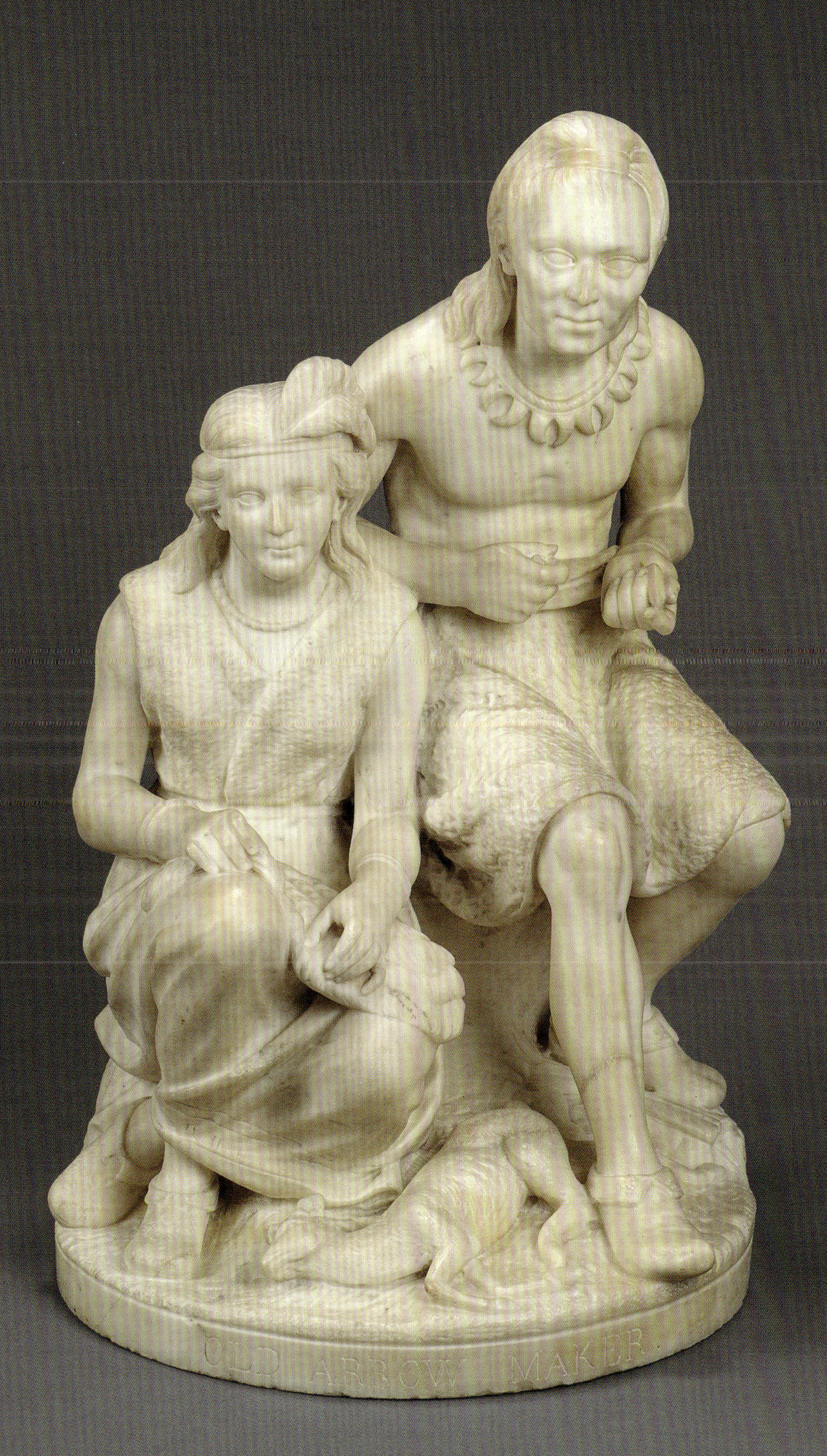

OLD ARROW MAKER

Hiawatha and the general interest in Native American subjects during the late nineteenth century allowed Lewis to create works that were simultaneously part of the dominant artistic market and a direct challenge to it. Through these works, she demanded that Black and Native American people be seen as complex, dignified, and deserving of artistic representation—at a time when both groups were often marginalized and misunderstood.

The dignity and introspection of Lewis's subjects countered the stereotypical depictions of Native Americans as either subjugated or uncivilized. In this sense, the busts stand as both artistic achievements and political statements about the possibility of Indigenous presence and survival within a national mythology that had otherwise consigned them to the margins. The busts are at once commemorative in nature but functional for instilling fresh visual insight in a three-dimensional form to a mythic narrative. Lewis's *Hiawatha* and *Minnehaha* sculptures represent more than just technical achievements in marble. They are part of a larger effort to redefine the possibilities of representation in art, asserting the dignity, complexity, and resilience of both Black and Native American peoples. Lewis's work occupies a unique space within the history of American sculpture, operating within and against the confines of European neoclassicism to create works that are as politically significant as they are aesthetically accomplished. In doing so, she not only challenged the racial and gendered boundaries of nineteenth-century art but also set the stage for future generations of artists to continue the struggle for visibility, representation, and cultural pride. By reimagining figures from *The Song of Hiawatha* as subjects capable of sophistication in the marble medium, Lewis expanded the possibilities of artistic

representation and offered a counternarrative to the dominant cultural myths of her time.

As *Contemporary Anishinaabe Art: A Continuation* demonstrates, Lewis's practice was not an anomaly but part of an enduring lineage of Anishinaabe creativity—one that persists today in a wide array of artistic media, from sculpture and painting to beadwork, birchbark artistry, and digital design. By situating Lewis within this broader tradition, the exhibition reclaims her as an essential figure in the evolving story of Anishinaabe art, bridging the historical and contemporary in ways that reaffirm the vitality of Native artistic expression.

Endnotes

1. In 1862, she faced accusations of poisoning two of her classmates, a charge that sparked a highly publicized and racially charged trial. Although Lewis was acquitted, the incident profoundly disrupted her studies. Shortly afterward, she was accused of stealing art supplies, leading to her departure from Oberlin before completing her degree. This story has been repeated multiple times in the literature on the artist, based largely on the account from her attorney John Mercer Langston, who alludes to the trial. See Geoffrey T. Blodgett, "John Mercer Langston and the Case of Edmonia Lewis: Oberlin, 1862," *Journal of Negro History* 53, no. 3 (1968): 201–18.

2. Kirsten Pai Buick, *Child of the Fire: Mary Edmonia Lewis and the Problem of Art History's Black and Indian Subject* (Durham, NC: Duke University Press, 2010), pp. 117–18.

3. Romare Bearden and Harry Henderson, *A History of African-American Artists: From 1792 to the Present* (New York: Pantheon Books, 1993), p. 70.

4. See, for example, *National Anti-Slavery Standard*, June 12, 1869, p. 3.

5. Buick, *Child of the Fire*, pp. 125–27.

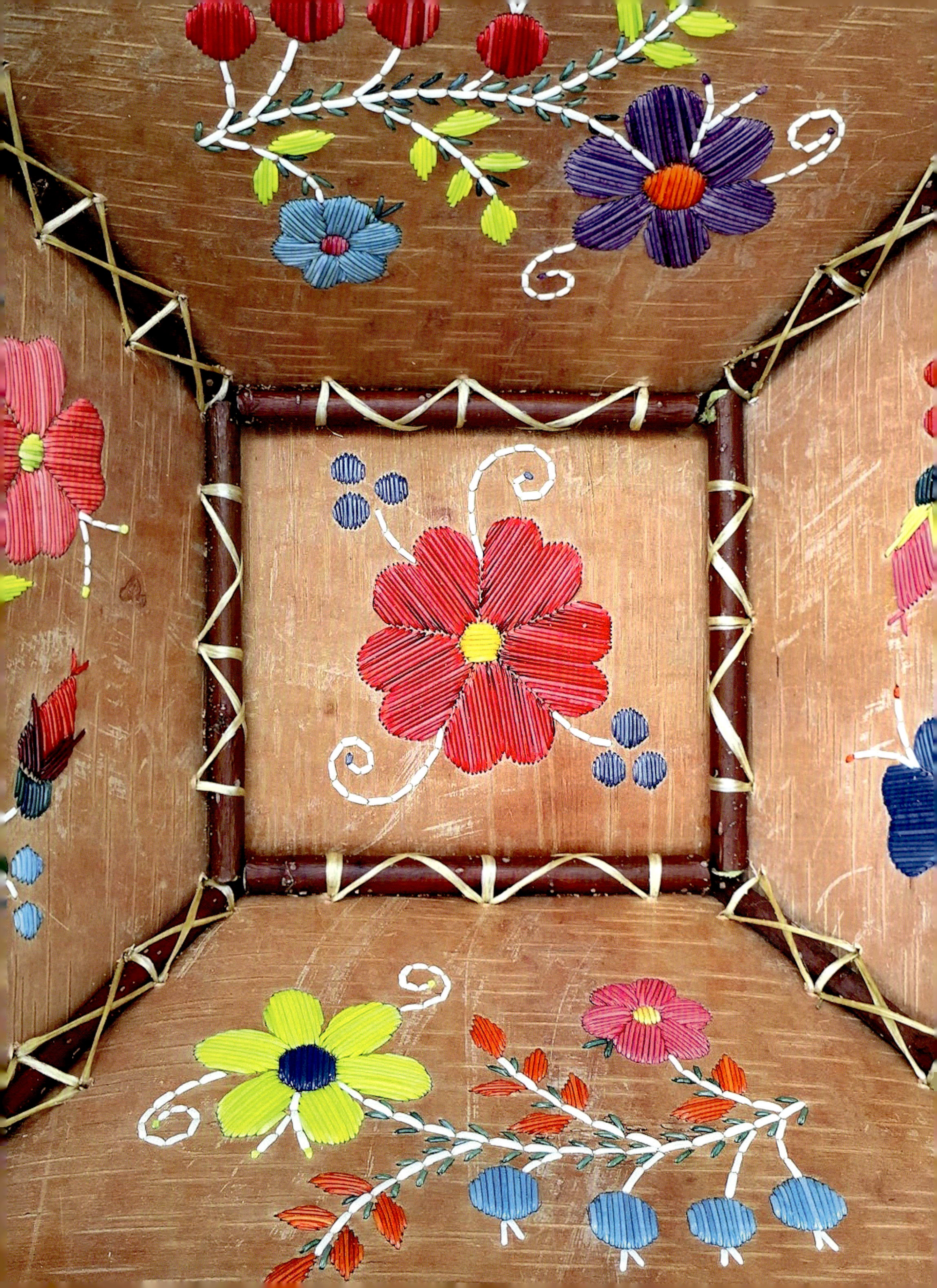

Honoring *Wiigwaas:* A Spiraling Anishinaabe Continuance

Kendra Greendeer, PhD (Ho-Chunk Nation; Red Cliff Band of Lake Superior Chippewa [Descendant])

"Birchbark and the culture goes hand in hand." —Pat Kruse[1]

No artistic medium sounds as authentically Great Lakes to me as the sound of birchbark peeling away from the tree. The look of *wiigwaas,* or birchbark, commands an ancestral presence within its textured papery surface with inside layers that expose various shades of brown. It symbolically and spiritually offers warmth in its beautifully imperfect features of parallel asymmetrical lines that glorify the humility of nature and Indigenous people. It carries a spirit while evoking the beauty of the woods around Lake Superior.[2]

The geographical range of paper birch or white birch growing within the United States is primarily in the Northeastern and Great Lakes regions and is intertwined with the culture of the Ojibwe, who have inhabited this area from time immemorial, and continues to provide numerous gifts to the Anishinaabe. Birchbark acts as an ancestral teacher, our first canvas, a vessel, and shelter, and through its use contemporary Anishinaabe artists are honoring those who came before them and securing their teachings for the future. While many Indigenous arts recognize the coalescence of various periods, the art form that uses birchbark disrupts the parameters of "traditional" or "contemporary" Native art due to the spiral temporality that exists within it.[3]

While Indigenous understandings of time often consider a circle or cyclical nature, the spiral allows for change or recognizing previous events at the same time as honoring our connection to cycles like the seasons and the ways in which we exist within a place. The spiral acknowledges the teachings learned through honoring ancestors and the importance of ensuring that we preserve them for future generations. Indigenous scholar Kyle P. Whyte (Citizen Potawatomi Nation) discusses spiraling time with the Anishinaabe expression *aanikoobijigan,* meaning ancestor and descendent at the same time, in his essay "Indigenous Science (Fiction) for the Anthropocene: Ancestral Dystopias and Fantasies of Climate Crises."[4] Whyte elaborates on our roles as participants within these varied spaces of time: "The spiraling narratives unfold through our interacting with, responding to and reflecting on the actual or potential actions and viewpoints of our ancestors and descendants. They unfold as continuous dialogues. The narratives also involve the dramas related to our own transformations as we move from being descendants to ancestors through our own lives."[5]

Within a birch tree there is the physical transformation and growth; however, because

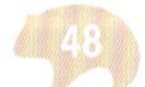

it and those interacting with it engage in actions of our ancestors, we (human and tree) are entangling ourselves within a spiraling time.

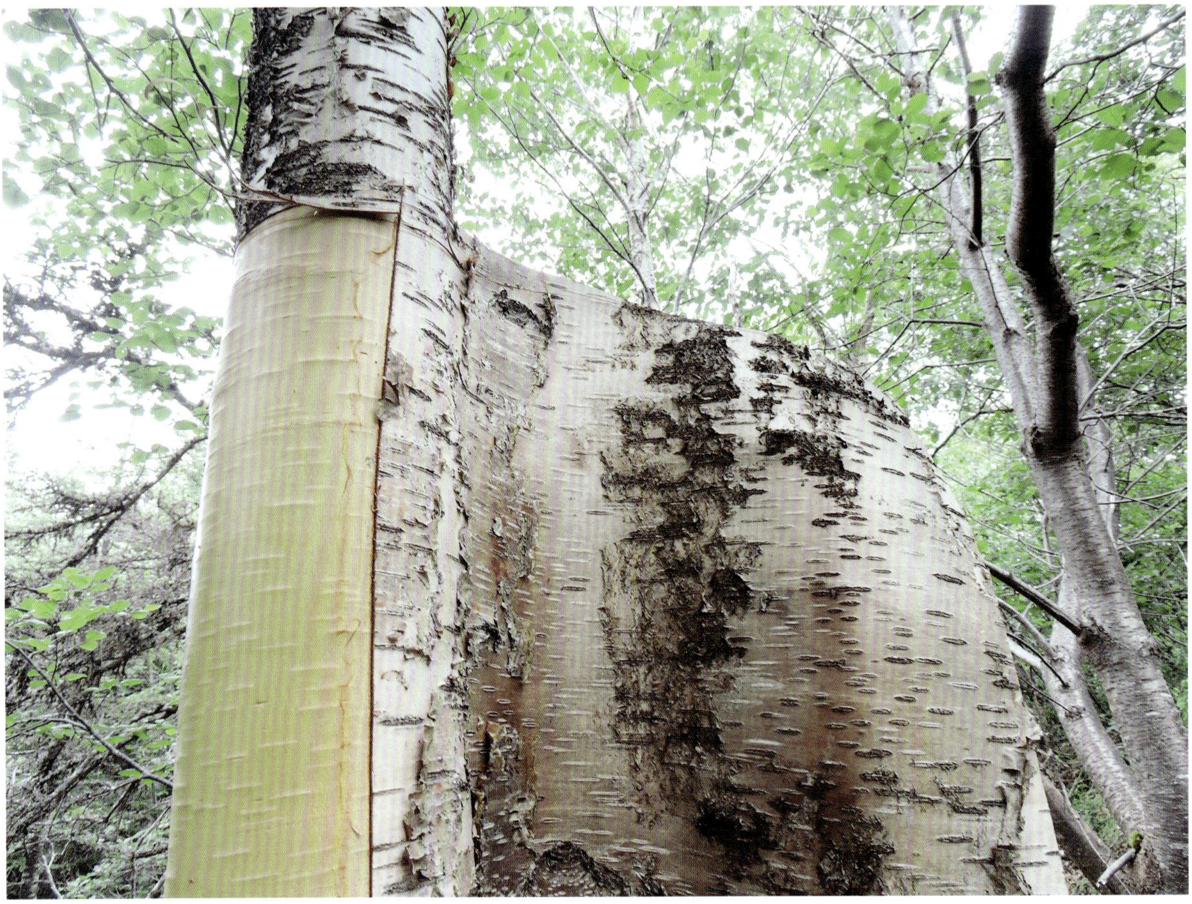

We are thus inquiring *with* ancestors and other living beings when it comes to stories that are a part of oral histories. A character often mentioned within Anishinaabe storytelling and oral history is Nanabozho, a trickster spirit. Anishinaabe stories recount the history of *wiigwaas* in which Nanabozho sought refuge, in a hollow birch tree, from angry thunderbird parents after Nanabozho harmed a nest of baby thunderbirds.

> The thunderbirds gave up their attack, knowing that they could not get to [Nanabozho] through the birchbark. After the thunderbirds left, [Nanabozho]

came out of the log and proclaimed that the birch tree would forever protect and benefit the people. [Nanabozho] made short marks on the birchbark to commemorate the sharp claws of the thunderbirds that almost killed him. The thunderbirds put "pictures" of their babies on the bark so that the sacrifice of their children would not be forgotten.[6]

These markings on the outside of the birch tree commemorate this event according to the stories and highlight how this tree will attend to Anishinaabeg (the Anishinaabe people's) needs.

Wiigwaas provided the necessary foundations for Anishinaabe survival. The outside of homes were covered in layers of it, which also provided the outer layer of canoes. Because

Contemporary Anishinaabe Art: A Continuation

of its pliability and naturally antimicrobial properties, its material is still utilized after the process of boiling maple sap down to maple sugar, among many other uses and needs. The entire tree offers medicinal use from its birth to its death. Due to its generous nature, Anishinaabeg show great care in harvesting and preparing birchbark.

The use of harvested bark varies since it is a material intertwined with health, foodways, origin stories, and identity. It serves as a record keeper for the generations of Anishinaabeg who have learned from the visual stories they hold. Birchbark scrolls were used as the first paper to document or help record what needed to be remembered. Despite settler interruptions in the continued use of *wiigwaas* art forms, it still serves the same purpose of memorializing how ancestral Anishinaabe made cultural items.

Continuing Anishinaabe lineages and learning from the items our ancestors left behind has been instrumental in contemporary birchbark artists' practice. These practices reflect on the significance of placemaking incorporated within the motifs that decorate the outside surface, the representation of stories of significance depicted on birch pieces, and the role birchbark canoes had in both migration and maintaining a connection throughout Anishinaabe territories. There is a spiraling temporality between Anishinaabe and *wiigwaas*. This relation goes beyond a tangible sensory experience into one of a spiralic embodied spiritual space. Here, we should acknowledge the role of dreams and dreaming in the connection between person and spirit.[7] Many of our first teachings that allowed for such a medium to be utilized were the teachings that came to Indigenous people through dreaming—a realm where

temporality transcends linear understanding to spiraling time. And since the process of harvesting birchbark today is the same as the ancestral practices used to harvest it, the ways in which birchbark artistic practice was attained and continues through spiralic encounters is derived from the spiritual realm in the sense noted above. This same metaphysical understanding continues in the ways Anishinaabe interact with land.

Birchbark artists featured in this exhibition, including Wayne Valliere, Ronald J. Paquin, Wanesia Misquadace, Pat Kruse, and Terri Hom / Binesikwe, consider their relationship to the materials by recognizing the surrounding environment and when it is an appropriate and respectful time to harvest. There is an honoring of the landscape that *wiigwaas* exists within. Along with knowing where one may find birch trees, there is a consideration that those harvesting from a living tree only collect a portion so as not to kill the tree and not to cut too deeply so as not to disrupt its ability to regrow. The tree regenerates its layers of birch as long as it's harvested with care and during appropriate periods. An offering of *asemaa* (tobacco) is also a part of this process, providing appreciation and respect to the spirit that the material is still connected to. Even with the availability of the tools of today, few are utilized, and so this ancestrally gifted act is not altered. This continued traditional harvesting practice illustrates a form of art making that connects the Anishinaabe artists and *wiigwaas* with an enduring bond.

As art history and museums contend with the timeframe for situating Indigenous artistic practices rooted in culture, materials like birchbark are often just labeled as "traditional" with no acknowledgment of the role this material and its continued use play in contemporary practice and contemporary

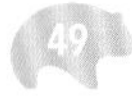

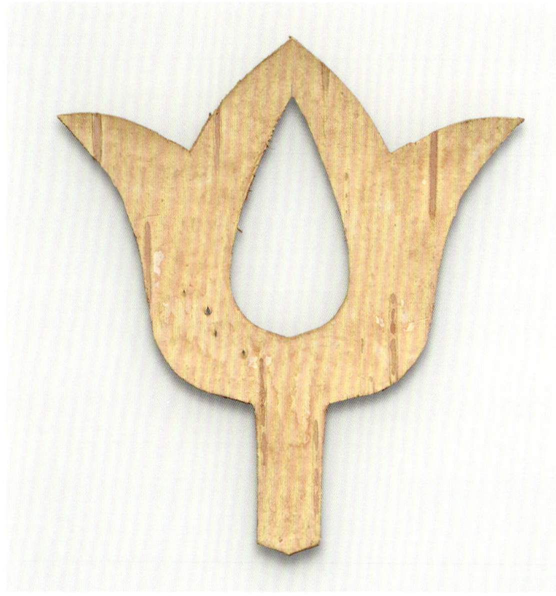

culture. Not only is the material relegated to the past, but the practices involved with and the relationship between the birchbark and the artists and their community is also treated as historical—which couldn't be further from the truth. In addition to looking at birchbark through a narrow art-historical lens, there is a bias in arts institutions that has yet to accept Anishinaabe and Great Lakes art forms as fully being a part of contemporary Native American art.[8]

In birchbark art making, a spiral temporality is recognized in its continued use. So, does this medium not entitle it to a fluid timeframe, one in which it can be traditional or contemporary, or both?[9] The practice of honoring the agency of a material based on its legacy and connection to Anishinaabeg is maintained (for contemporary culture) through the temporal layers of Indigenous artistic practice immersed in Indigenous placemaking symbolized within *wiigwaas.*[10] Additionally, the presence of ancestor-made works are contributing to and sharing their spirit within the present.

Those who harvest birchbark pay attention

to the seasonal cues that suggest it is time to harvest. These seasonal changes force the gatherer to pay attention to other plant and animal relations to know when the birch can offer a piece of bark without harming the tree.[11] The ancestral connections to this material and its spirit are still recognized within Anishinaabe arts and can be seen in the approach to the construction of the objects made from birchbark. Many artists value *wiigwaas* agency by allowing the object to speak: a piece of birchbark that has been harvested may bend a certain way, a way that does not suit the needs of the artist and so does not want to be manipulated as the artist intended. It is thus used for something else.

Today, this continued connection and ability to engage with birchbark are represented by the works of Anishinaabe artists. Contemporary birchbark works often feature designs and are etched, bitten, quilled, or layered atop a base or foundation of *wiigwaas.* Designs reinforce the connection of foliage, animals, or *doodem* figures onto the canvas-like being of *wiigwaas.* Etched designs are created with the thicker spring-harvested bark, and often bone is used to carve into the layer—echoing practices that have existed for millennia.

Birchbark canoe maker Wayne Valliere (Lac du Flambeau Band of Lake Superior Chippewa) has exercised his cultural and artistic practice in various mediums throughout his life. His most known medium is birchbark canoes, which incorporate narrative etching designs that exemplify an understanding of the land and its life. Valliere's father used paper grocery bags to cut patterns to

Contemporary Anishinaabe Art: A Continuation

use in birchbark work, and Wayne Valliere continues this method.[12] This same approach to communal teaching continues in his current practice, in which he works with youth to teach them how to construct a canoe, which in parallel teaches this art form that allows for community healing through cultural practices while also reinvigorating canoe traditions within Lac du Flambeau and beyond. The site at which Valliere's canoes are launched is the same place his ancestors used, thus incorporating a reenactment of the spiraling continuum of Anishinaabe creation stories. Valliere has stated: "The greatest blessing I have as a Native artist is having the opportunity to be in the forest harvesting materials. It keeps me in balance with her as well as remembering the teachings of my elders."[13]

Valliere's father left behind traces of that tradition for his son to reignite in the form of narrative cutouts of recyclable material. Recognizing the disconnect and interruptions Anishinaabeg faced during the cultural genocide and era of boarding schools, which sought to eradicate Indigenous languages and traditions, some of the efforts made by a new generation offer an opportunity for personal healing while rekindling a connection to ancestral heritage.[14]

One such artist is Ronald J. Paquin (Sault Ste. Marie Tribe of Chippewa), a self-taught artist specializing in birchbark and antler mediums, mainly in the form of canoes and baskets. Paquin has constructed several canoes since he first learned the art while working at the Museum of Ojibwa Culture in St. Ignace, Michigan, in the mid-1980s.[15] While he is versed in an art form with long ancestral ties, applying pitch, layers of birchbark, and sown spruce roots as a contemporary Anishinaabe, Paquin invokes a sculptural understanding of material enviable of any modern artist.

Paquin is an active teacher and shares his skills with children, adults, apprentices, and grandchildren.[16] He explains: "Birchbark canoes are no longer used for survival, but understanding their value will help connect our ancestors to our grandchildren in a way that encourages respect for our natural environment, respect for our traditions, and respect for ourselves."[17] In this active conservation of Indigenous knowledge, Paquin recognizes the interconnectedness of creating cultural artworks from the land and our continued self-understanding.

While embedded within tradition, the birchbark canoe is a sculptural work of art. These works often include etching motifs and subtle patterns in their construction as well as seams painted in pitch. Valliere notes that "canoe building is the apex of Anishinaabe crafts."[18] Such sculptures incorporate so many elements to master, which include cultural value and Indigenous knowledge as well as community engagement. Valliere explains the aspects of time we interact with by our movements in the canoe: "The front is called *niigaan jiimaan,* which means the future. And the stern of the canoe is *ishkiyaon jimaan,* meaning the past. Ripples of water, that's the past."[19] Thus, the action of rowing a canoe already encompasses elements of spiral temporality within it.

Birchbark is present throughout Ojibwe food sovereignty practices, which are the individual and community ways to preserve and continue ancestral foods and foodways. For example, the canoe is used for fishing and can move easily through wild rice growing areas. The shape of the front of the canoe aids in the minimal disturbance of the plants, while birchbark trays are used for winnowing. During maple sugar processing, birch sticks are used to stir the cooking maple syrup, and after it is cooked down to sugar, birchbark cones are used in its shaping. Birchbark is used to make baskets that could hold anything, including food. Historically, many of these containers had designs, some of which acted as labels for what they stored.[20]

The birchbark container is a vessel constructed similarly to our ancestor-made works and those that have incorporated other mediums into its construction. Wanesia Misquadace (Fond du Lac Band of Lake Superior Chippewa in Minnesota) is a jeweler, basket maker, and birchbark biting artist. While Misquadace currently resides in a region with no birchbark, she visits a birchbark area once a year to gather, and this period brings back memories shared with her grandmother, mother, and son when they gather berries and bark together. She explains: "It's my time to heal and share new memories that are told in my sculpture metal baskets. . . . My great-great-grandfather, Chief Misquadace, chose not to sign a treaty that would sell timber rights. Intrinsically, it's the DNA of our people, the strength and the stories that are told; those connections and bonds can never be broken."[21] In her birchbark containers reinforced in silver, she recreates and decorates ancestral containers into a material form secured for a future generational connection.

Misquadace incorporates the oldest form of patternmaking, birchbark biting. *Mazinibaganjigan*,[22] or birchbark bitings, also referred to as "transparencies" or "chews," acted as original patterns for quills and, later, beads.[23] The process of stripping thin interior sheets and folding them numerous times to create a pattern requires the artist to carefully bite as they visualize the design. The result of the defined bites will not be fully realized until the sheet is carefully pulled apart to expose the pattern, creating a bitten pattern that is a work of art.

This historical relationship to quilled birchbark and patternmaking is practiced by Pat Kruse (Red Cliff Band of Lake Superior Chippewa; Mille Lacs Band of Ojibwe [Descent]), who creates birchbark "paintings" (two-dimensional layered and sewn narrative images) and baskets with designs based on local wildlife. Within the sinew-sewn birchbark cutout compositions, Kruse highlights *wiigwaas* kin, other beings, and narratives through a flattened birchbark that brings out a canvas-like quality. Aside from cutting out patterns, he does not manipulate the material in any way. Incorporating the various shades that naturally occur allows one to recognize the beauty and qualities of the multiple layers found in birchbark. He states: "There's no perfection . . . things crack, things break, things happen . . . and it's like you're trying to perfect something that's an imperfect thing."[24] This humility reflected in birchbark reminds us of the beauty in imperfection. The *wiigwaas* works he designs are art rooted in the Great Lakes, the northern United States, and the Anishinaabeg's significant connection to this being, birchbark. Kruse also recreates older-style baskets inspired by works found in museum collections. While he may still consider himself a novice after practicing this art form for decades, Kruse's exploration of *wiigwaas* into three-dimensional and two-dimensional surfaces that he calls paintings suggests an understanding of birchbark that commemorates ancestrally made works.

In 2018, Kruse and apprentice Terri Hom / Binesikwe (Lac Courte Oreilles Band of Lake Superior Chippewa) visited the Bess Bower Dunn Museum of Lake County in Libertyville, Illinois, to view historic works featuring birchbark. They found a birchbark cradle in the museum's collection during this visit. This

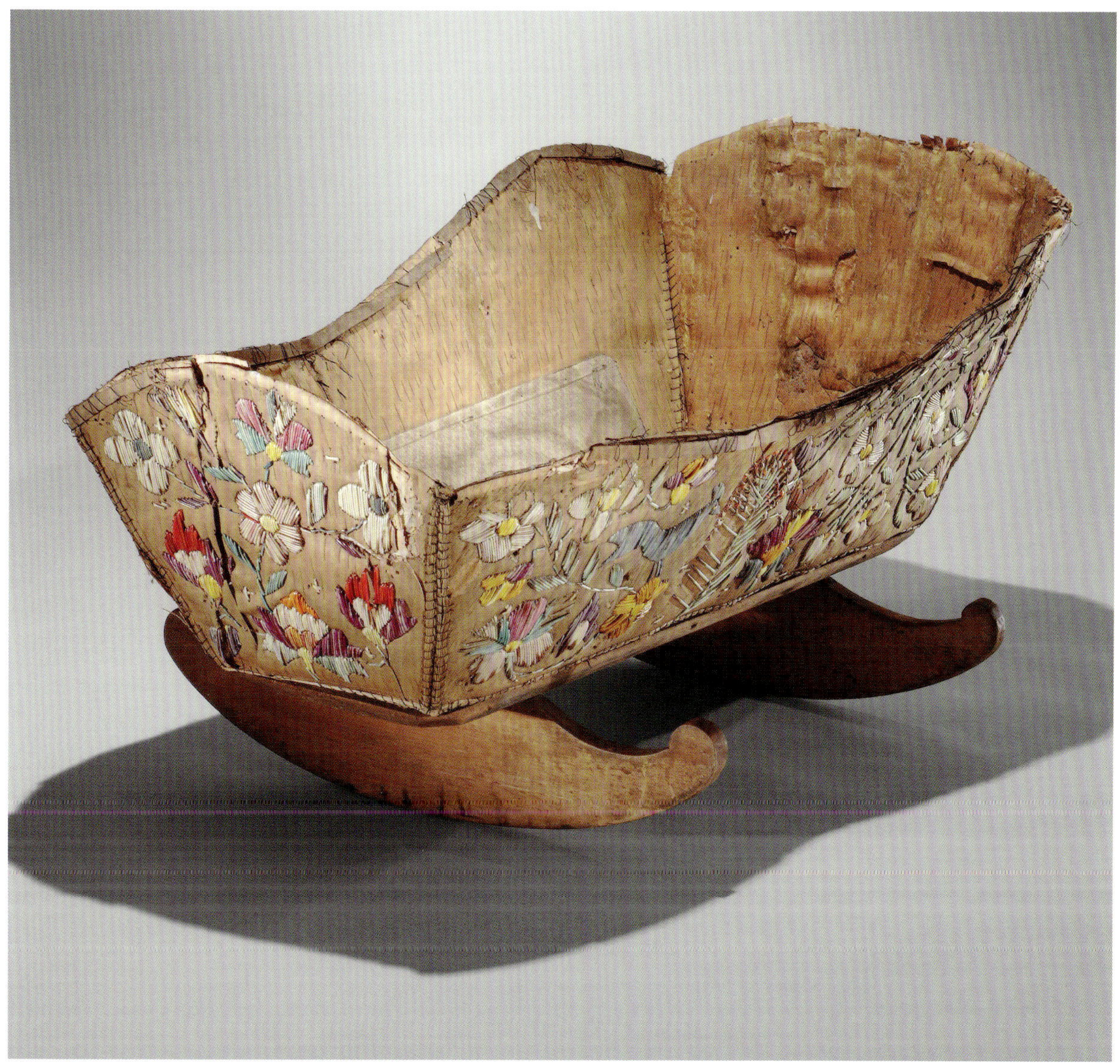

style of quilled birchbark cradle was last made in the nineteenth century, so it was significant for Hom and Kruse to reinstate this work of art into the community. After returning home, Kruse spent three months designing and creating a pattern. Hom then incorporated floral beadwork patterns done with dyed quills. Hom explains: "Our project on display at the Dunn Museum is a celebration of the past, present, and future of our children and grandchildren."[25] While the museum symbolizes a space based on freezing cultures in time, the efforts done by Indigenous artists breathe new life into works and practices that were removed, or attempted to be removed, from the community.

Terri Hom's practice as a beadwork and quillwork artist focuses on preserving and commemorating traditional Ojibwe floral patterns. Hom's birchbark quill art merges original materials with ancestral design. She creates baskets in the old style with birchbark, sinew, quills, red willow, and sweetgrass. Many of her baskets are based on those stored in collections in numerous museums. Hom acts as an intermediary to reconnect these baskets' spirit to the people whose ancestors created them. As Hom notes, "Working with my hands connects me to the ancestors."[26] In her efforts to engage with various temporal fragments, Hom replenishes Ojibwe art forms.

The continued Anishinaabe forms of artistry in the Great Lakes incorporate tradition, cultural values, language, and a reclaiming of territory-specific practices. We are reclaiming our homeland one piece of birch at a time; through this activity, we are aiming to create something to engage with the teachings of our ancestors. Birchbark was used to convey a way of life through its use in scrolls, canoes, containers, and shelters, and continues to depict a way of life more subtly in contemporary art. Birchbark art is a testament to the fact that art does not need to move away from tradition and cultural values to be considered "contemporary." The Anishinaabeg still practice art forms that many settlers only allow to exist within the past— as evidenced by where and how museums have kept cultural belongings and how they are typically labeled "traditional." Its use and validity as a material of contemporary artistic practice is not to be merely reserved as an artifact for anthropological inquiry. It's meant to remind us that ancestors and future generations benefit from its teachings and presence. We exist within a spiralic temporality, continuously engaging with our ancestors through materials and actions that connect us to ancestral places. By continuing to incorporate birchbark into contemporary works of art, Anishinaabe artists maintain this relationship with *wiigwaas* and the seasonal care it provides to us and provided to our ancestors.

Birchbark art illustrates a more profound memory within me and touches on the ancestral place memory that I hold. It expresses a place that my ancestors knew and are still present within. I can picture, wear, and surround myself with it; I know it connects me because it is acting as a means of entry to a spiralic space. It holds a piece of beauty conveyed with short parallel lines. Its inclusion within a pattern resembles Anishinaabeg and their relationship with the land in the past, present, and future—and always.

Endnotes

1. *Prairie Mosaic | Pat Kruse: Birch Bark Artist,* Facebook video, 5 min., 54 sec., uploaded by Prairie Public, February 19, 2022, https://www.facebook.com/prairiepublic/videos/prairie-mosaic-pat-kruse-birch-bark-artist/289574699942898/.

2. Lake Superior is the current site of my Anishinaabe relatives, who live on the lakefront at the northern tip of the state of Wisconsin, and who are in the band of Red Cliff Ojibwe. I can't say that I have had much experience harvesting or creating from the birch tree. Still, I know it has always been a material that adorned home decor and jewelry and is symbolic of my Ojibwe family in northern Wisconsin.

3. Laura Marie De Vos, "Spiralic Time and Cultural Continuity for Indigenous Sovereignty: Idle No More and the Marrow Thieves," *Transmotion* 6, no. 2 (Winter 2020): 1–42. Spiralic temporality as defined by non-Native scholar Laura Maria De Vos refers to an Indigenous experience of time that is informed by a people's particular relationships to the seasonal cycles on their lands, and which acknowledges the present generations' responsibilities to ancestors and those not yet born.

4. Kyle P. Whyte, "Indigenous Science (Fiction) for the Anthropocene: Ancestral Dystopias and Fantasies of Climate Change Crises," *Environment and Planning E: Nature and Space* 1, nos. 1–2 (March 2018): 224–42, here 228.

5. Ibid., 229.

6. Ziibiwing Center of Anishinabe Culture & Lifeways, "*Wiigwaas* (Birchbark)," part 5 of a series of *Kinoomaagewin Mzinigas,* Little Teaching Books (Mt. Pleasant, MI: Ziibiwing Center of Anishinabe Culture & Lifeways, n.d.).

7. I want to acknowledge the work of Nadine Morsette and her publication *Cree Writing,* printed by Rocky Boy Tribal Schools. Nadine discusses the story of teachings that came to a man through a dream. In these series of dreams, he was taught how to make an ink to write on birchbark, and, later, spirits taught him how to make a book. There are endless resources that acknowledge the role of dreams as platforms for learning. For an example that bridges Indigenous art making and dreams, see Nancy Van Styvendale, J. D. McDougall, Robert Henry, and Robert Alexander Innes, eds., *The Arts of Indigenous Health and Well-Being* (Winnipeg: University of Manitoba Press, 2021),

pp. 45–58.

8. Conversations with curator Denene De Quintal have further supported this statement.

9. For example, pottery and clay traditions of the Southwest can exist within the sphere of both contemporary and traditional. Can we move past historical settler understandings of Indigenous culture and have this same understanding be applied to other regions?

10. Indigenous placemaking is a reorientation in space that asserts and describes an experience of boundlessness within ancestral lands still here, or as Indigenous scholar Kasey Keeler describes in *American Indians and the American Dream* (2023) as "places policy has long excluded them from." Indigenous placemaking in practices of Indigenous ancestral return can also be the embodied space that includes the memory attached to a place, making place more than a sensory experience that encompasses the landscape and aspects of nature that Native people came to understand through their cultural stories and practices.

11. While it may be encouraged to harvest summer bark in late spring or early summer, there are different Ojibwe markers on when it is best to harvest. Some may say it is also when the flies start to bite, among other wildlife indicators. In Native Harvest Ojibwe Products, a subdivision of White Earth Land Recovery Project. "Harvesting Birch Bark," June 10, 2017, https://nativeharvest.com/blogs/news/harvesting-birch-bark.

12. "Community Spirit Award Honoree Is Breathing Life Back into Traditions Set Forth by His Ancestors," First Peoples Fund blog, n.d., https://www.firstpeoplesfund.org/post/community-spirit-award-honoree-is-breathing-life-back-into-traditions-set-forth-by-his-ancestors.

13. "Wayne Valliere," First Peoples Fund website, n.d., https://www.firstpeoplesfund.org/community-spirit-award-honorees/wayne-valliere.

14. Meagan Francis, "The Ancient Art of Birchbark Canoes Lives On in Michigan," MyNorth.com blog, November 14, 2024, https://mynorth.com/2024/11/the-ancient-art-of-birchbark-canoes-lives-on-in-michigan/.

15. Ibid.

16. "Ronald J. Paquin," First Peoples Fund website, n.d., https://www.firstpeoplesfund.org/community-spirit-award-honorees/ronald-j-paquin.

17. Ibid.

18. *NEA National Heritage Fellows Tribute Video: Wayne Valliere (2020),* YouTube video, 6 min., 56 sec., uploaded by the National Endowment for the Arts, March 8, 2021, https://www.youtube.com/watch?v=PXd2wTcx3qA.

19. Ibid.

20. *Yvonne Walker Keshick | NEH/NEA 50th Anniversary,* YouTube video, 8 min., 52 sec., uploaded by Detroit PBS, December 19, 2016, https://www.youtube.com/watch?v=QCo5tsua40E.

21. Wanesia Misquadace in discussion with the author, December 2024.

22. Tribal Adaptation Menu Team, Dibaginjigaadeg Anishinaabe Ezhitwaad: A Tribal Climate Adaptation Menu, Great Lakes Indian Fish and Wildlife Commission, Odanah, Wisconsin (2019), p. 7.

23. "Wanesia Spry Misquadace," Harpo Foundation blog, January 29, 2020, https://www.harpofoundation.org/wanesia-spry-misquadace-native-american-residency-fellow/.

24. *Prairie Mosaic | Pat Kruse: Birch Bark Artist,* Facebook video.

25. Kim Mikus, "A Research Visit Turns into Exhibit Opportunity at Dunn Museum," *Daily Herald,* January 9, 2020, https://www.dailyherald.com/20200109/lifestyle/a-research-visit-turns-into-exhibit-opportunity-at-dunn-museum/.

26. *Convergence,* Madeline Island Museum, on display in the Capser Center during the 2023 season.

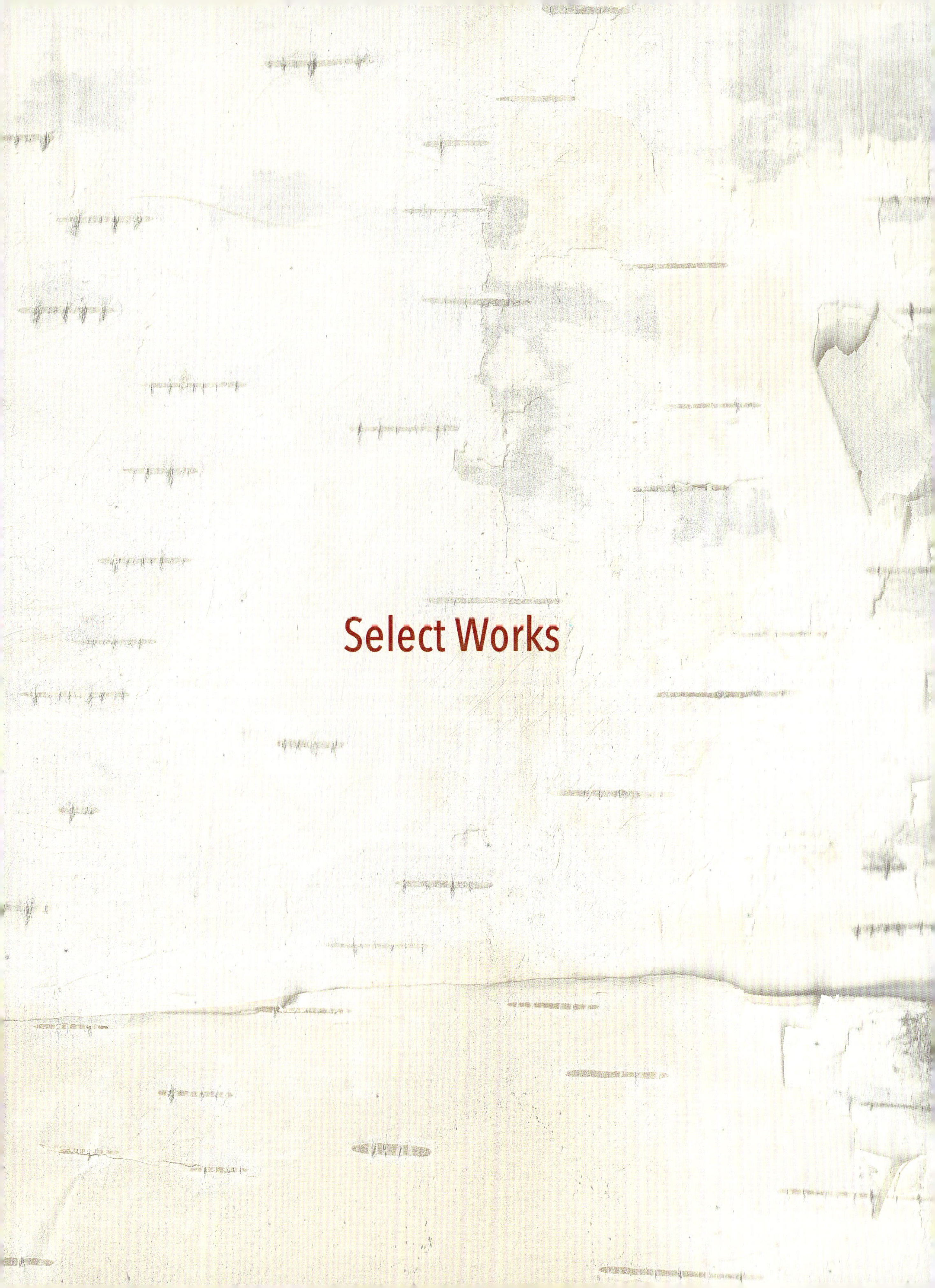

Select Works

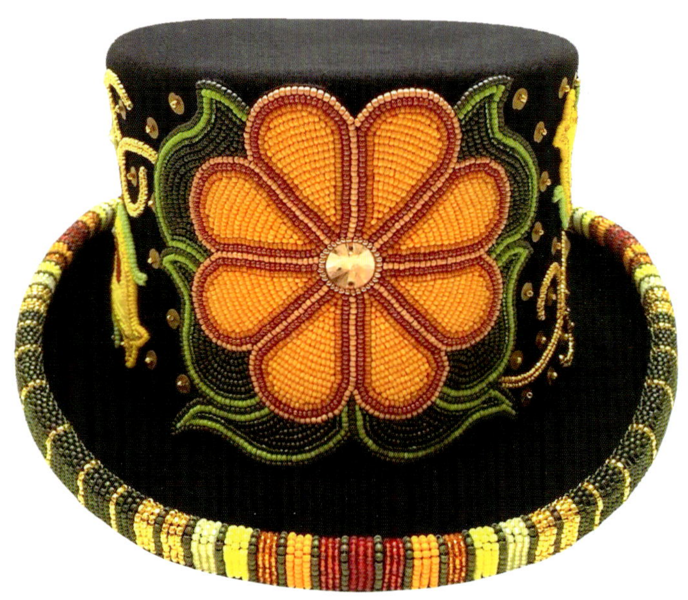

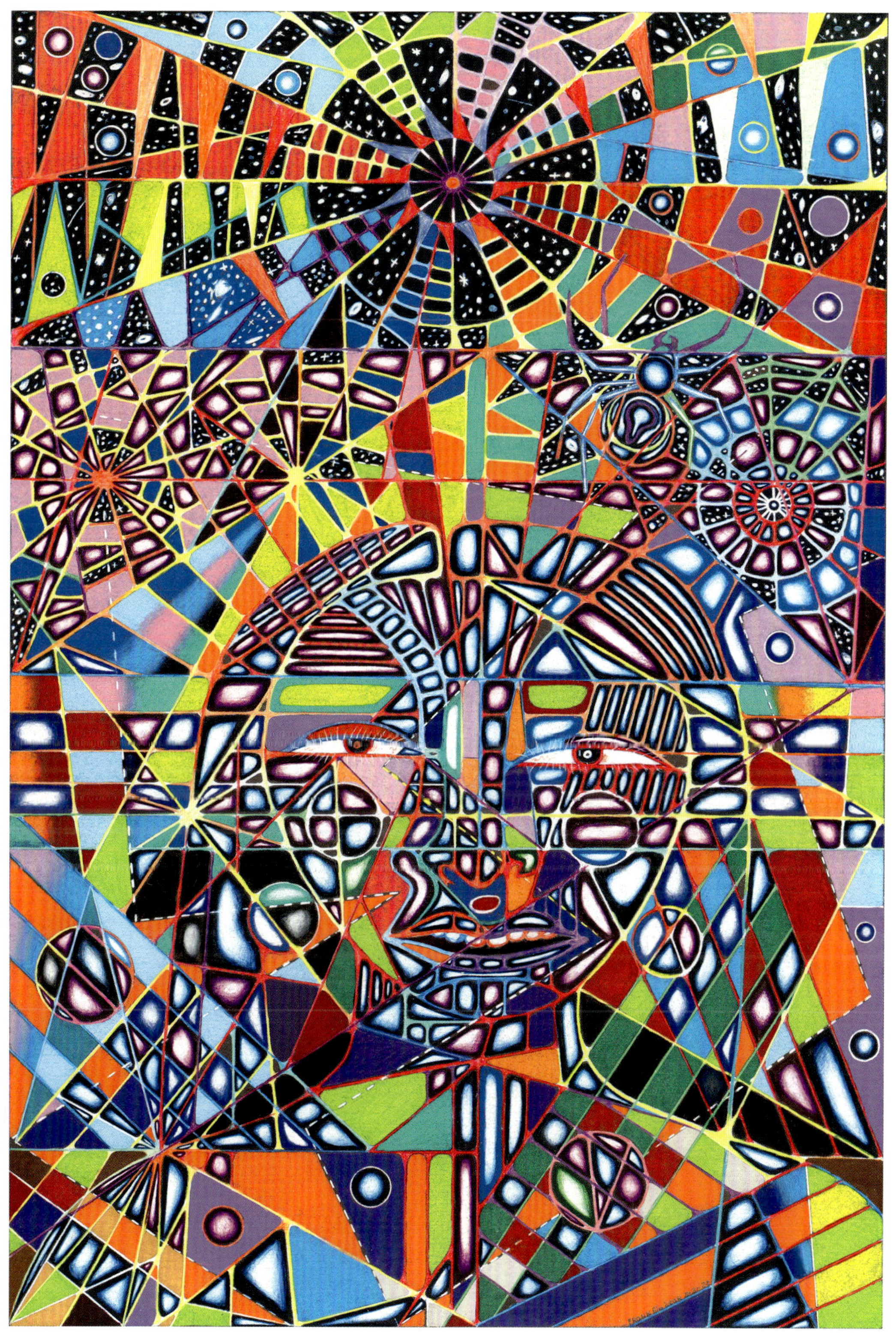

Frank Big Bear (White Earth Band of the Minnesota Chippewa; b. 1953), *Anishinaabe Man Trapped in a Trickster's Web,* 2023

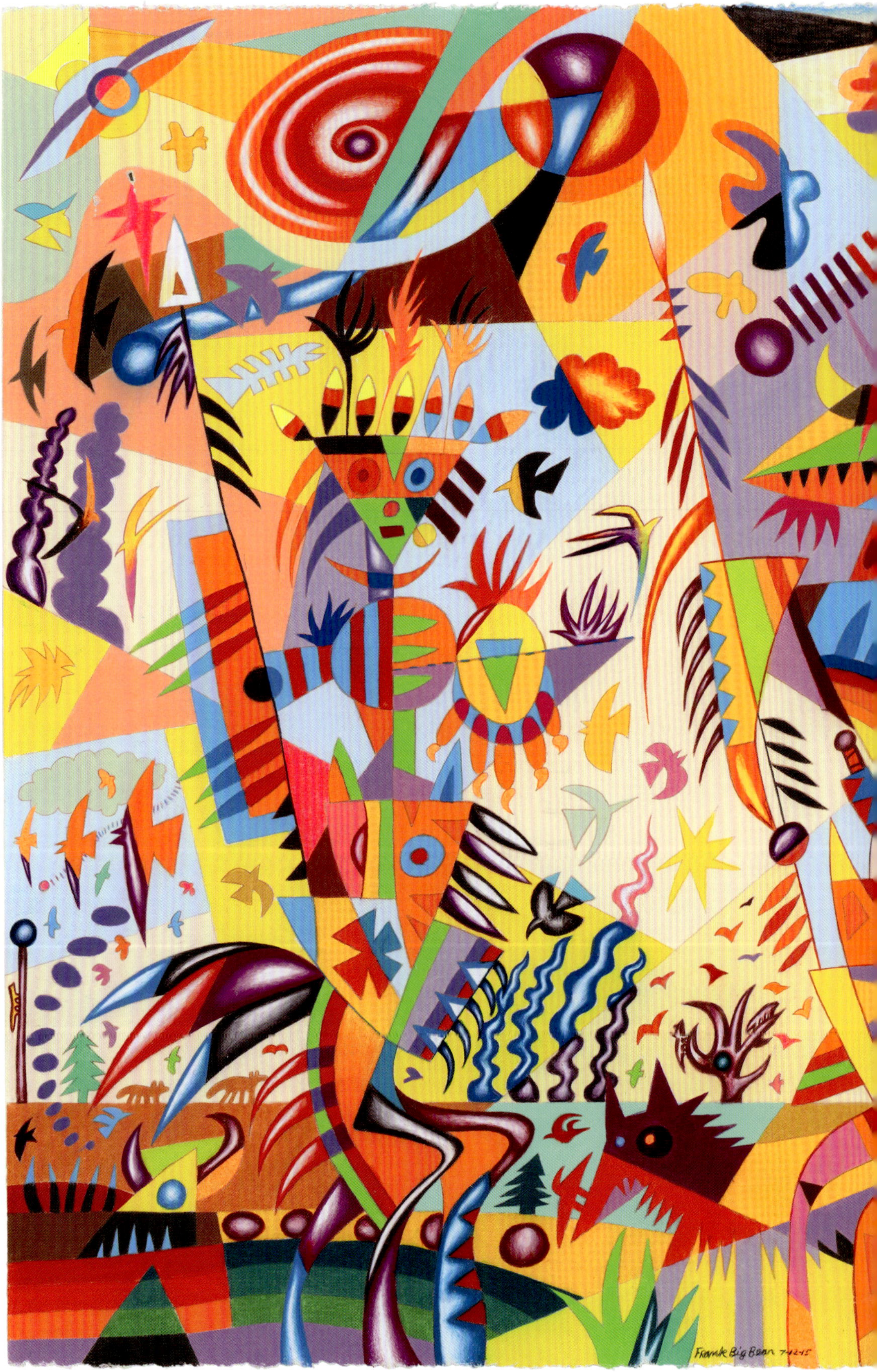

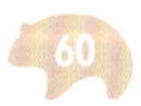

Contemporary Anishinaabe Art: A Continuation

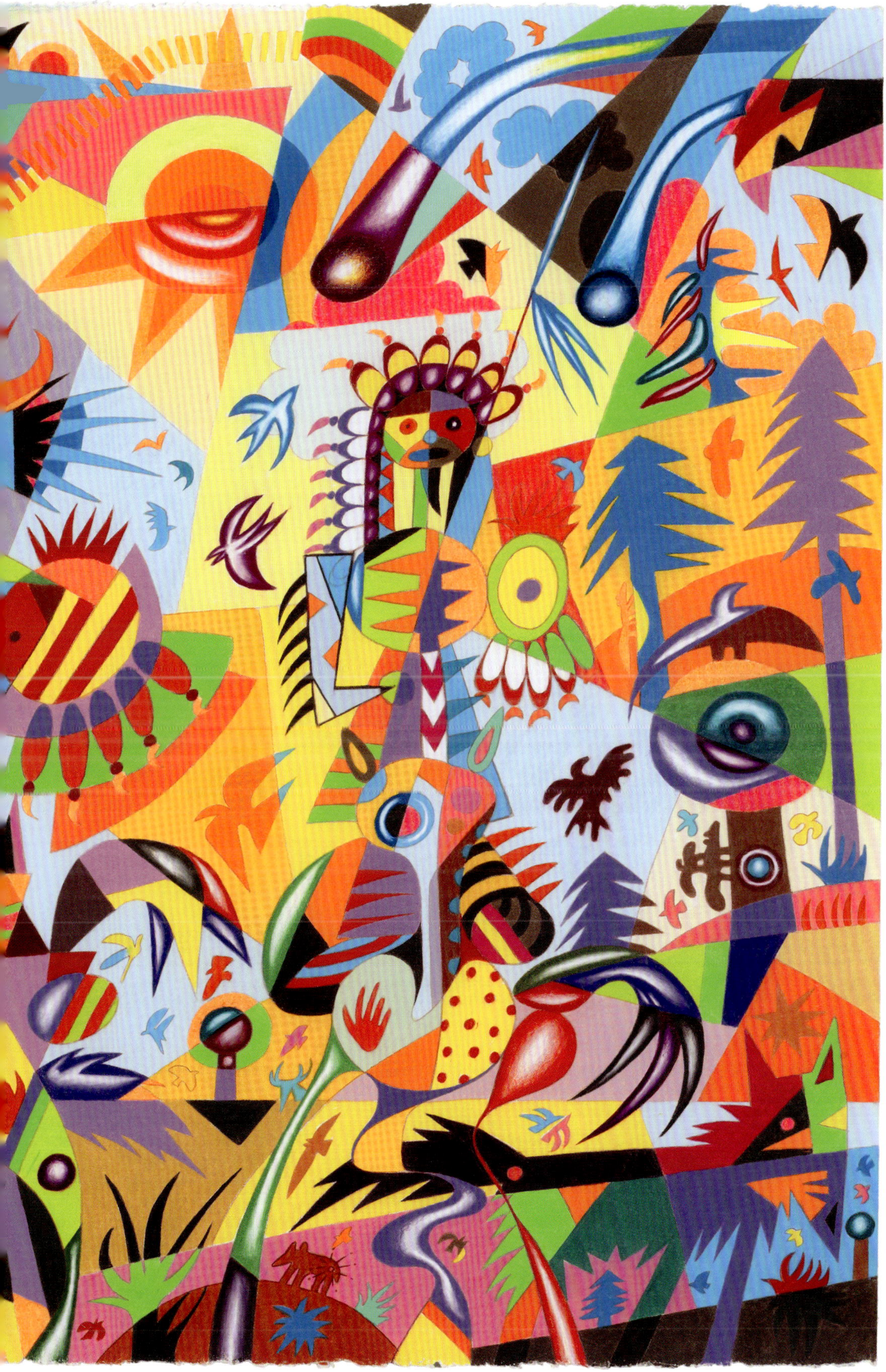

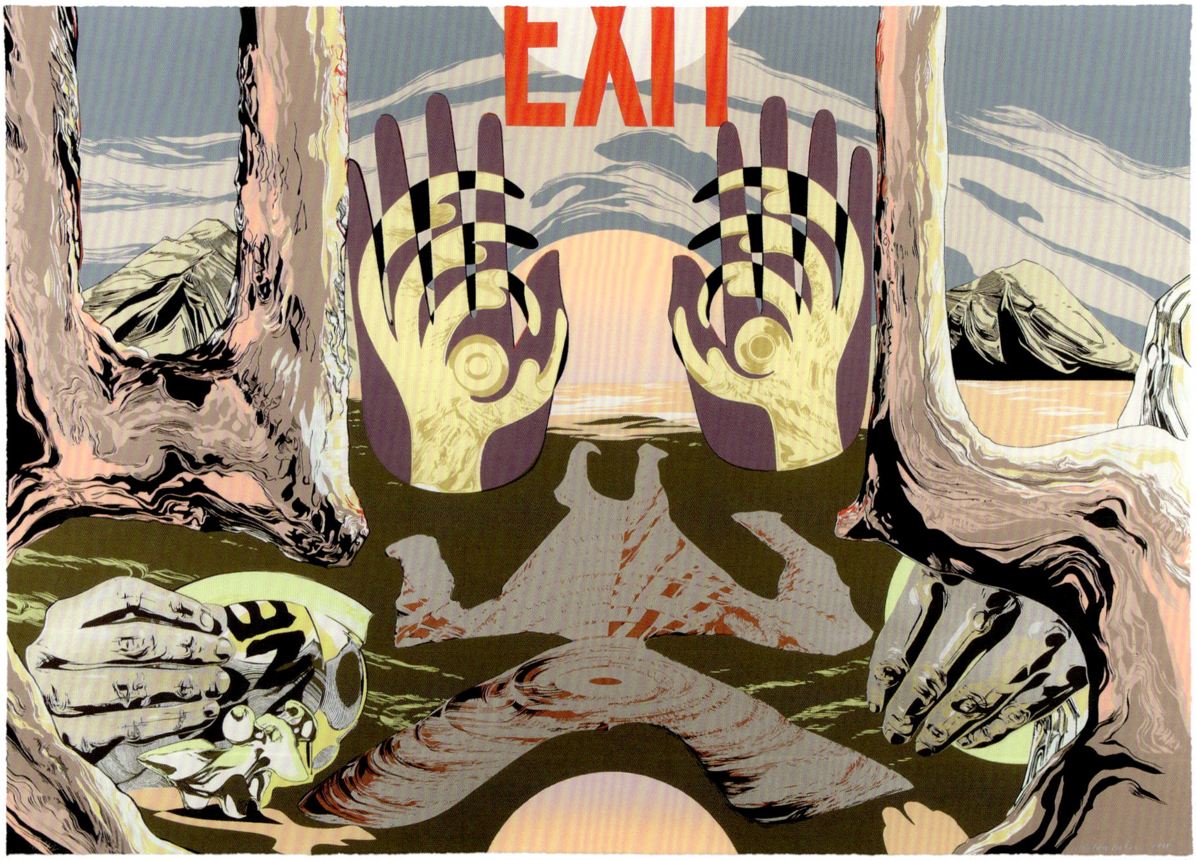

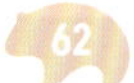

Previous Spread: Frank Big Bear (White Earth Band of the Minnesota Chippewa; b. 1953), *Three Warriors on Horses (During Climate Change),* 2015

Andrea Carlson (Grand Portage Band of Lake Superior Chippewa; b. 1979), *Exit,* 2018

Contemporary Anishinaabe Art: A Continuation

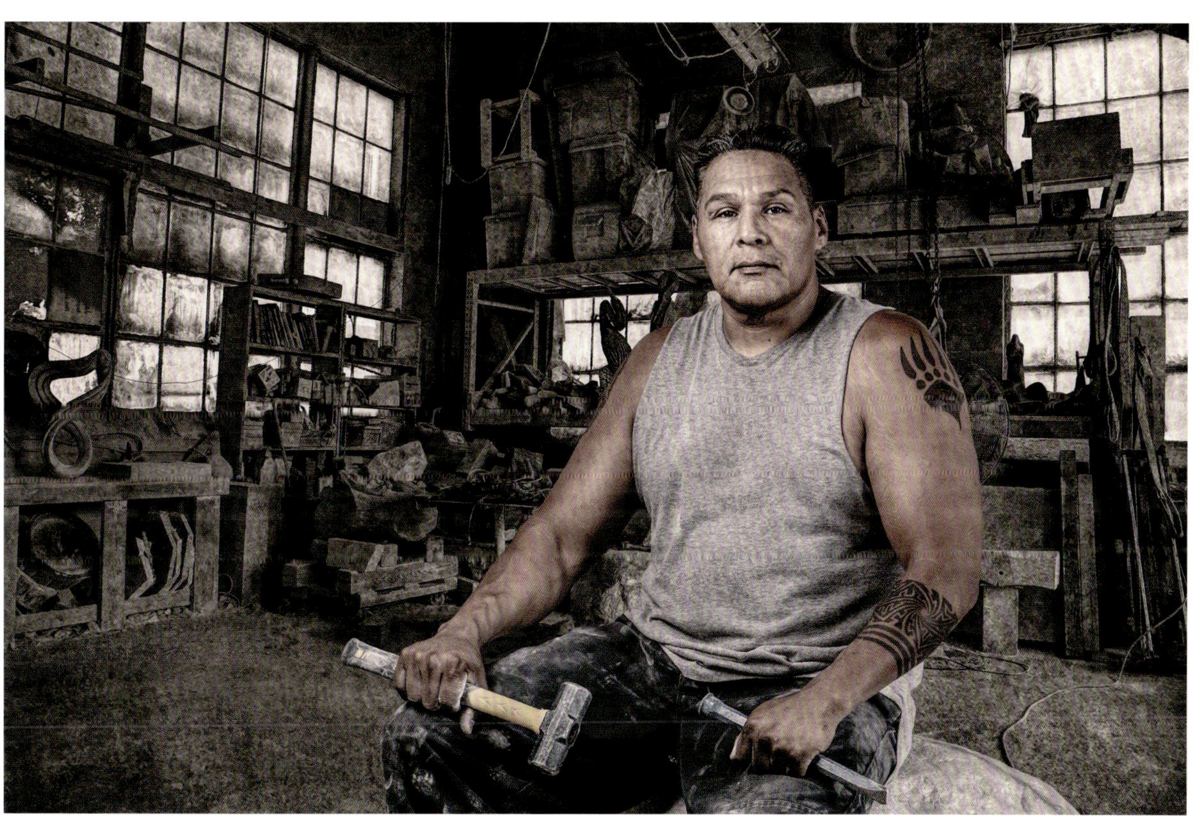

Richard Church (Match-E-Be-Nash-She-Wish Band of Pottawatomi; b.1947), *Asinaabe (Stone Man),* 2017

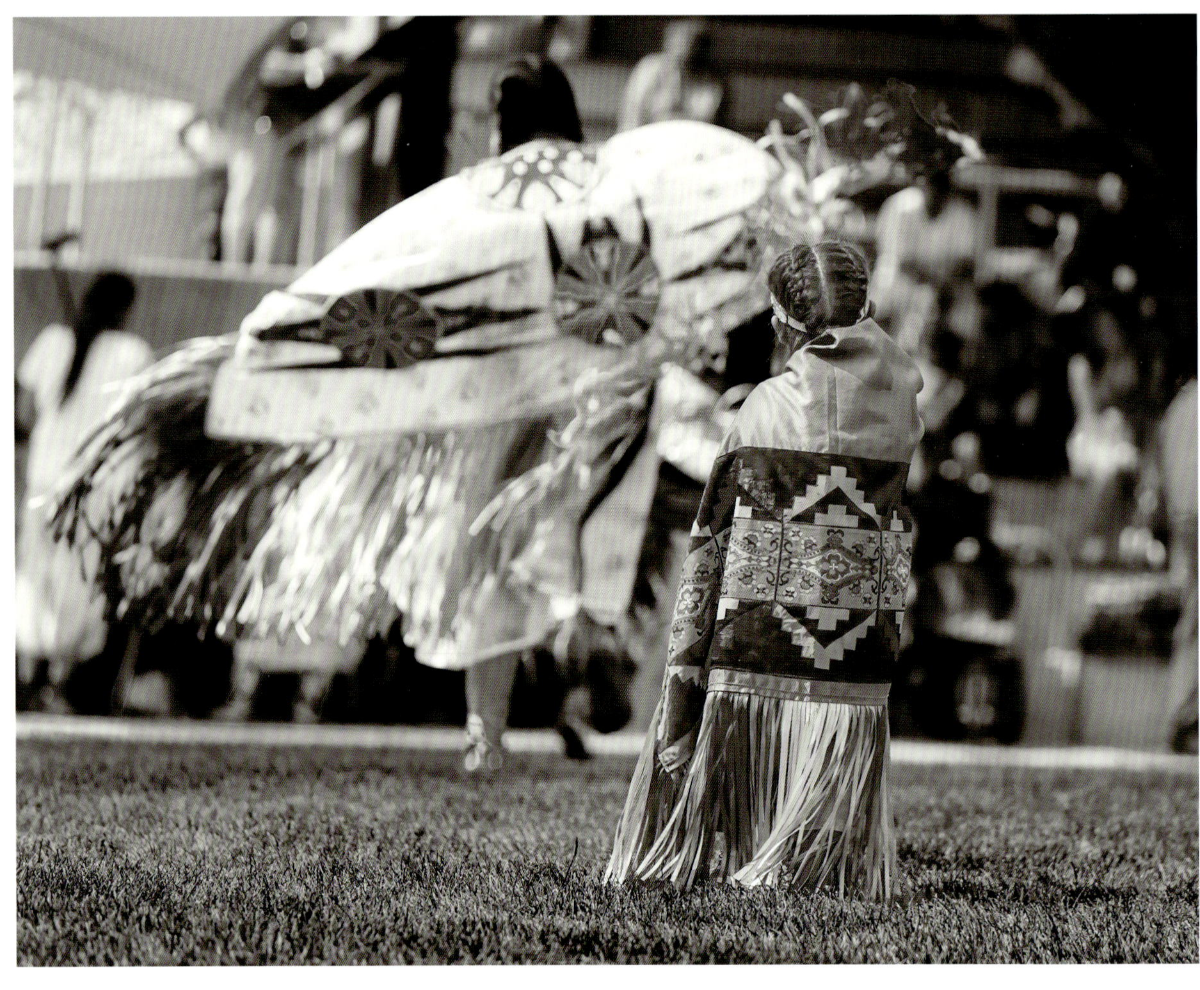

Richard Church (Match-E-Be-Nash-She-Wish Band of Pottawatomi; b.1947), *Young Shawl Dancer*, 2023

Contemporary Anishinaabe Art: A Continuation

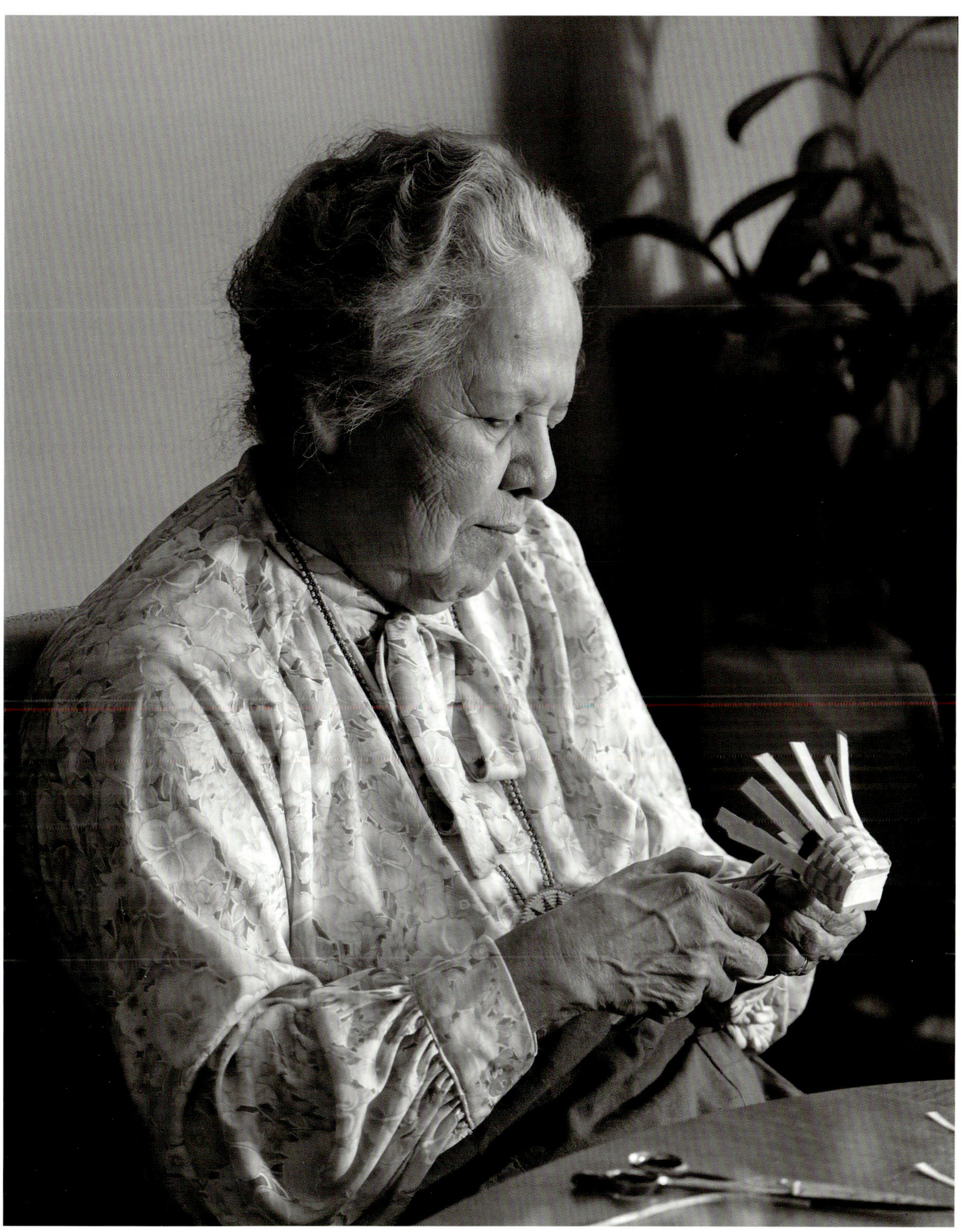

Richard Church (Match-E-Be-Nash-She-Wish Band of Pottawatomi; b.1947), *My Cuz,* 1978

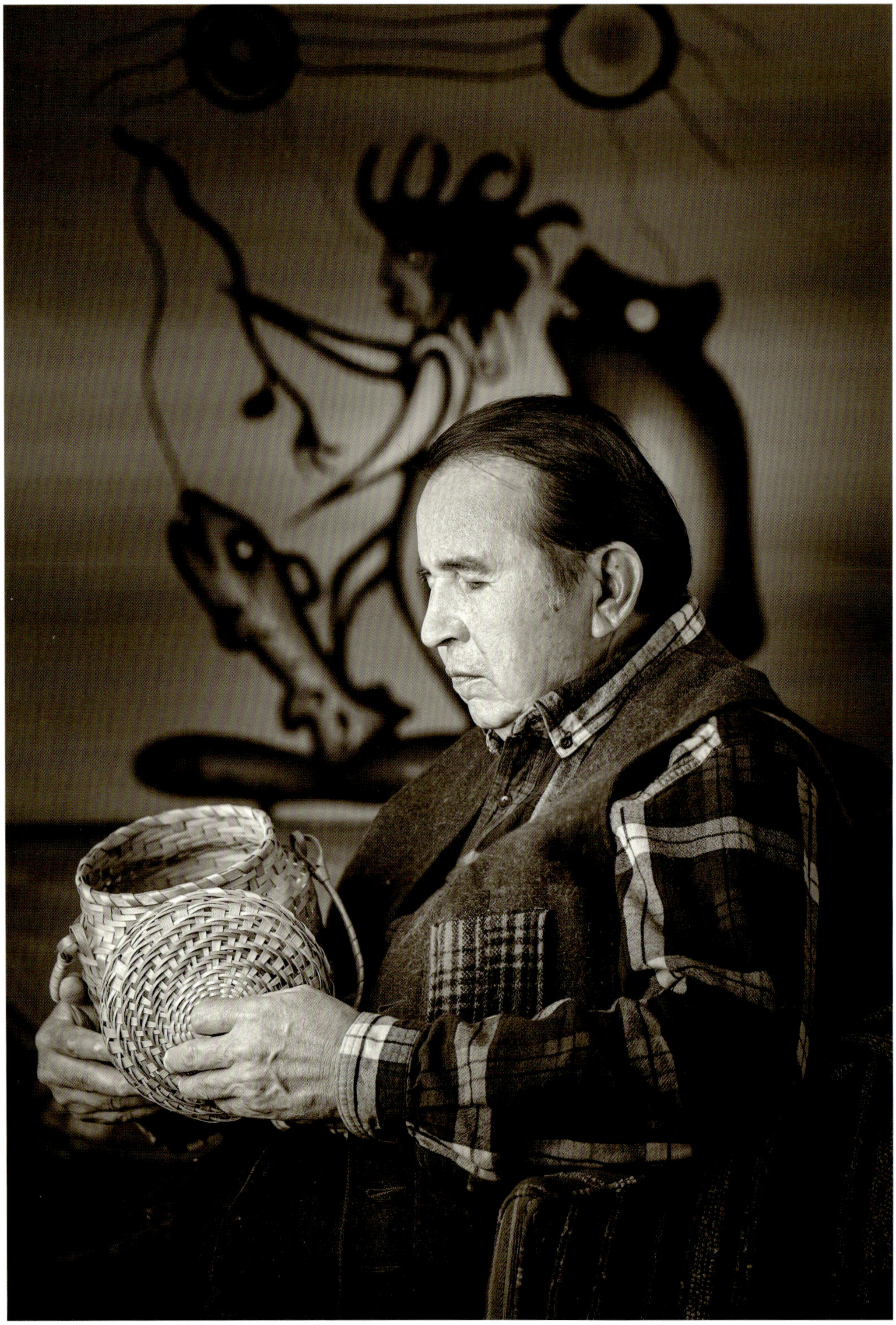

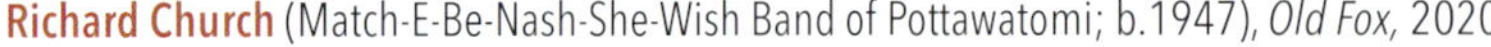

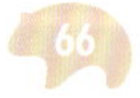

Contemporary Anishinaabe Art: A Continuation

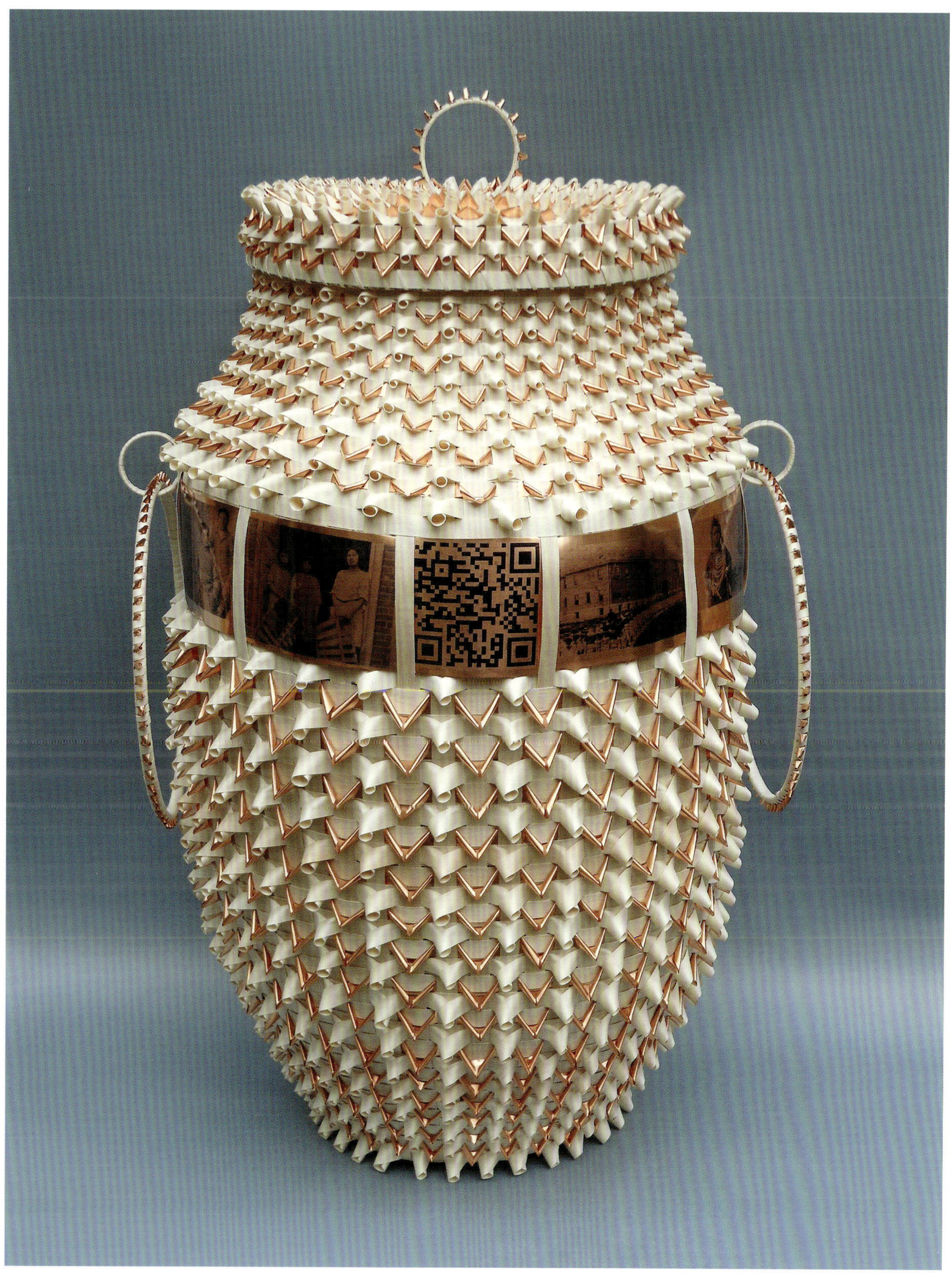

Kelly Church (Match-E-Be-Nash-She-Wish Band of Potawatomi; Grand Traverse Band of Ottawa and Chippewa Indians [Descent]; b. 1967), *Every Picture Tells a Story*, 2025

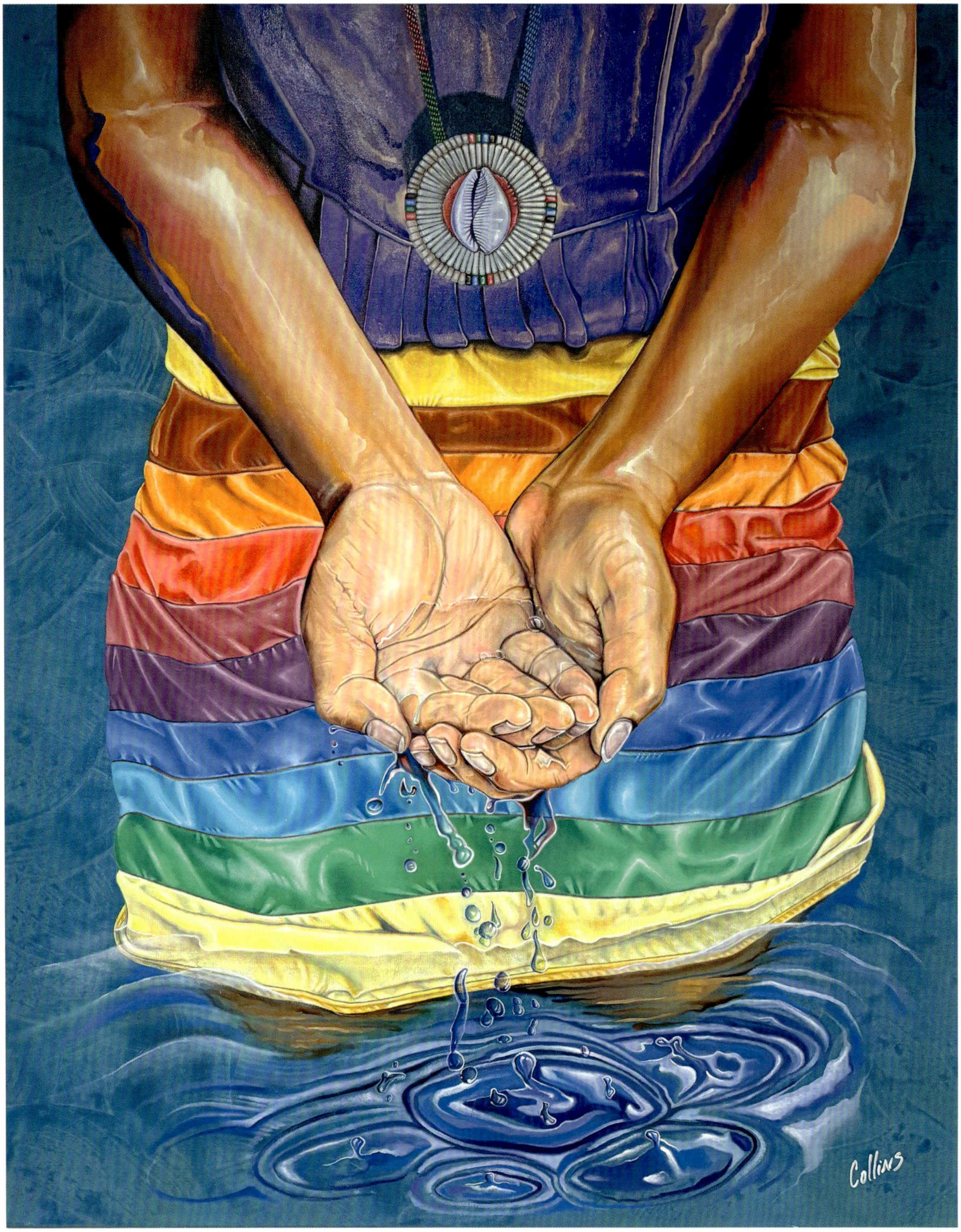

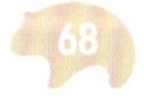

Patrick Collins (Saginaw Chippewa Indian Tribe; b. 1973), *Healing Hands,* 2024

Contemporary Anishinaabe Art: A Continuation

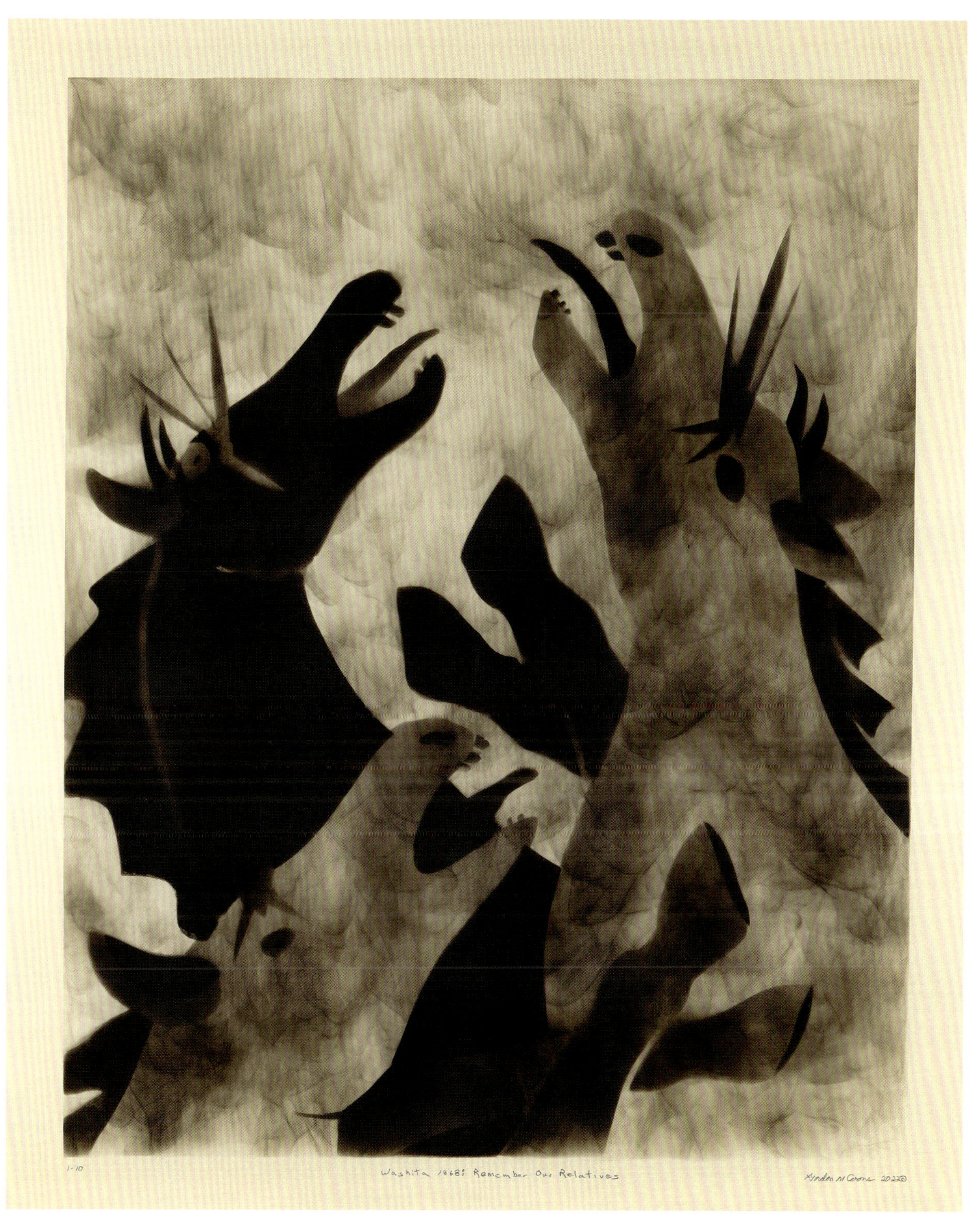

Gordon M. Coons (Lac Courte Oreilles Band of Lake Superior Chippewa; b. 1949), *Washita 1868: Remember Our Relatives,* 2022

Select Works

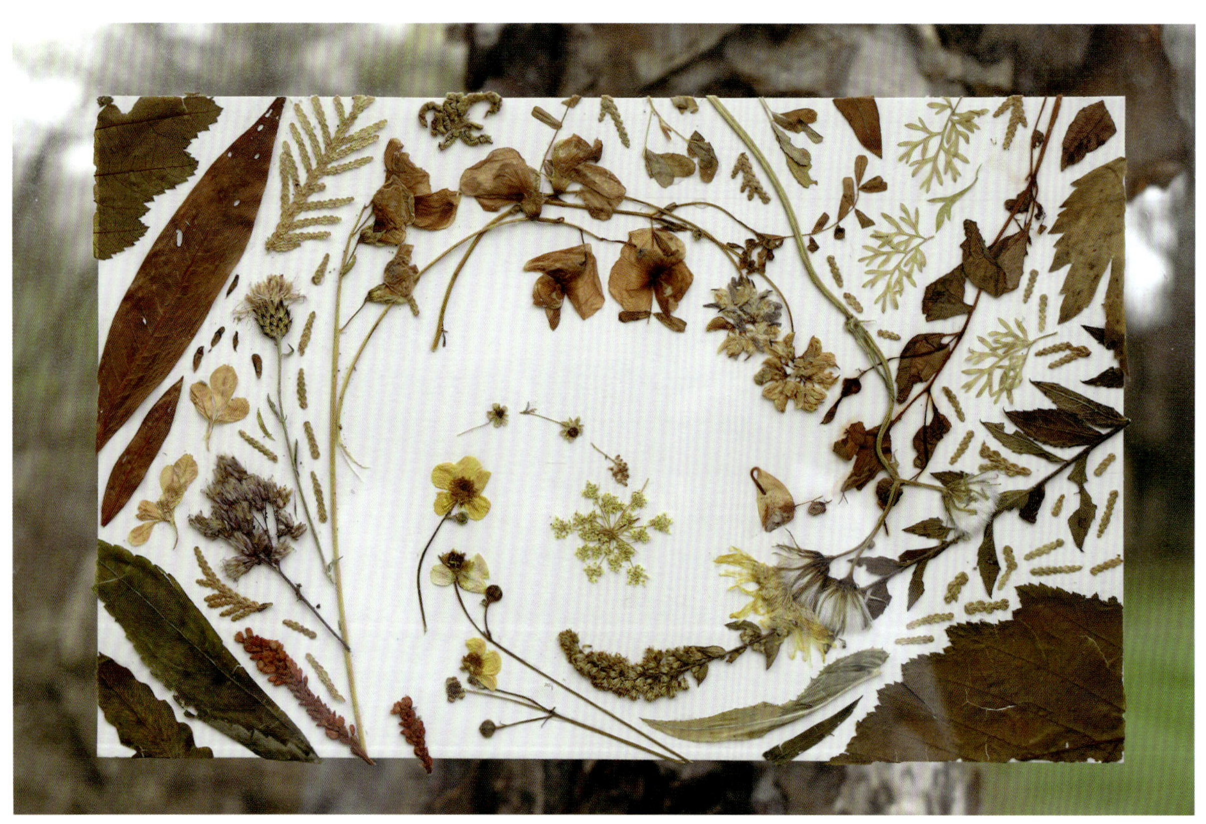

Zoi Crampton (Saginaw Chippewa Indian Tribe; b. 2001), *Exsiccata,* 2021

Contemporary Anishinaabe Art: A Continuation

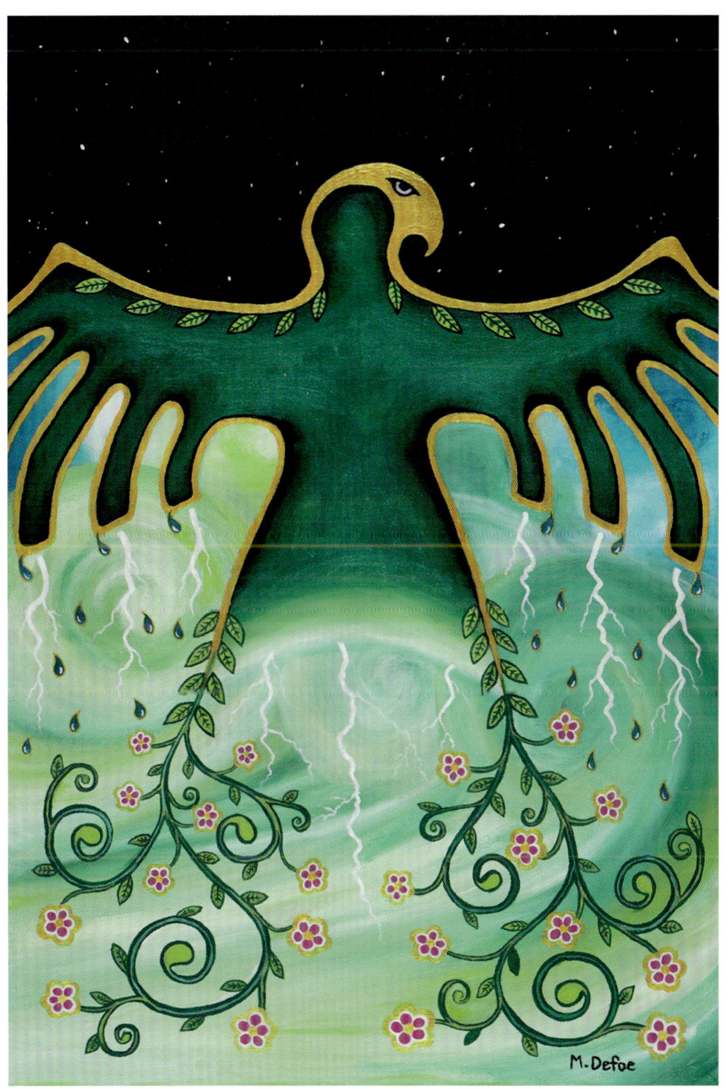

Michelle Defoe (Red Cliff Band of Lake Superior Chippewa; b. 1982), *Ziigwan Binesi – Spring Thunderbird,* 2018

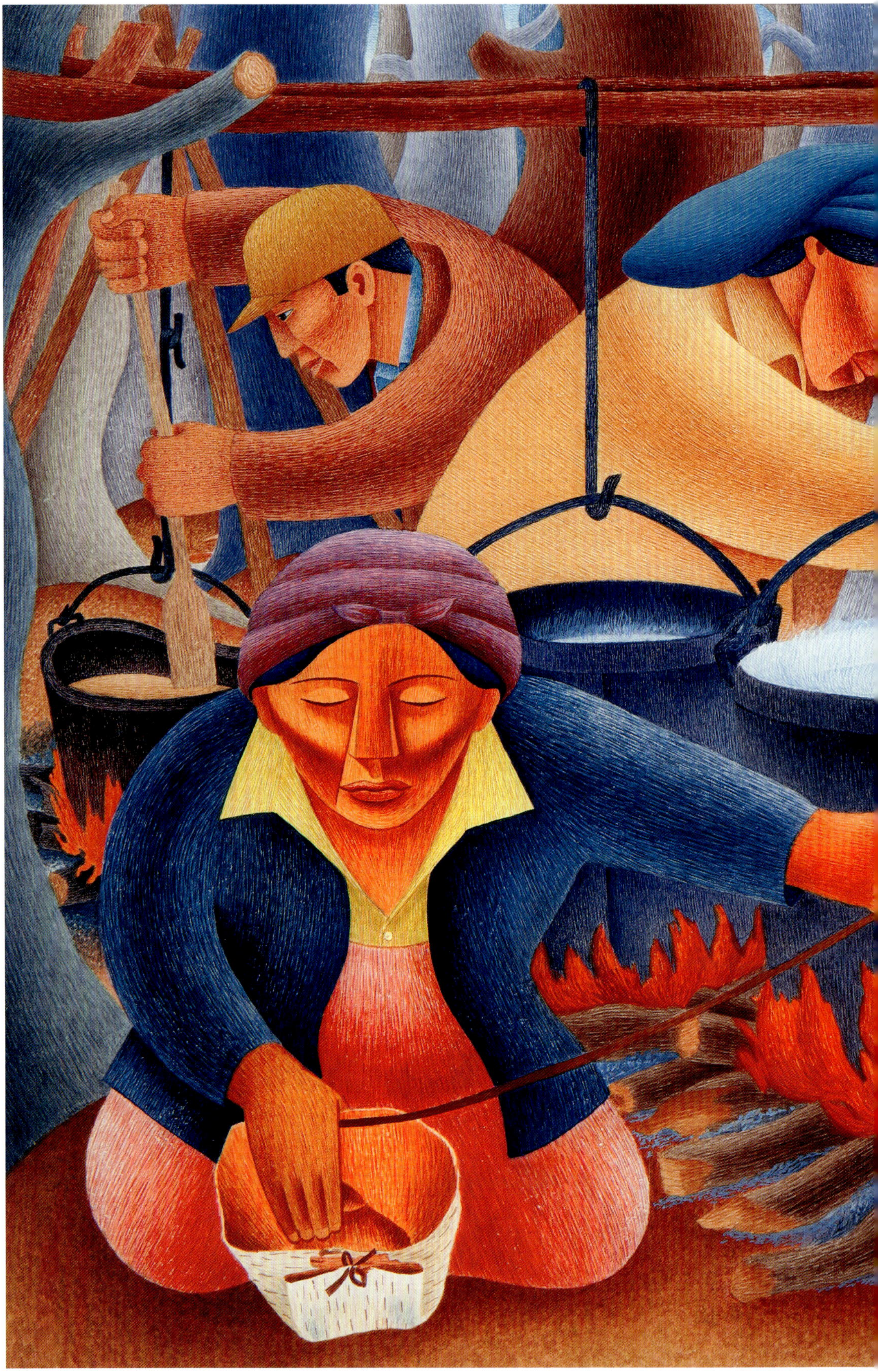

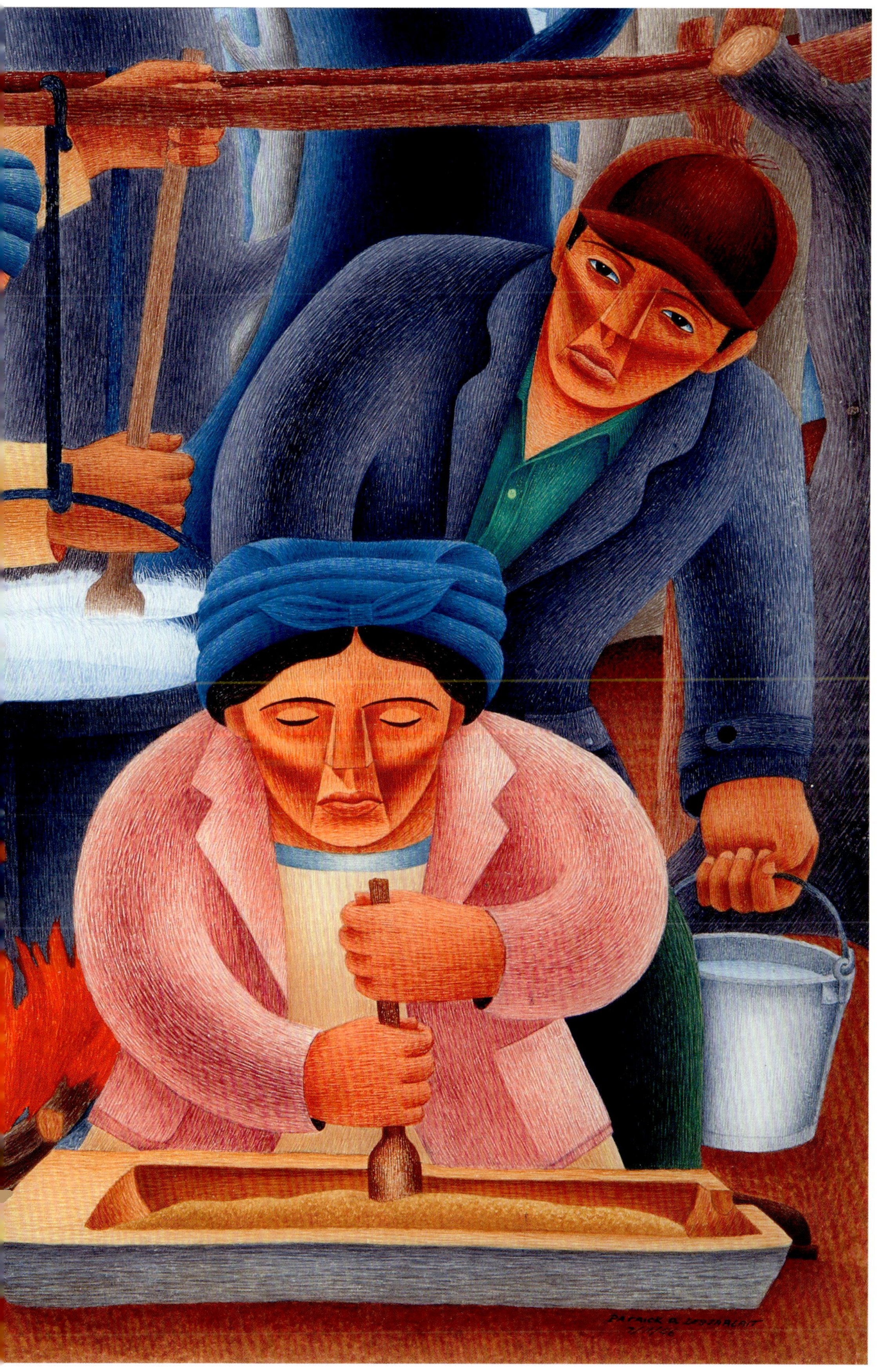

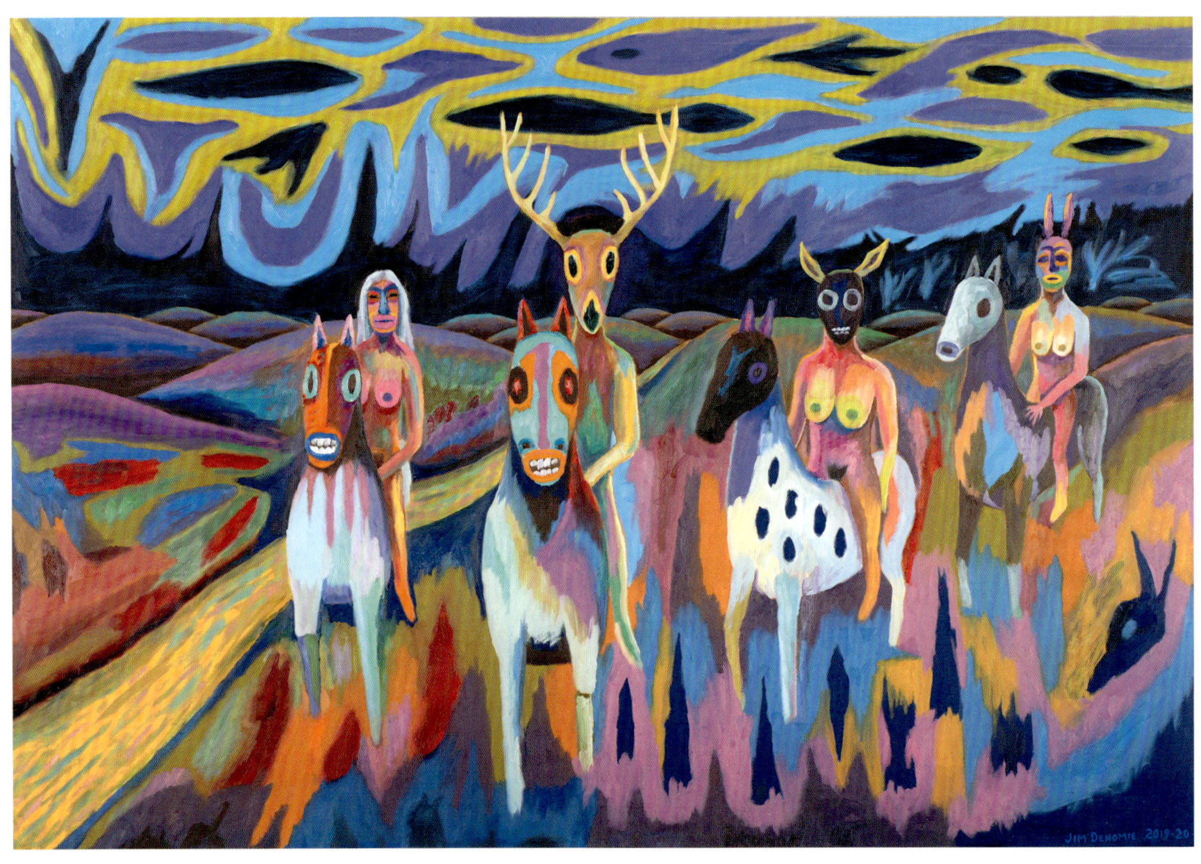

Previous Spread: Patrick DesJarlait (Red Lake Band of Ojibwe; 1921–1972), *Maple Sugar Time,* 1946

Jim Denomie (Lac Courte Oreilles Band of Lake Superior Chippewa; 1955–2022), *Four Days and Four Nites, Ceremony,* 2019–20

Contemporary Anishinaabe Art: A Continuation

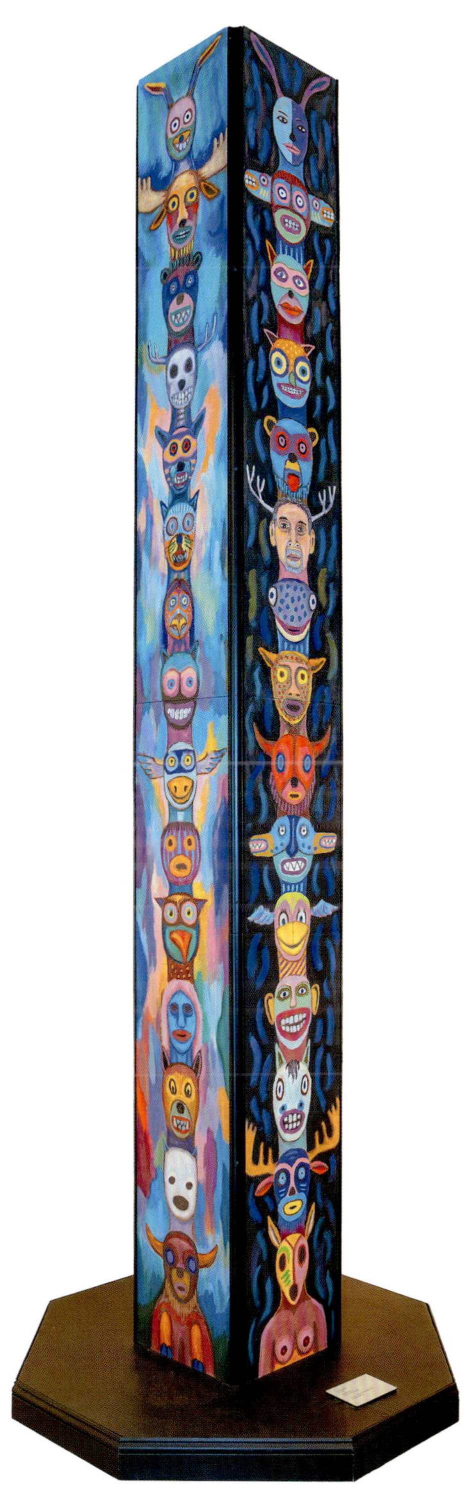

Jim Denomie (Lac Courte Oreilles Band of Lake Superior Chippewa; 1955–2022), *Untitled (Totem Painting),* 2016

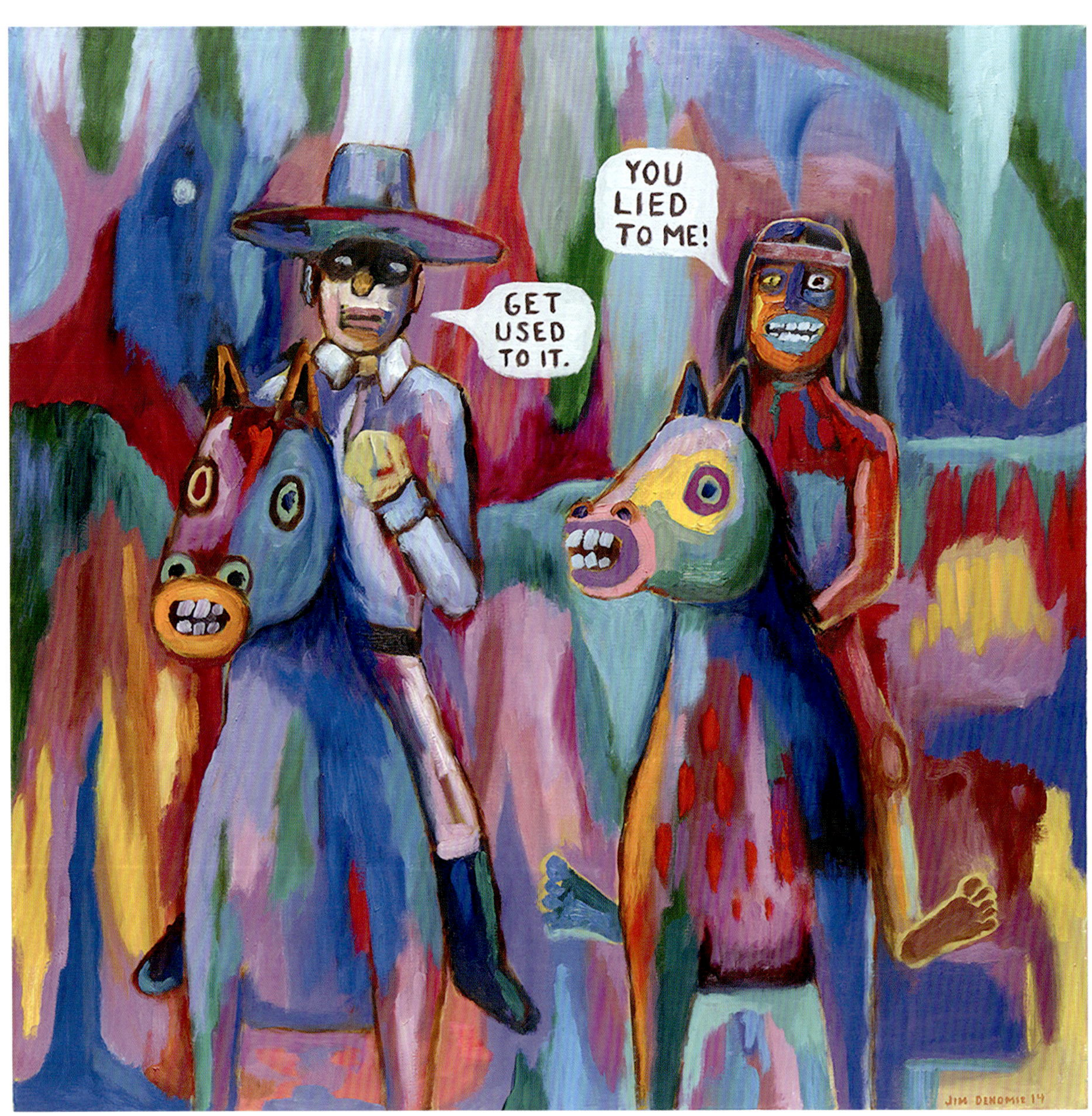

Jim Denomie (Lac Courte Oreilles Band of Lake Superior Chippewa; 1955–2022), *Untruthful,* 2014

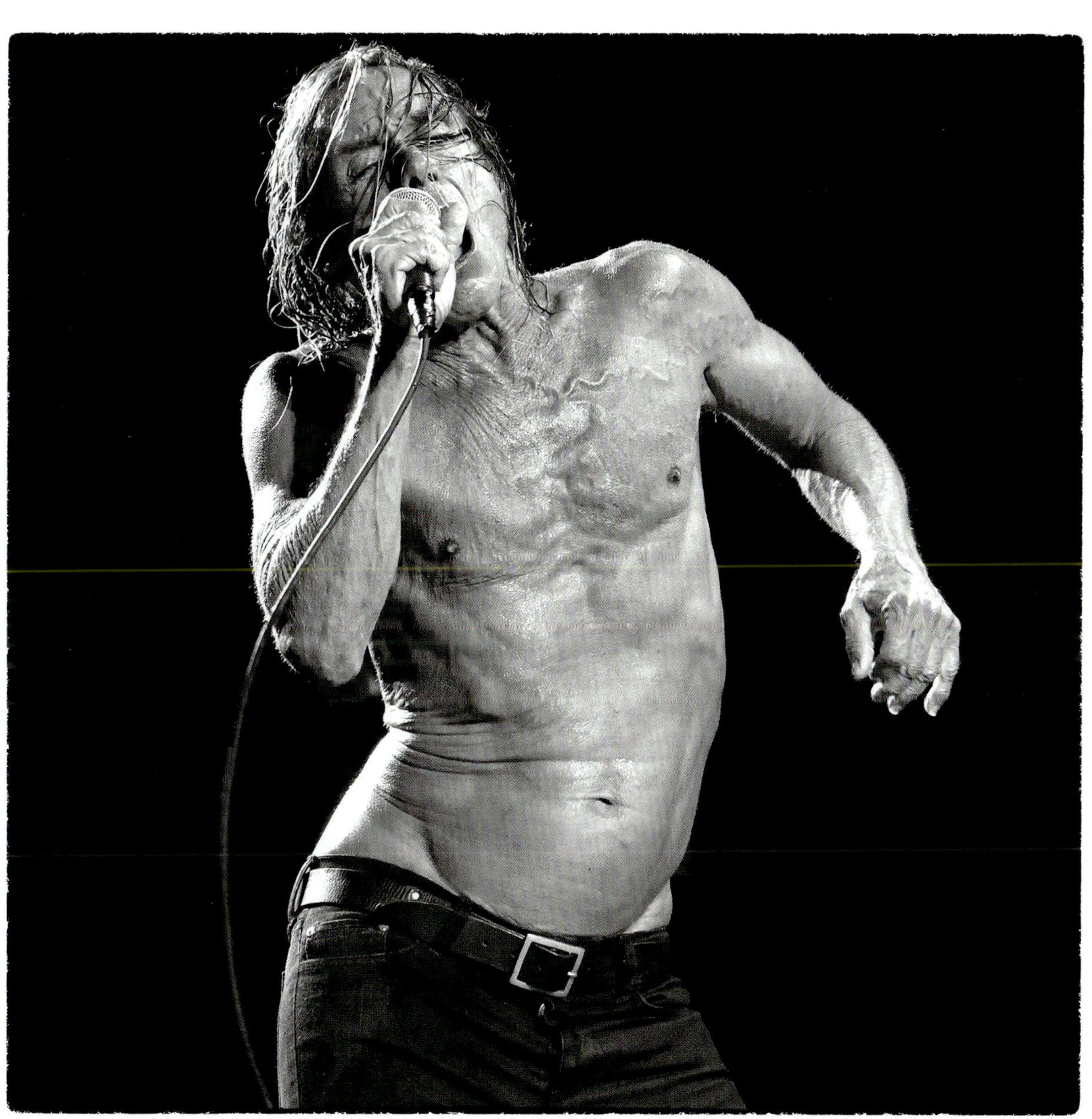

David Dominic, Jr. (Little Traverse Bay Bands of Odawa Indians; b. 1970), *Iggy Pop, Ann Arbor 2011,* 2011

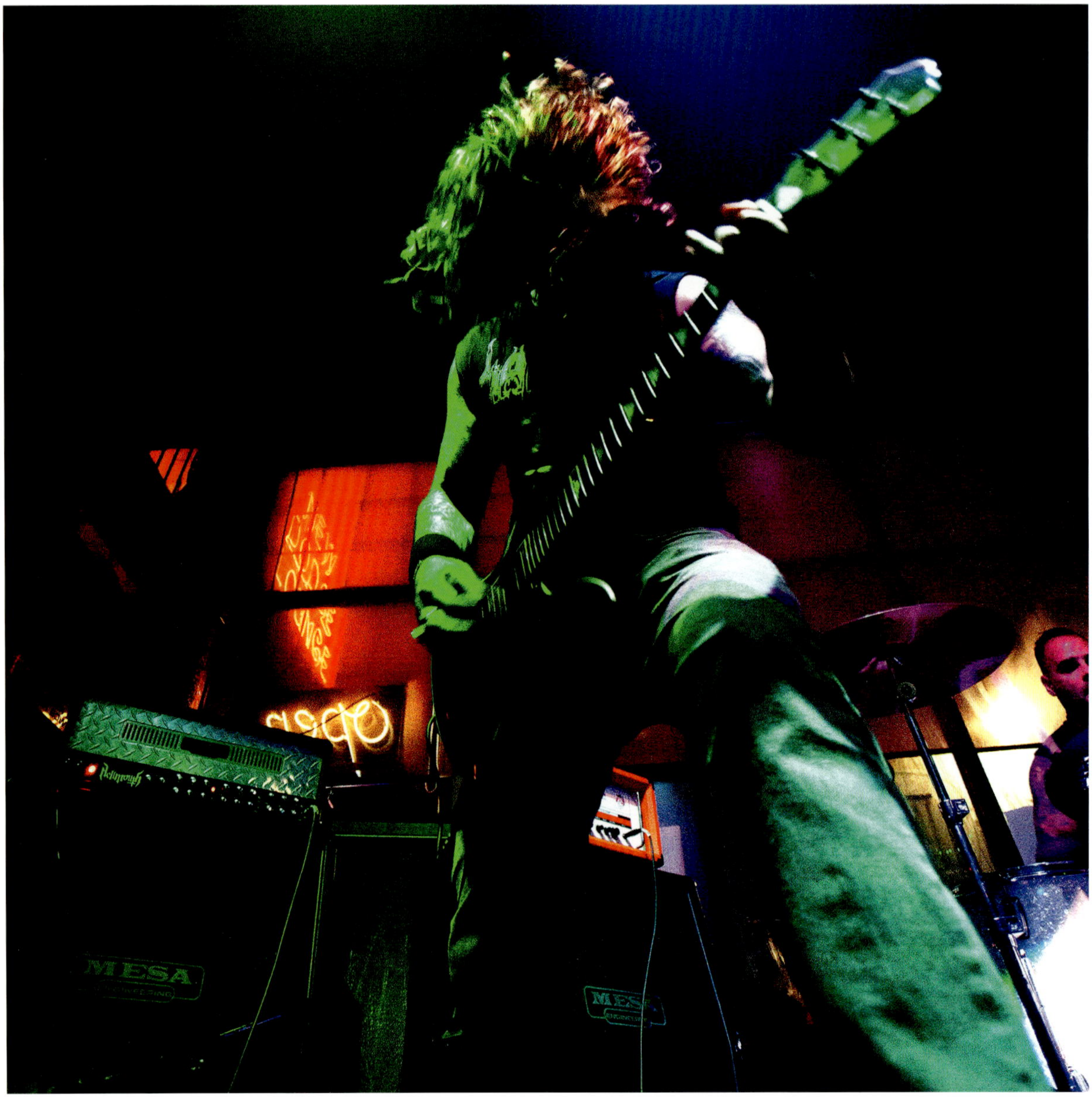

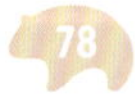

Contemporary Anishinaabe Art: A Continuation

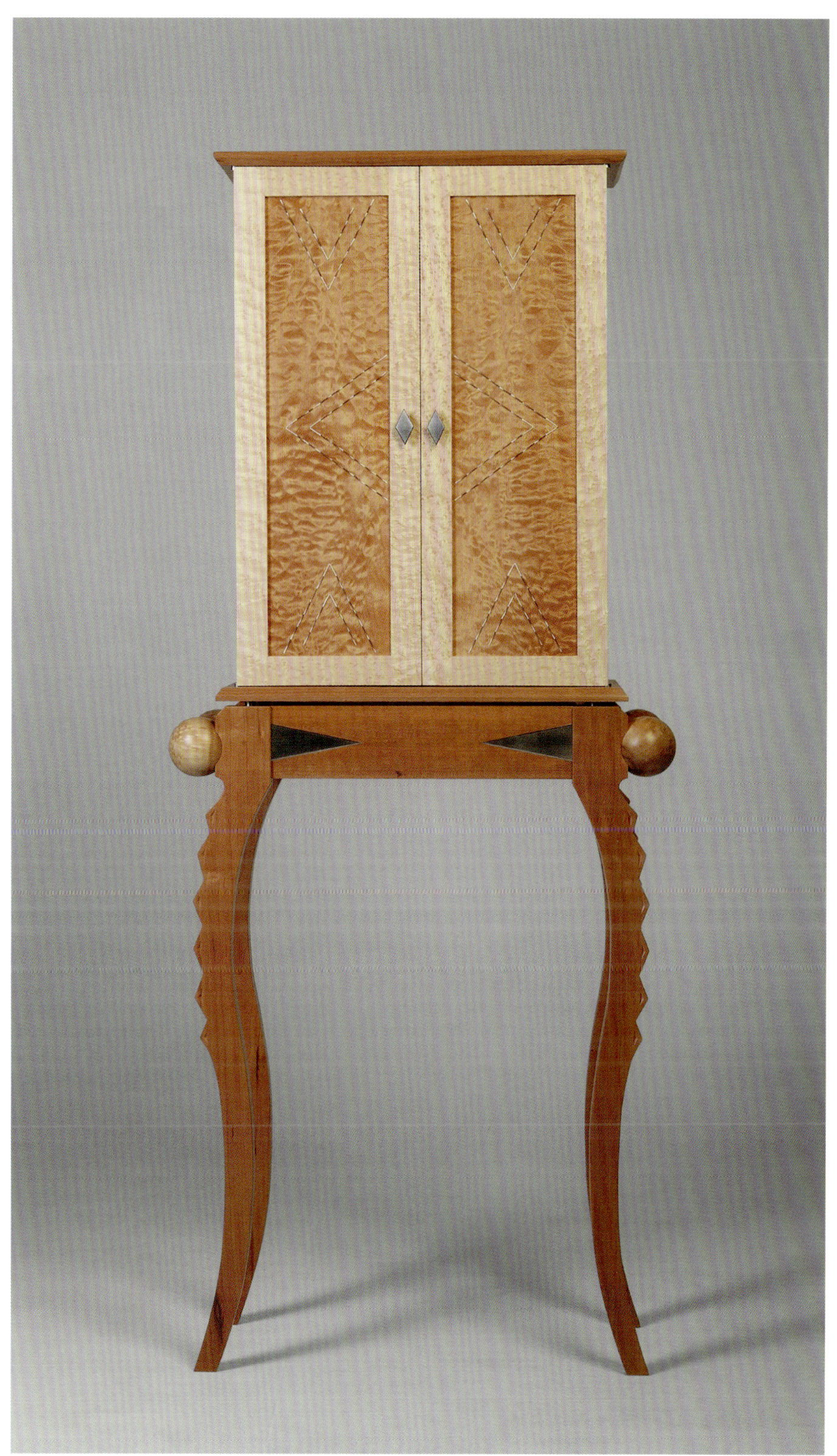

Dennis Esquivel (Grand Traverse Band of Ottawa and Chippewa Indians; b. 1961), *Out of the Woodlands: Standing Cabinet,* 2012

Select Works

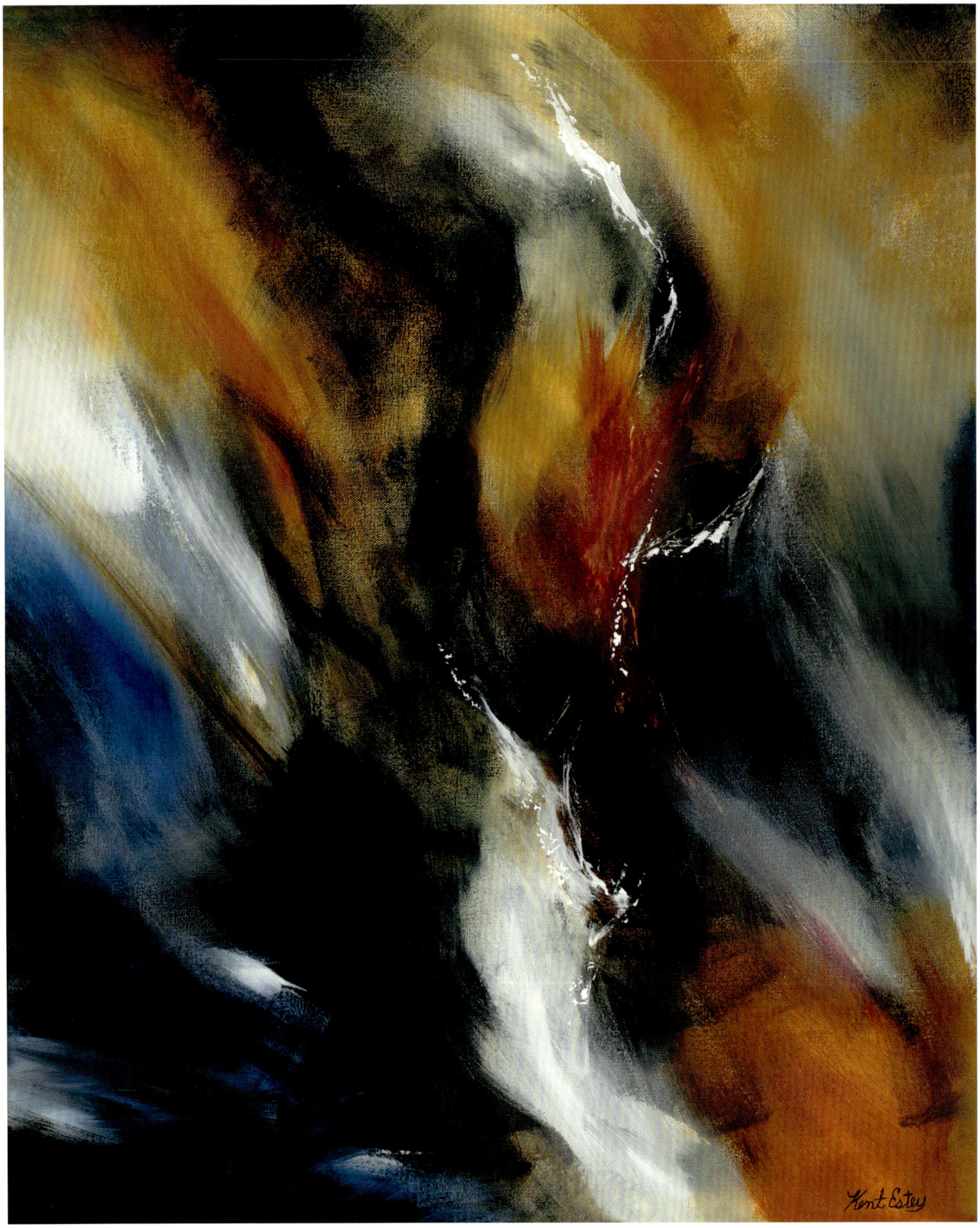

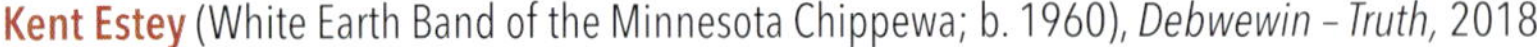

Kent Estey (White Earth Band of the Minnesota Chippewa; b. 1960), *Debwewin – Truth,* 2018

Contemporary Anishinaabe Art: A Continuation

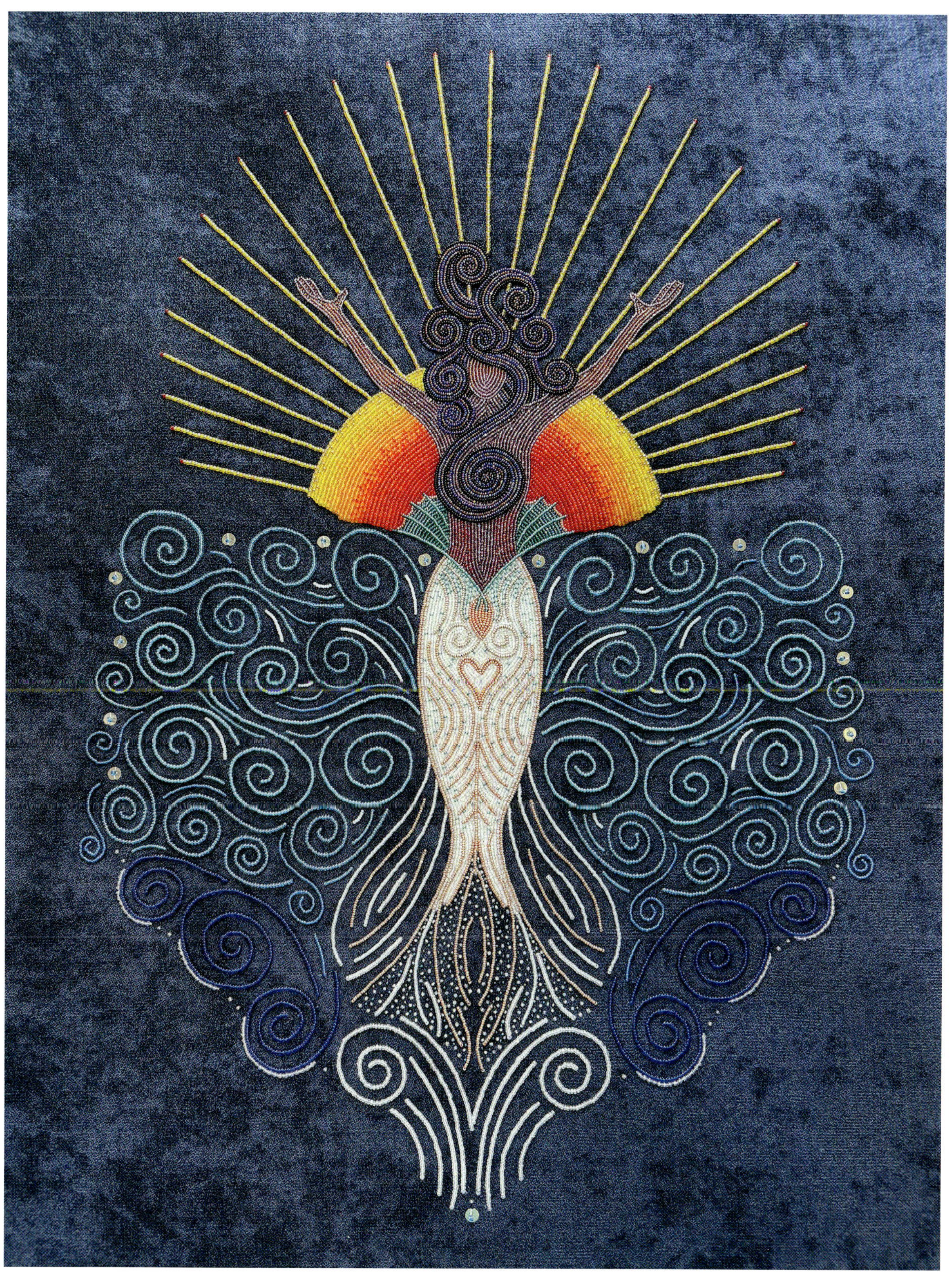

Jessica Leigh Gokey (Lac Courte Oreilles Band of Lake Superior Chippewa; b. 1985), *She Loves,* 2023–24

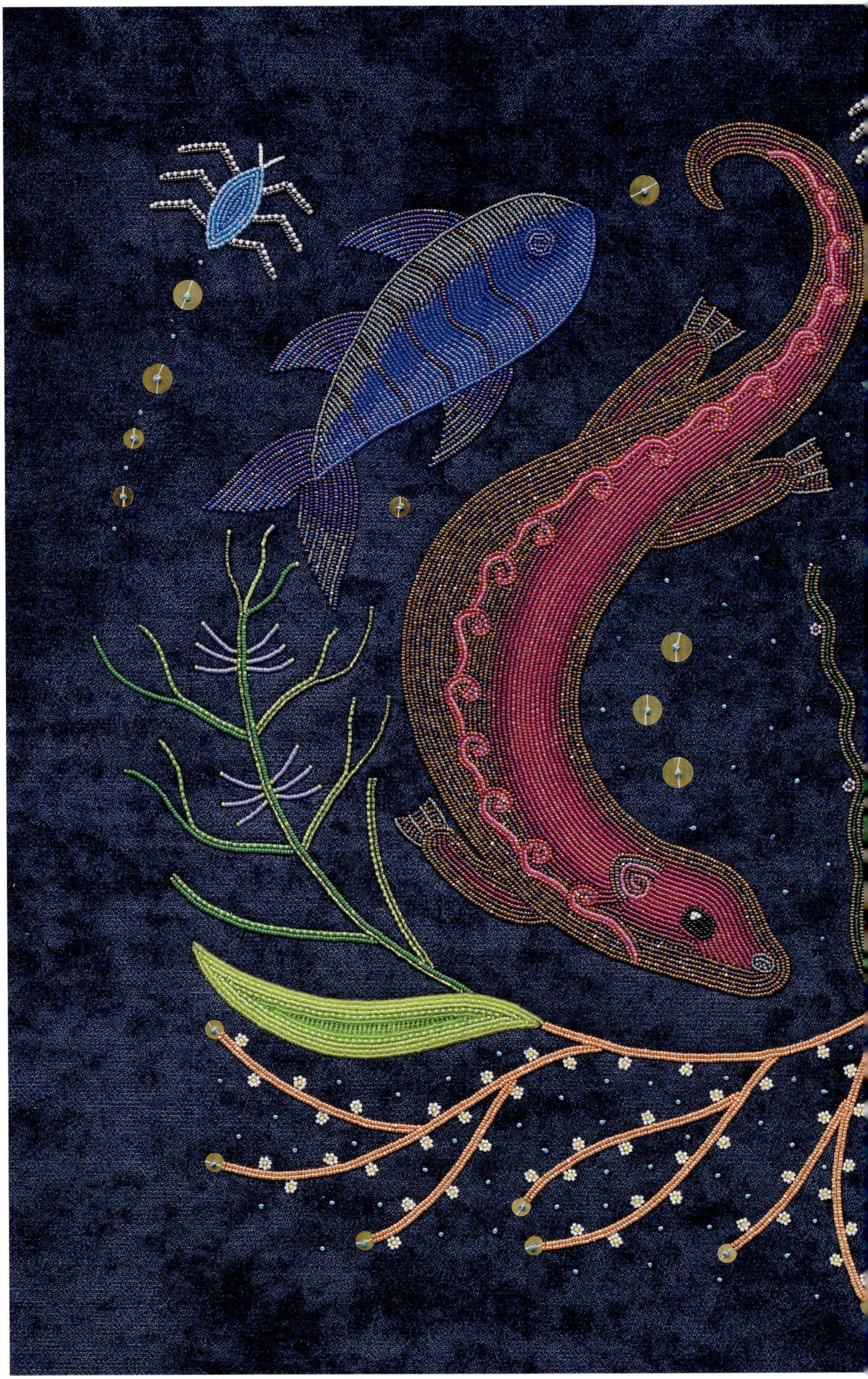

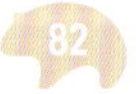

Contemporary Anishinaabe Art: A Continuation

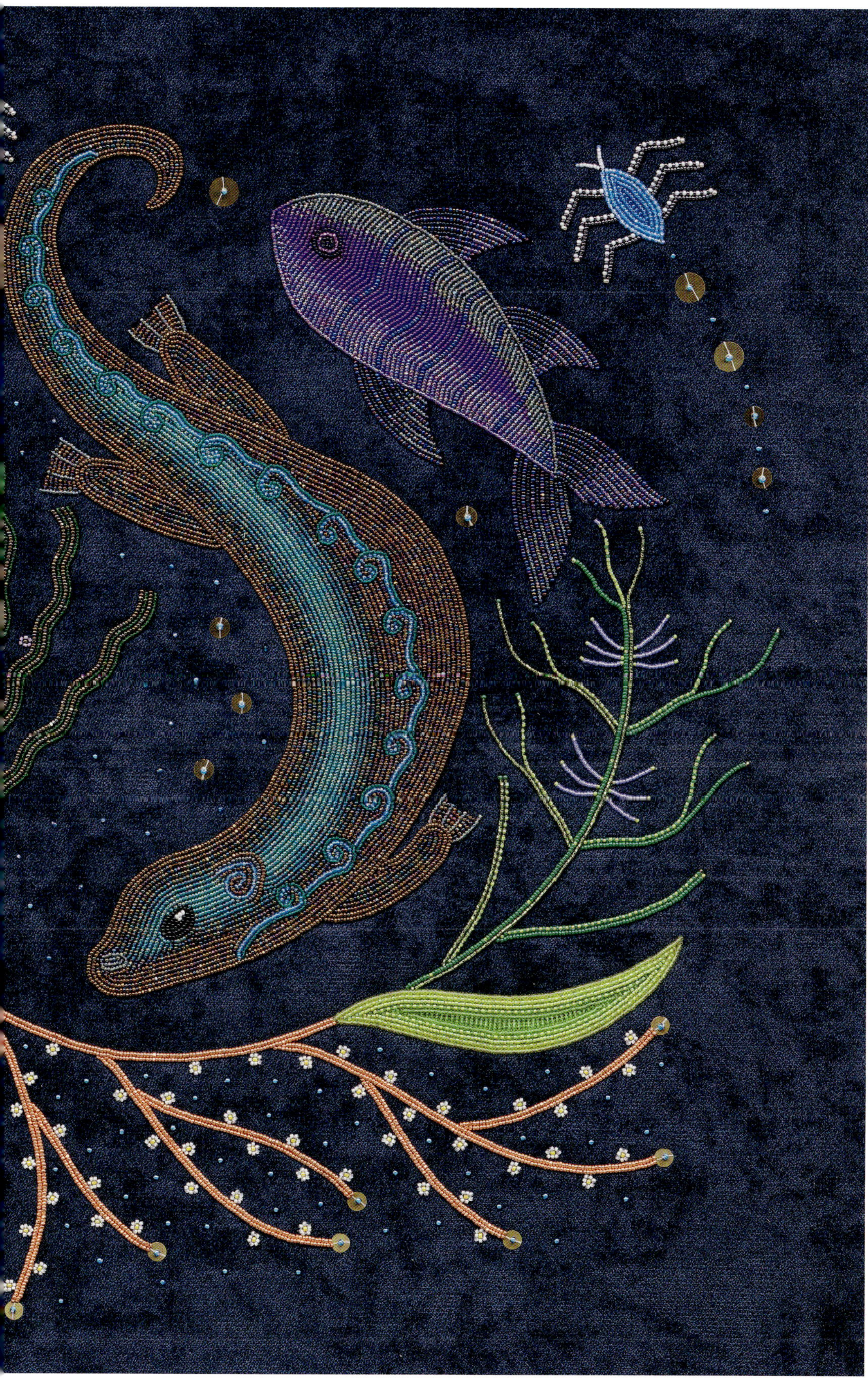

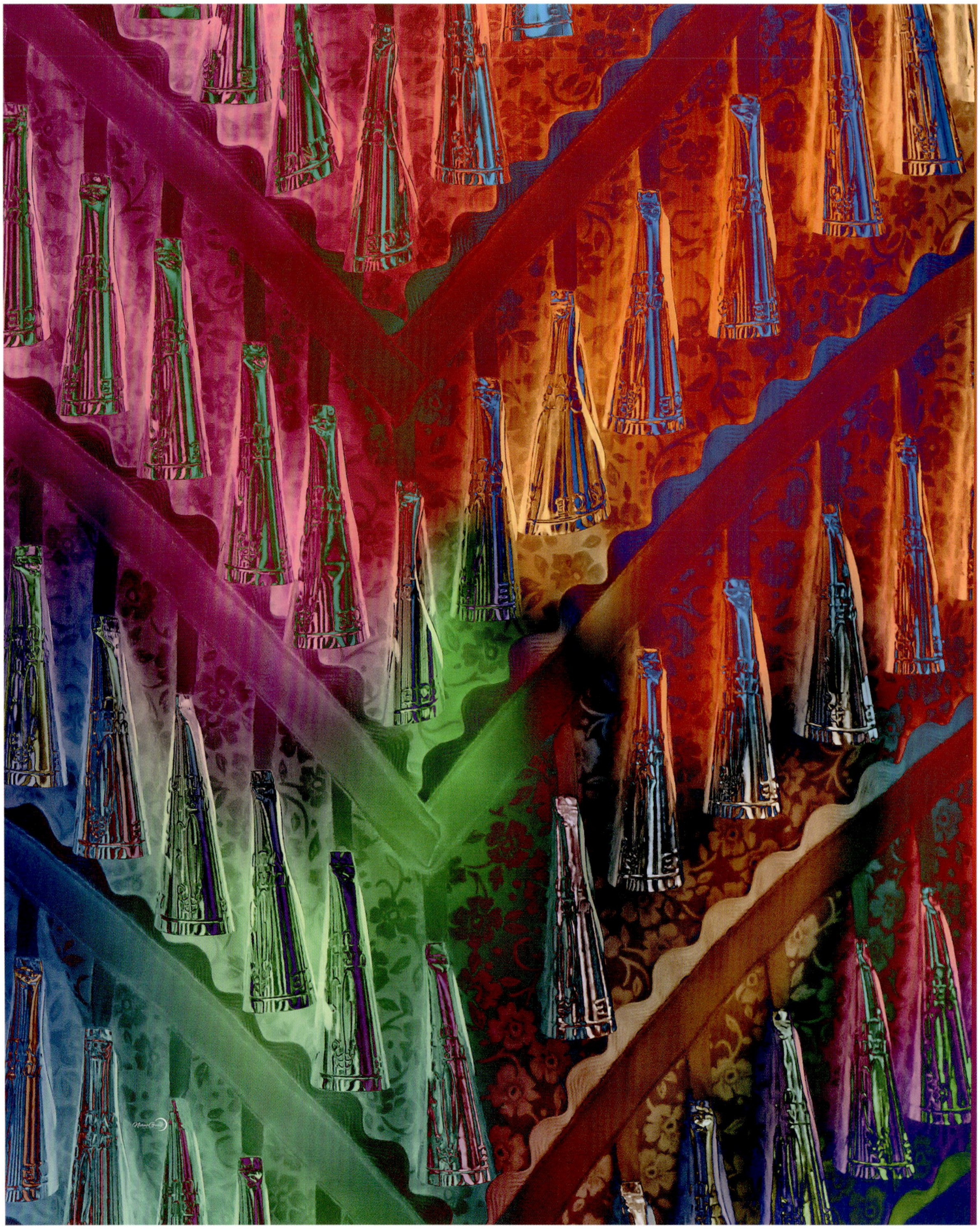

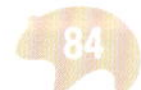

Previous Spread: Jessica Leigh Gokey (Lac Courte Oreilles Band of Lake Superior Chippewa; b. 1985), *Companions,* 2022

Marcella Hadden (Saginaw Chippewa Indian Tribe; b. 1961), *Jingle Dress,* 2020

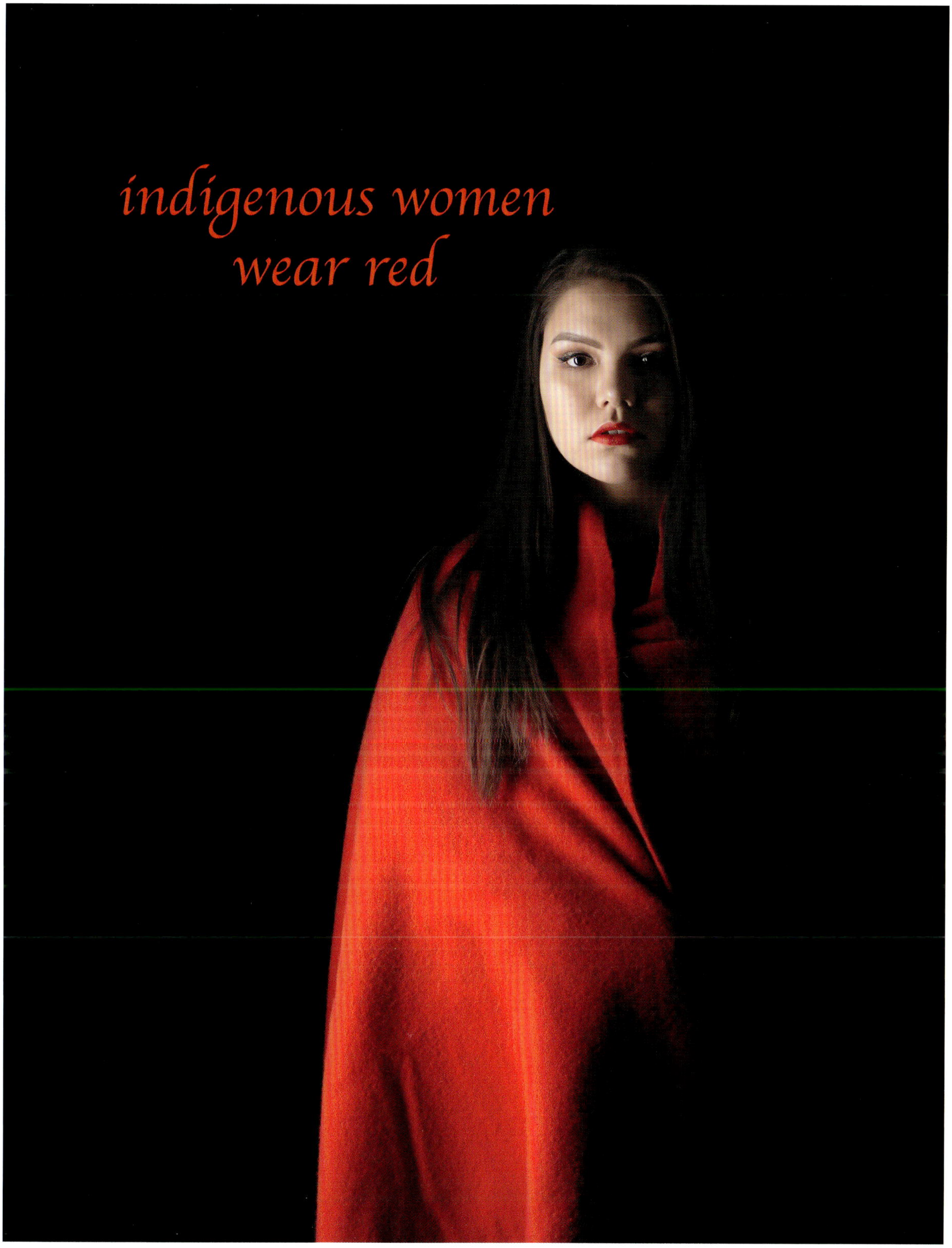

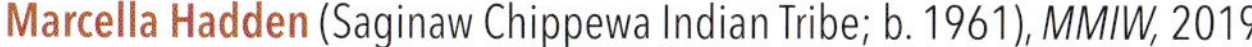

Marcella Hadden (Saginaw Chippewa Indian Tribe; b. 1961), *MMIW*, 2019

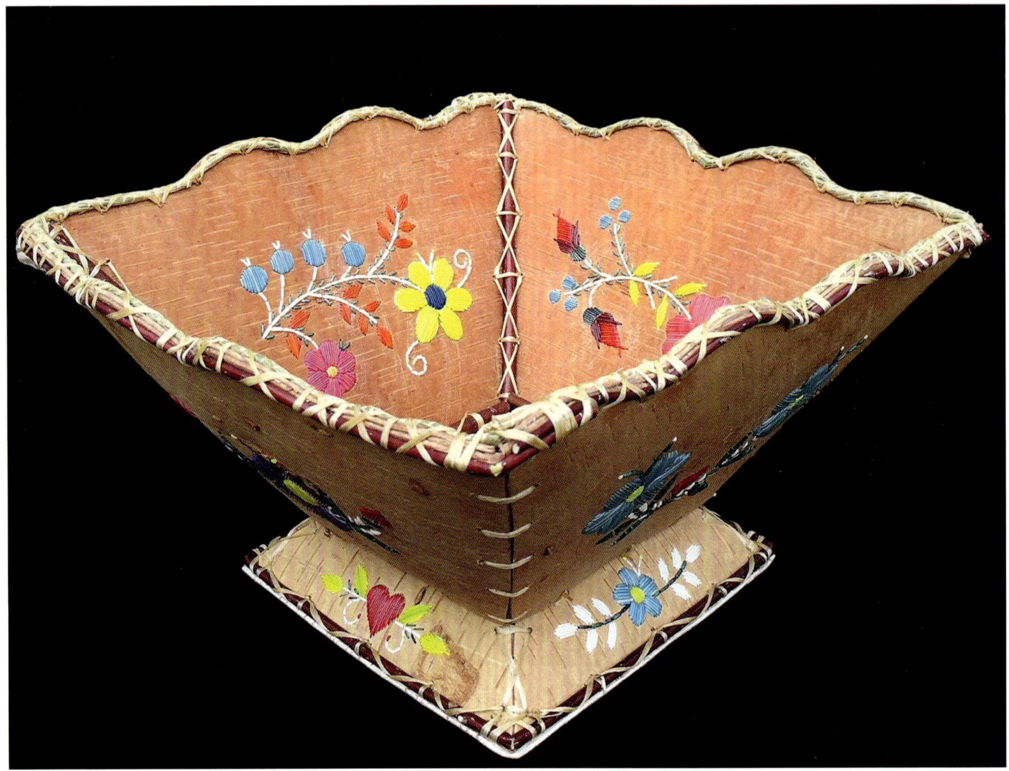

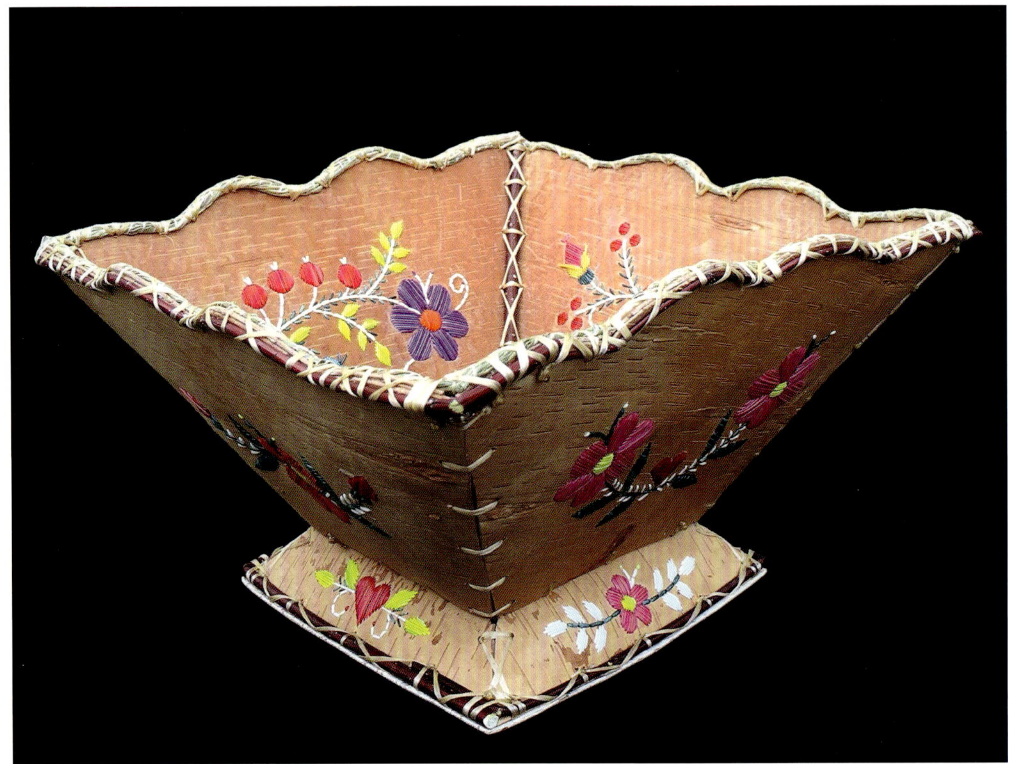

Terri Hom / Binesikwe (Lac Courte Oreilles Band of Lake Superior Chippewa; b. 1964), *My Brother's Basket,* 2020

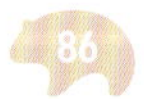

Contemporary Anishinaabe Art: A Continuation

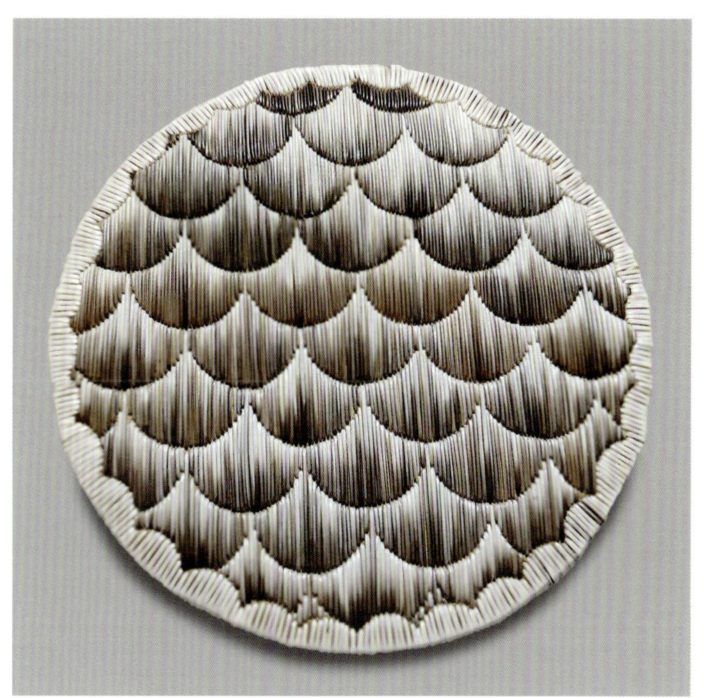

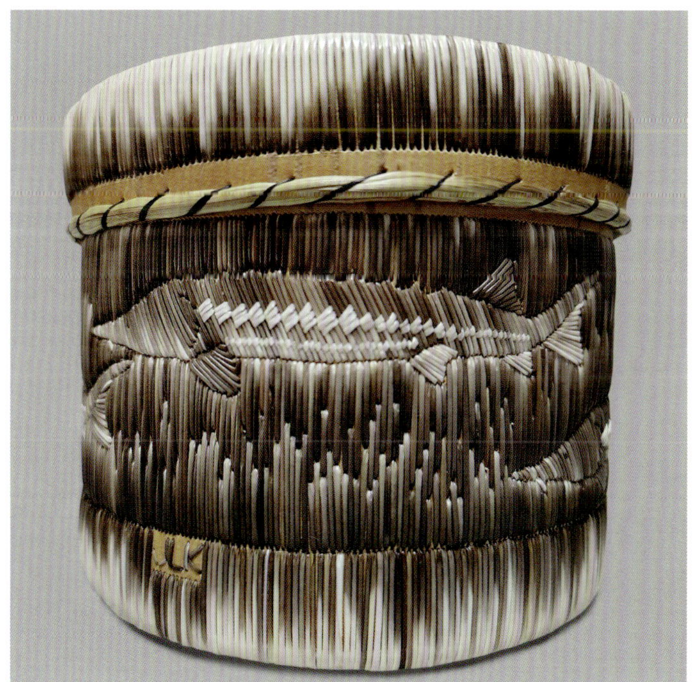

Jacob Keshick (Little Traverse Bay Bands of Odawa Indians; b. 1987), *Open Water,* 2025

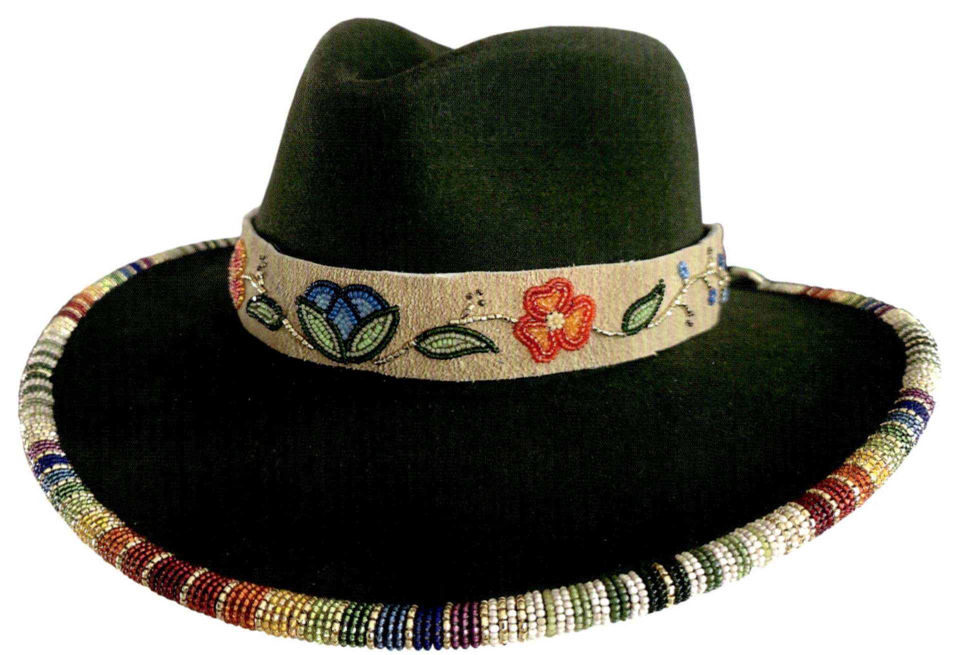

Heron Hill Designs–Joey Kennedy (First Descendant of Saginaw Chippewa Indian Tribe; b. 1990) and **Daniel Collazos** (b. 1990), *Baakaani-inaadizi: Their Actions Are Different,* 2025

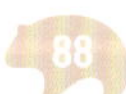

Contemporary Anishinaabe Art: A Continuation

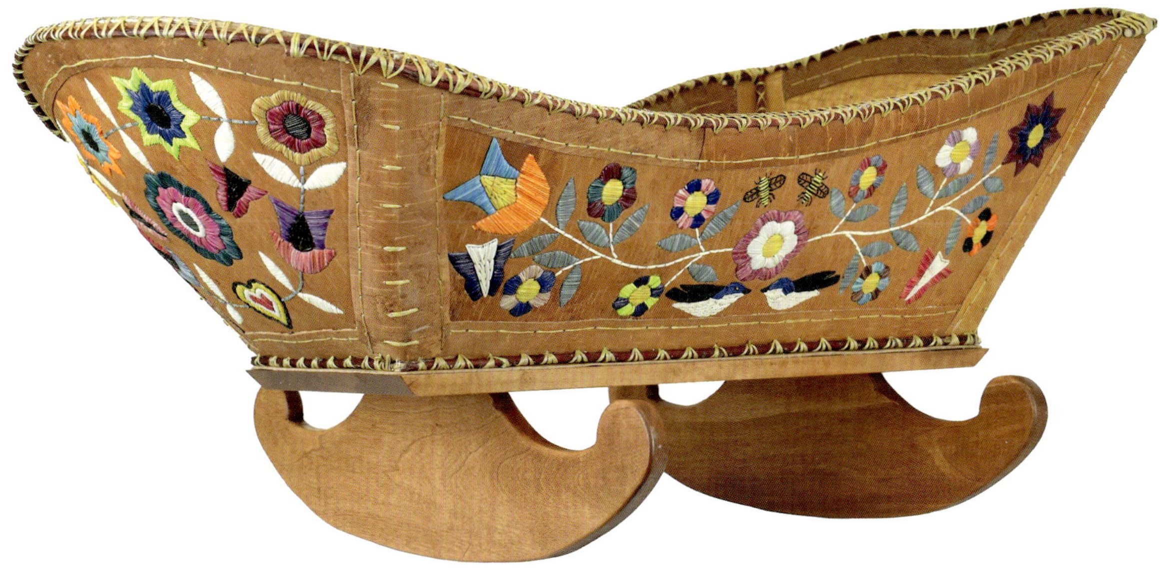

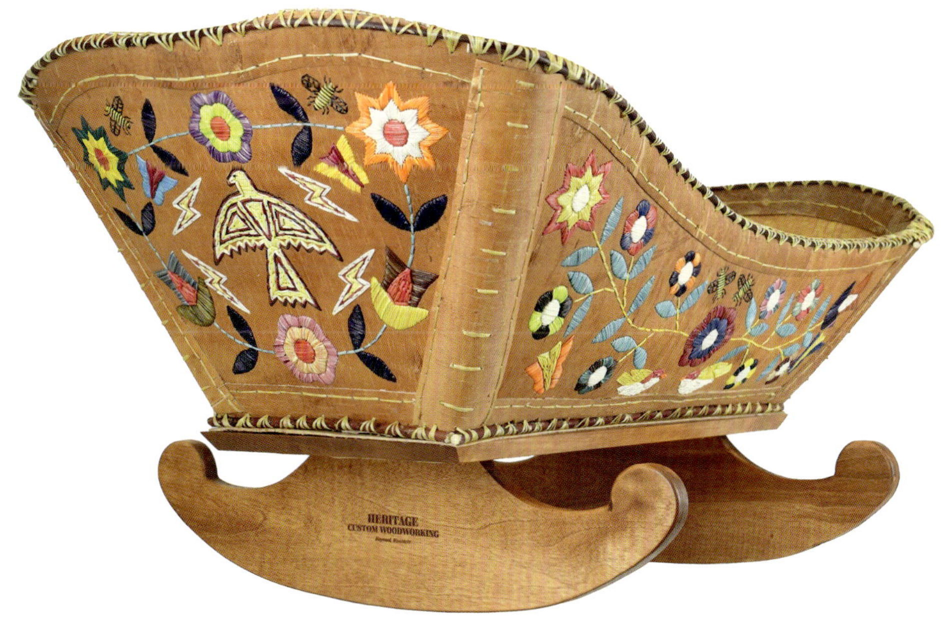

Pat Kruse (Red Cliff Band of Lake Superior Chippewa; Mille Lacs Band of Ojibwe [Descent]; b. 1971), *Cradle of All Colors,* 2019

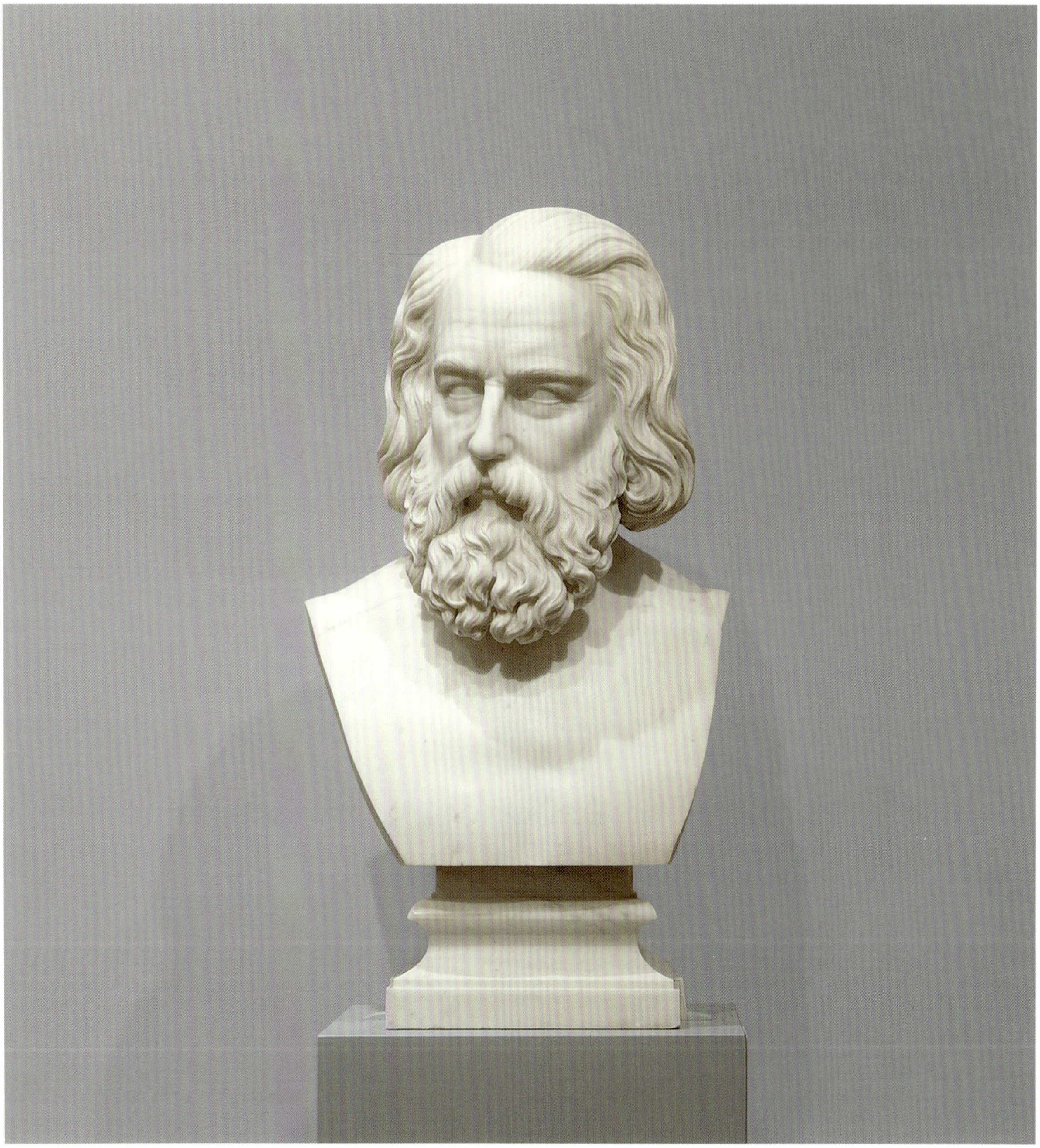

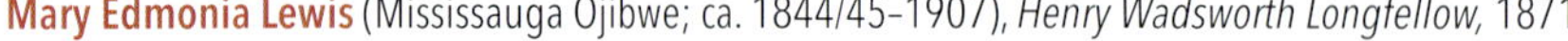

Mary Edmonia Lewis (Mississauga Ojibwe; ca. 1844/45–1907), *Henry Wadsworth Longfellow,* 1871

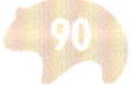

Contemporary Anishinaabe Art: A Continuation

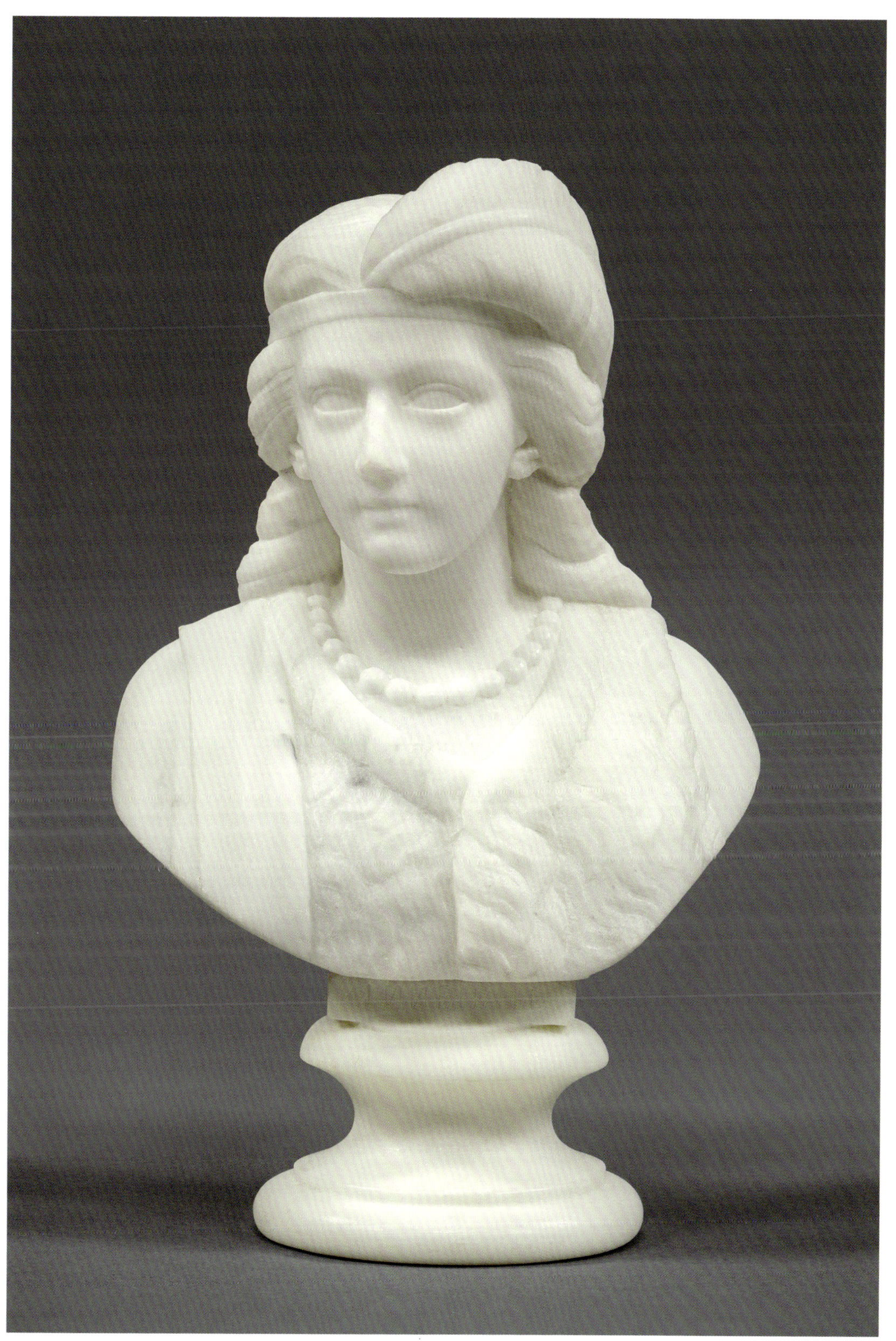

Mary Edmonia Lewis (Mississauga Ojibwe; ca. 1844/45–1907), *Minnehaha,* 1868

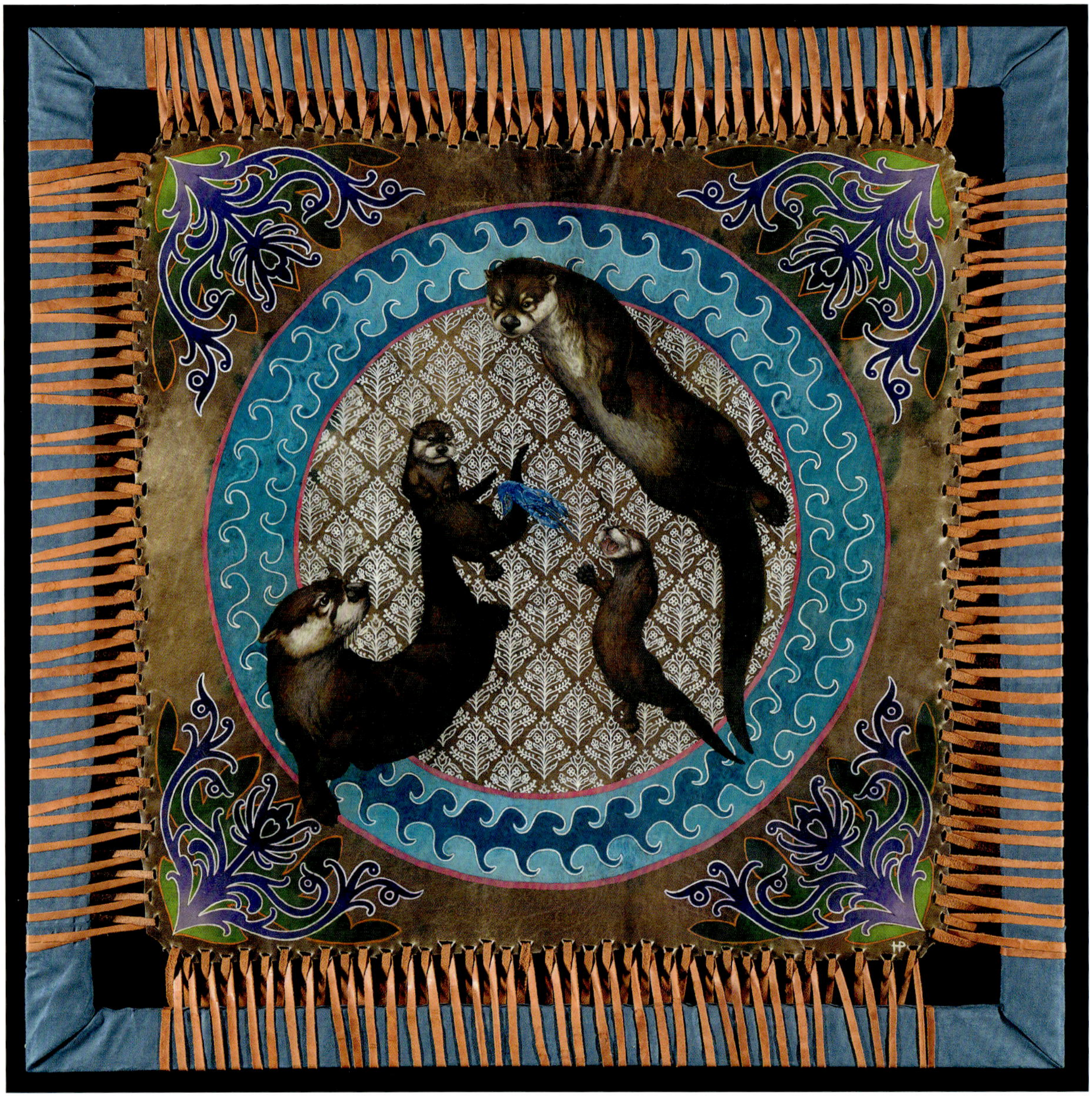

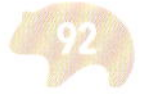

David Martin (Pokagon Band of Potawatomi; b. 1973), *Family Hunt,* 2024

Contemporary Anishinaabe Art: A Continuation

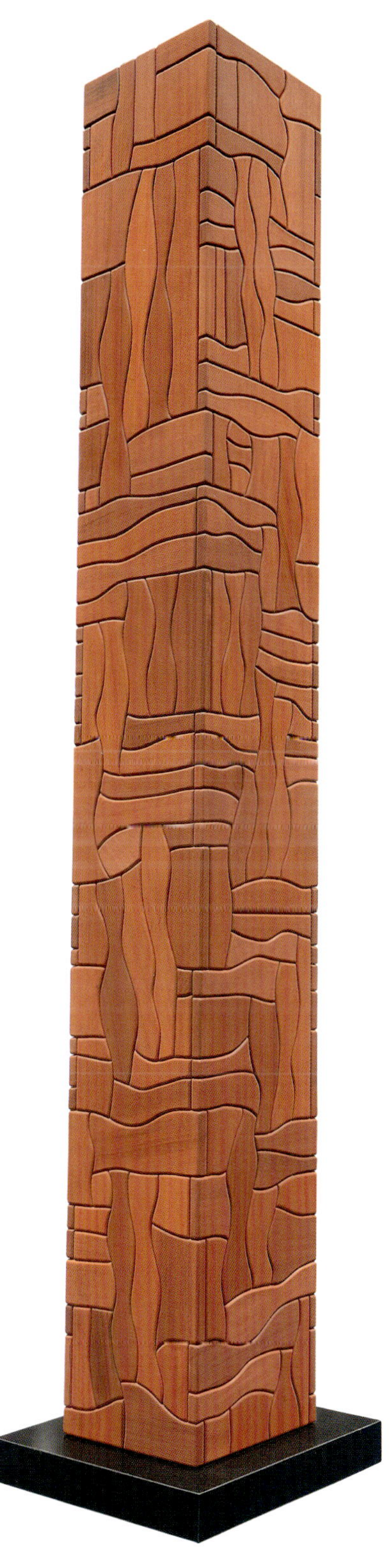

George Morrison (Grand Portage Band of Lake Superior Chippewa; 1919–2000), *Totemic Column, 1995–2024*

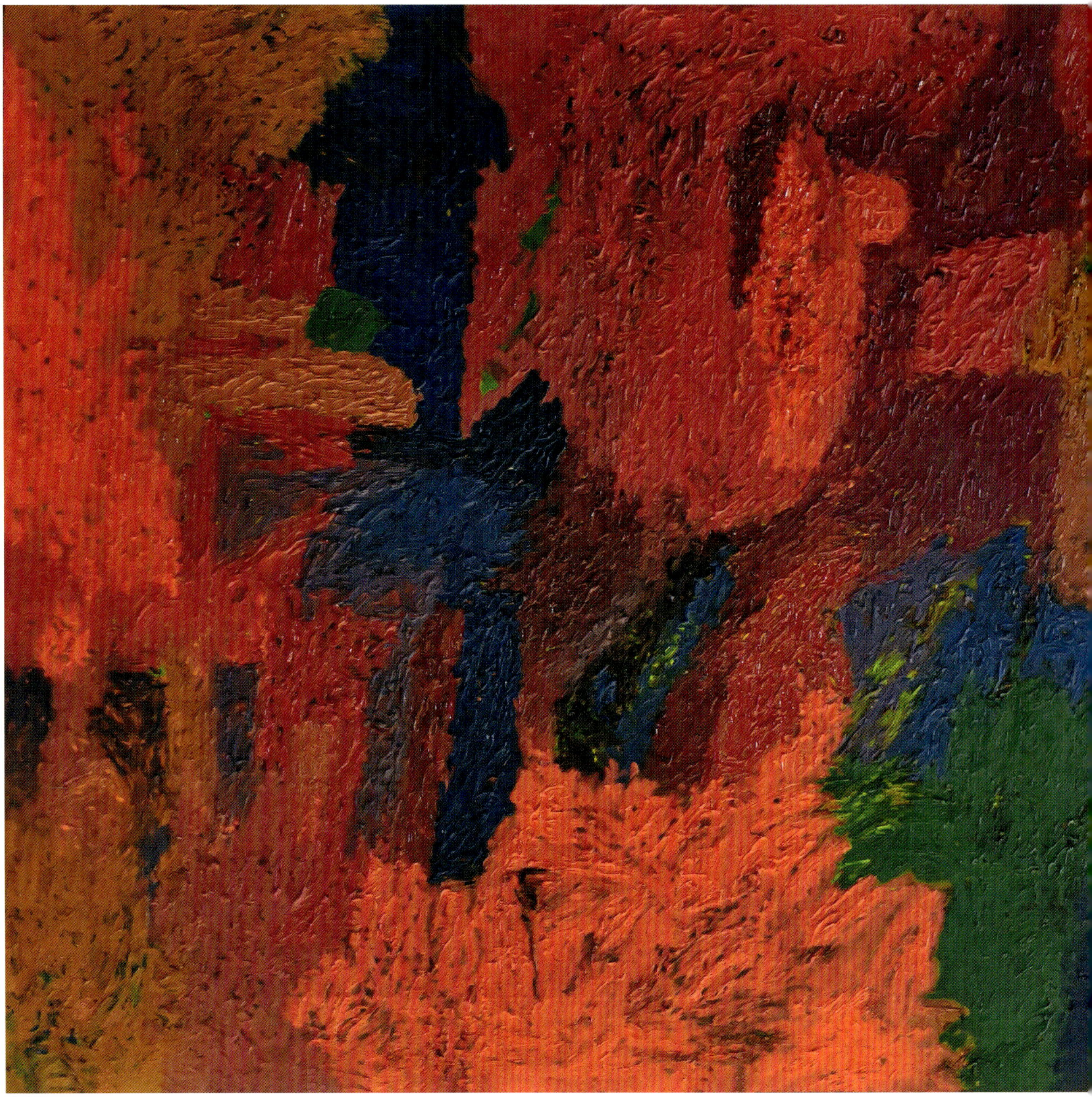

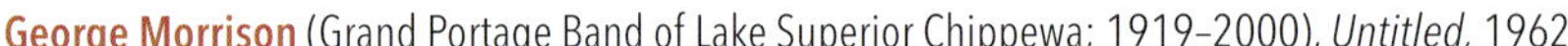

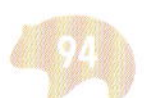

Contemporary Anishinaabe Art: A Continuation

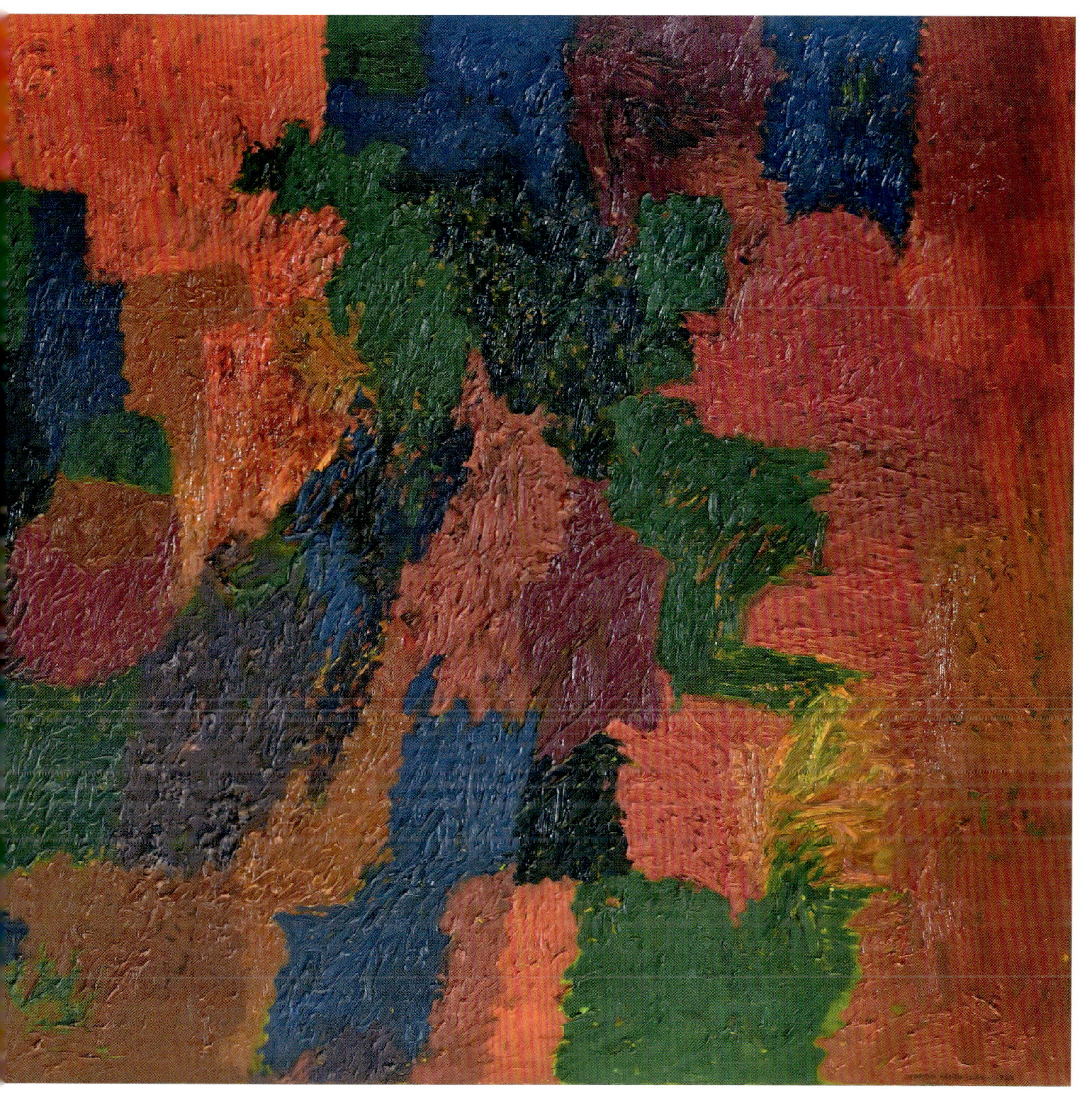

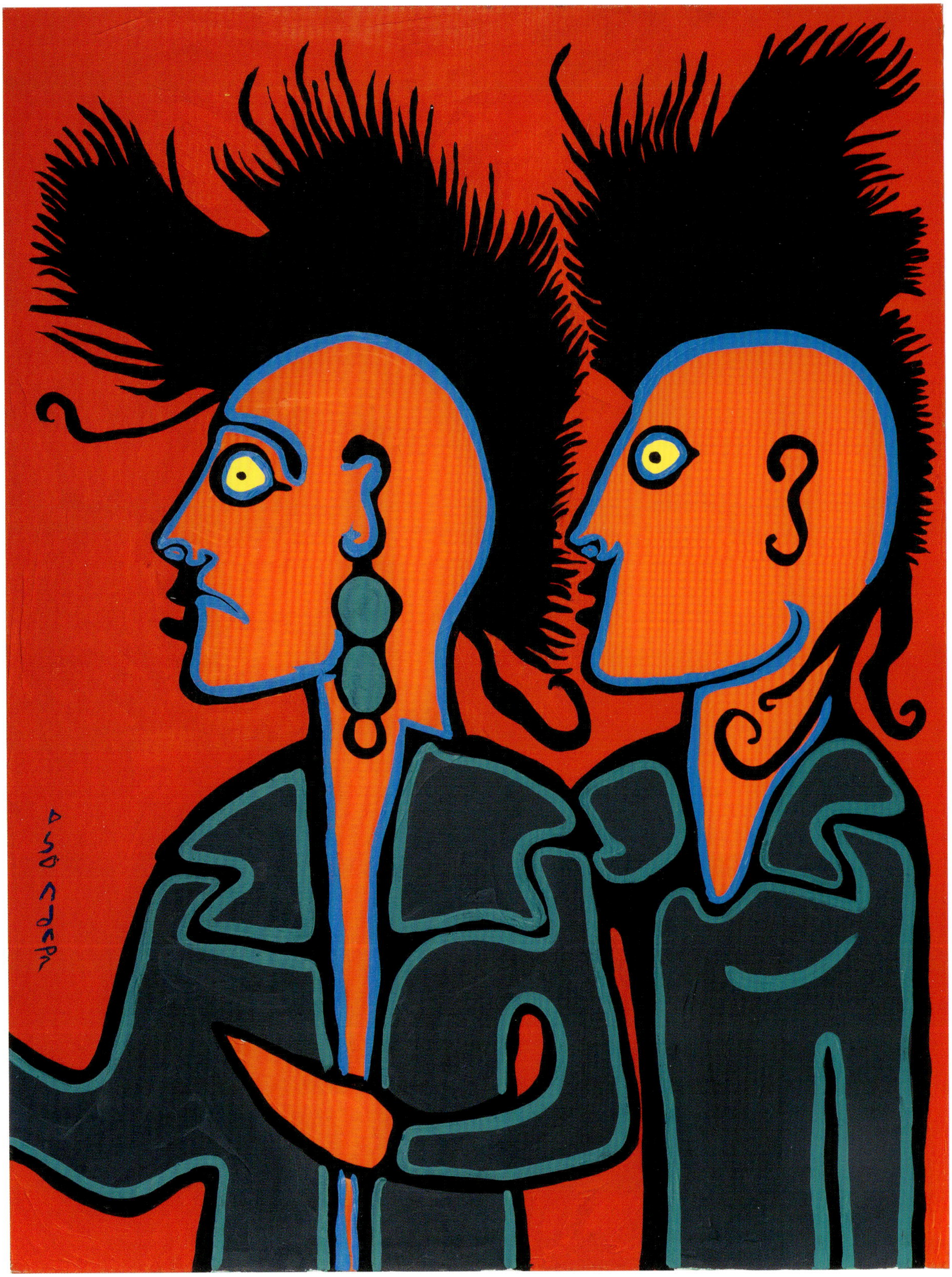

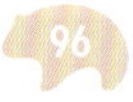

Norval Morrisseau (Bingwi Neyaashi Anishinaabek First Nation; 1932–2007), *Punk Rockers Nancy and Andy,* 1989

Contemporary Anishinaabe Art: A Continuation

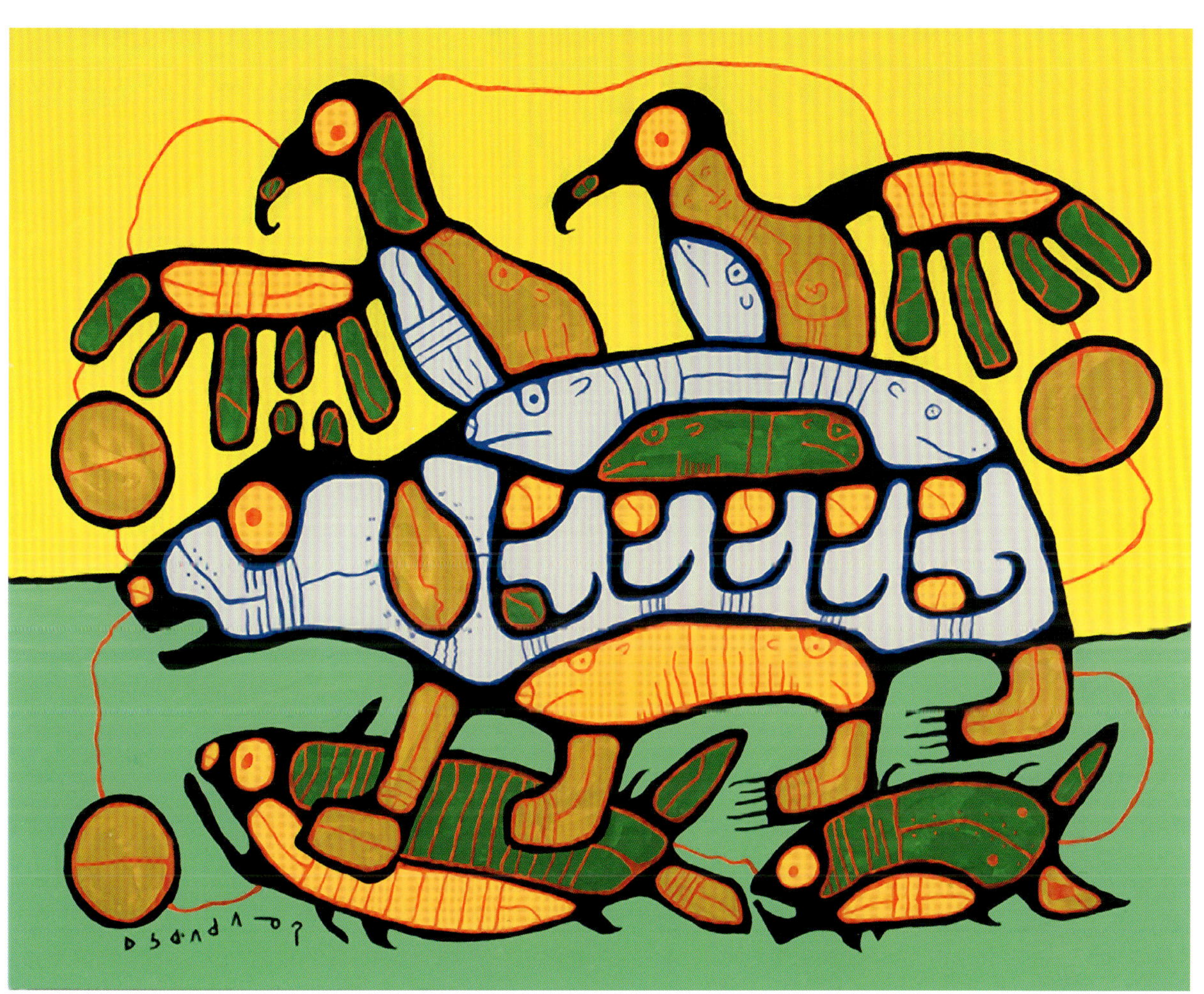

Norval Morrisseau (Bingwi Neyaashi Anishinaabek First Nation; 1932–2007), *Bear, Fish, Bird–Interdependence,* ca.1990

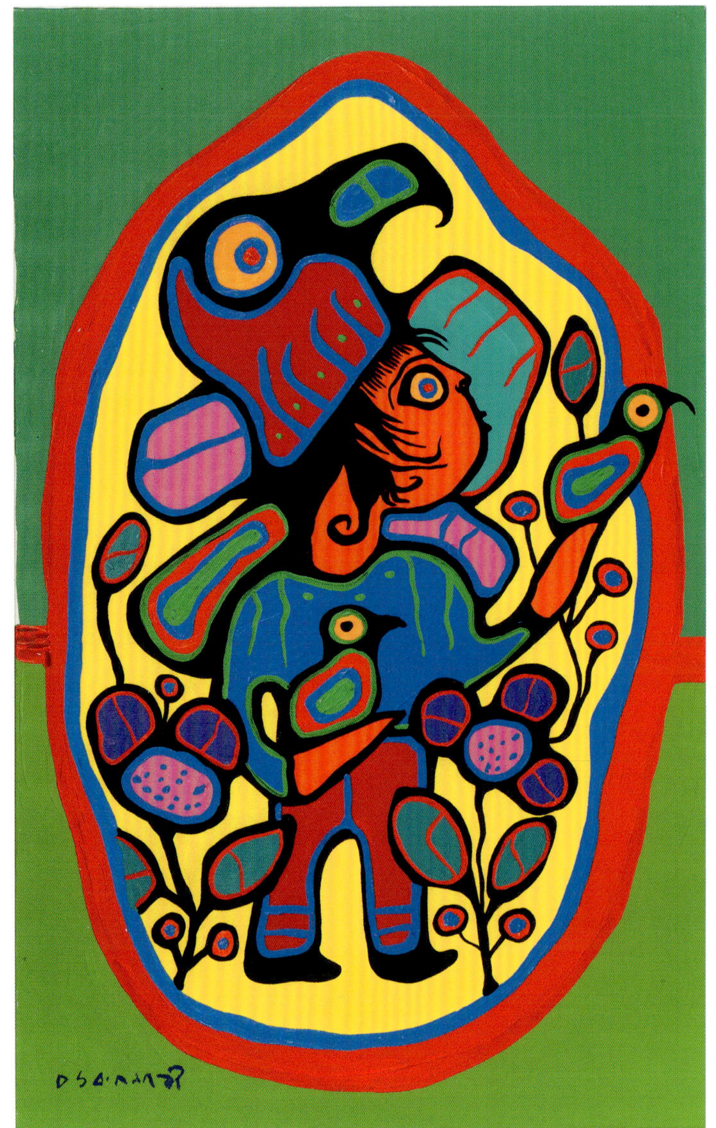 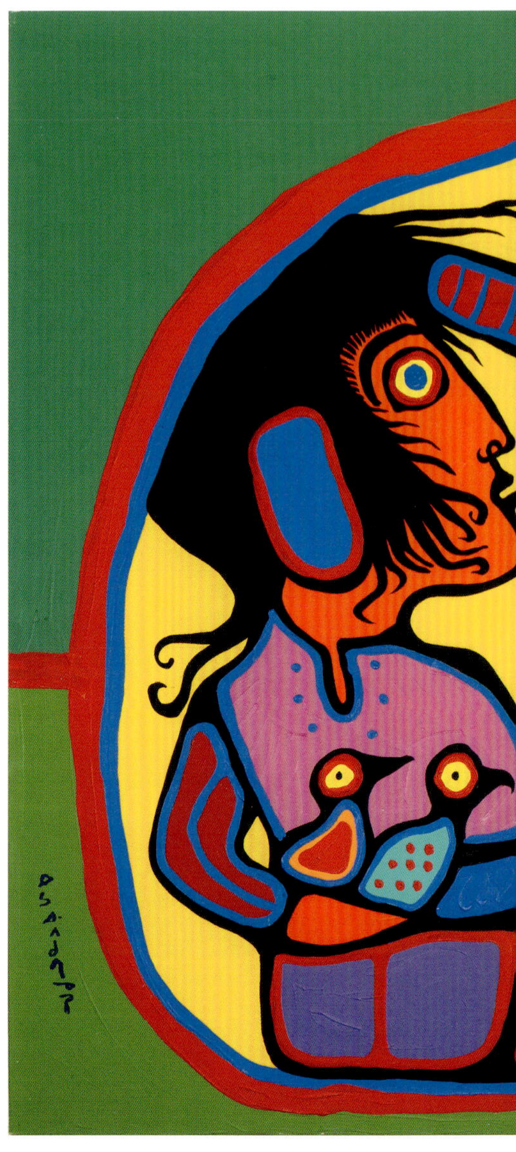

Norval Morrisseau (Bingwi Neyaashi Anishinaabek First Nation; 1932–2007), *Elder Teaching the Next Generation to Communicate in Harmony with All Living Beings,* 1991-92

Contemporary Anishinaabe Art: A Continuation

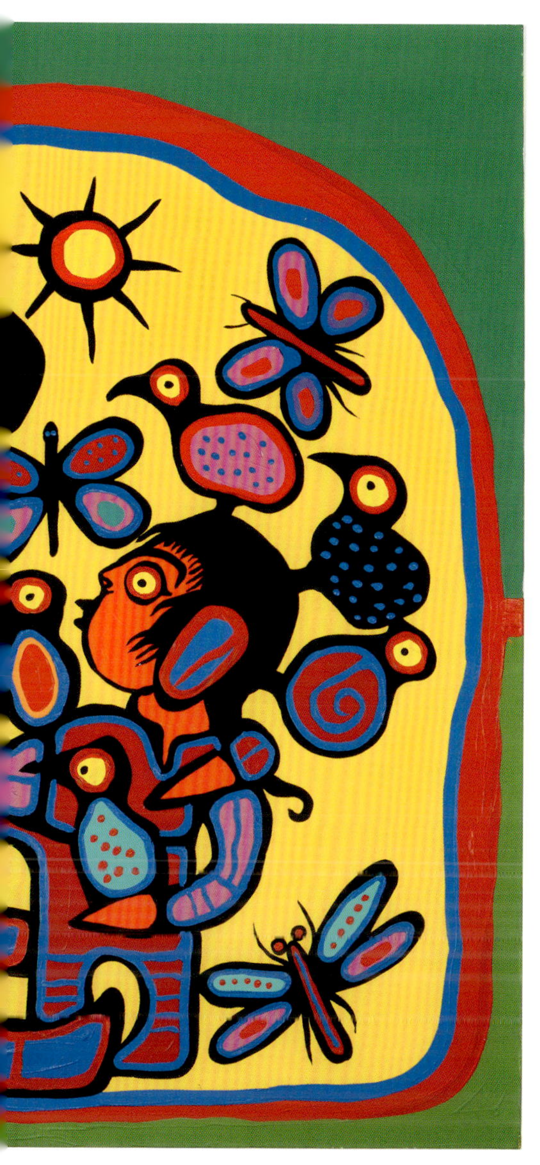

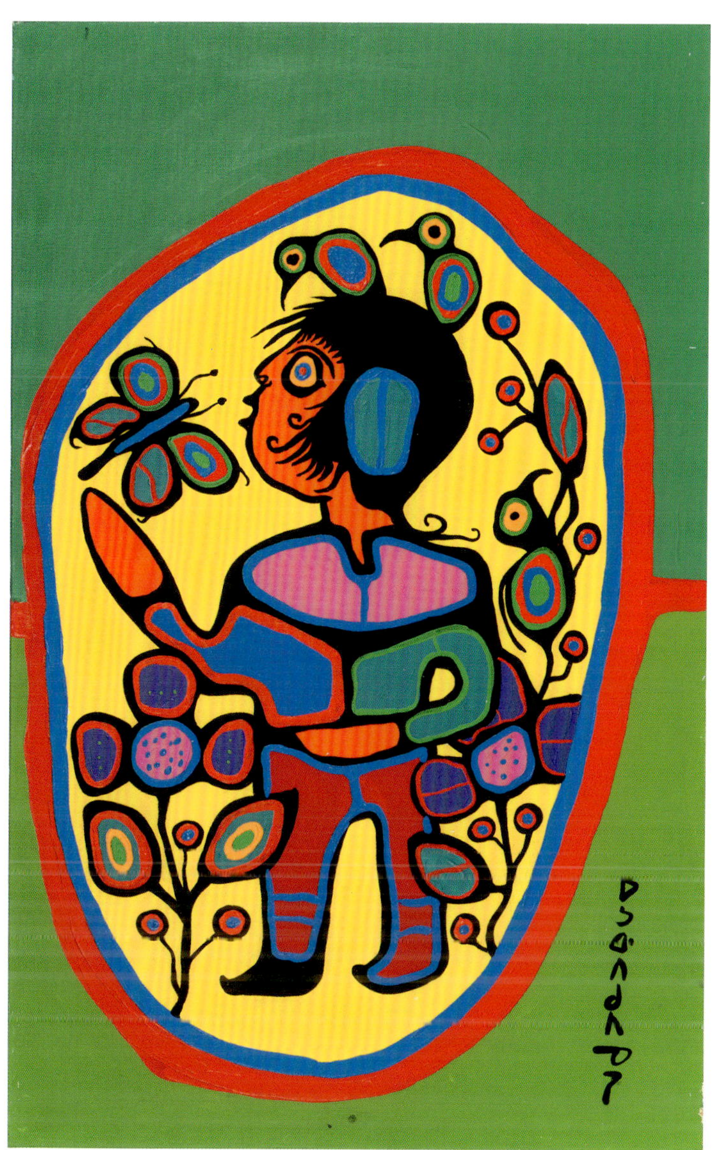

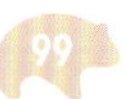

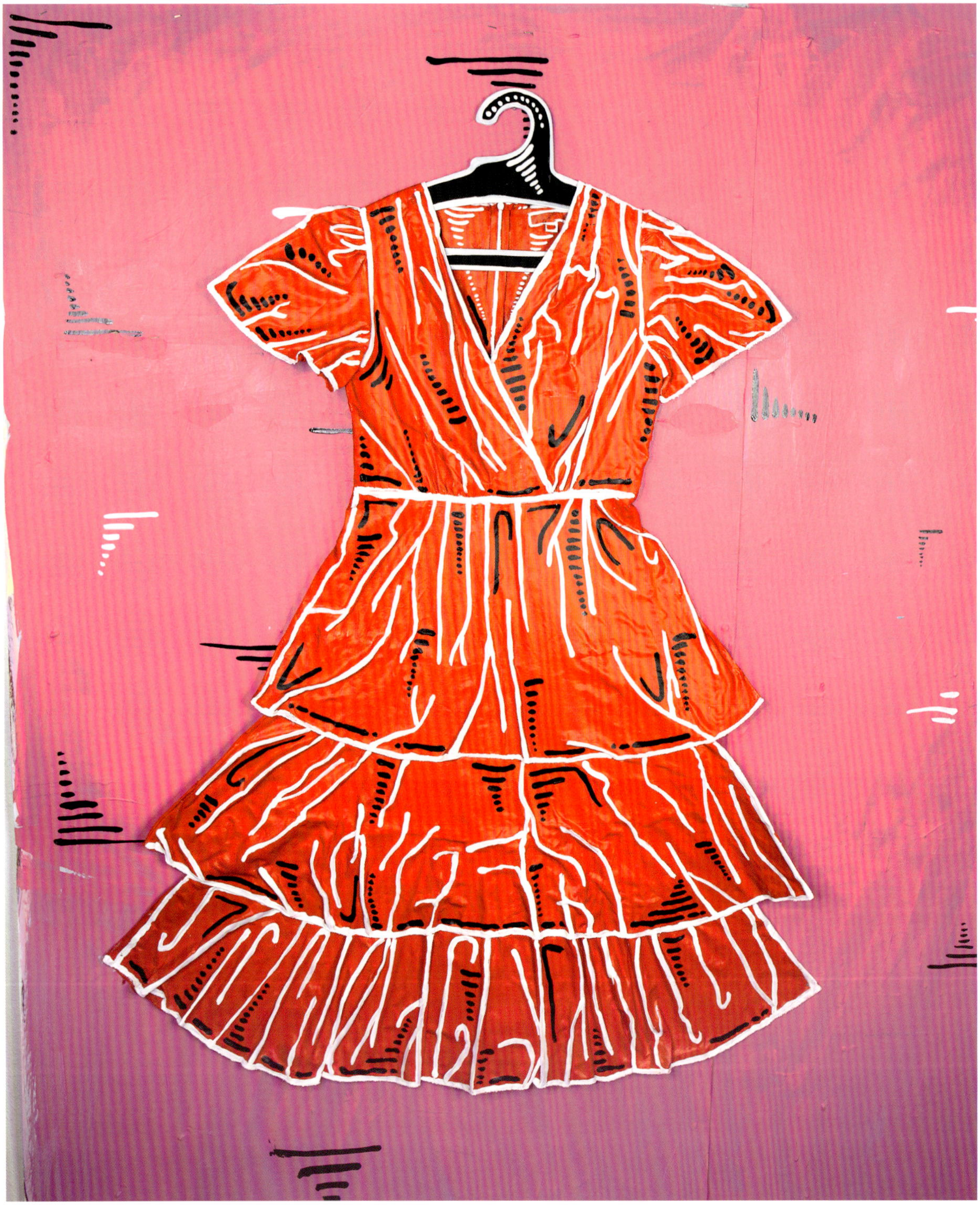

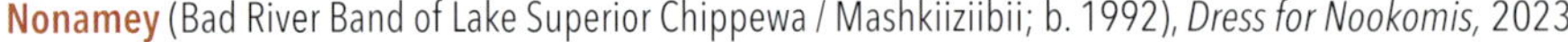

Nonamey (Bad River Band of Lake Superior Chippewa / Mashkiiziibii; b. 1992), *Dress for Nookomis,* 2023

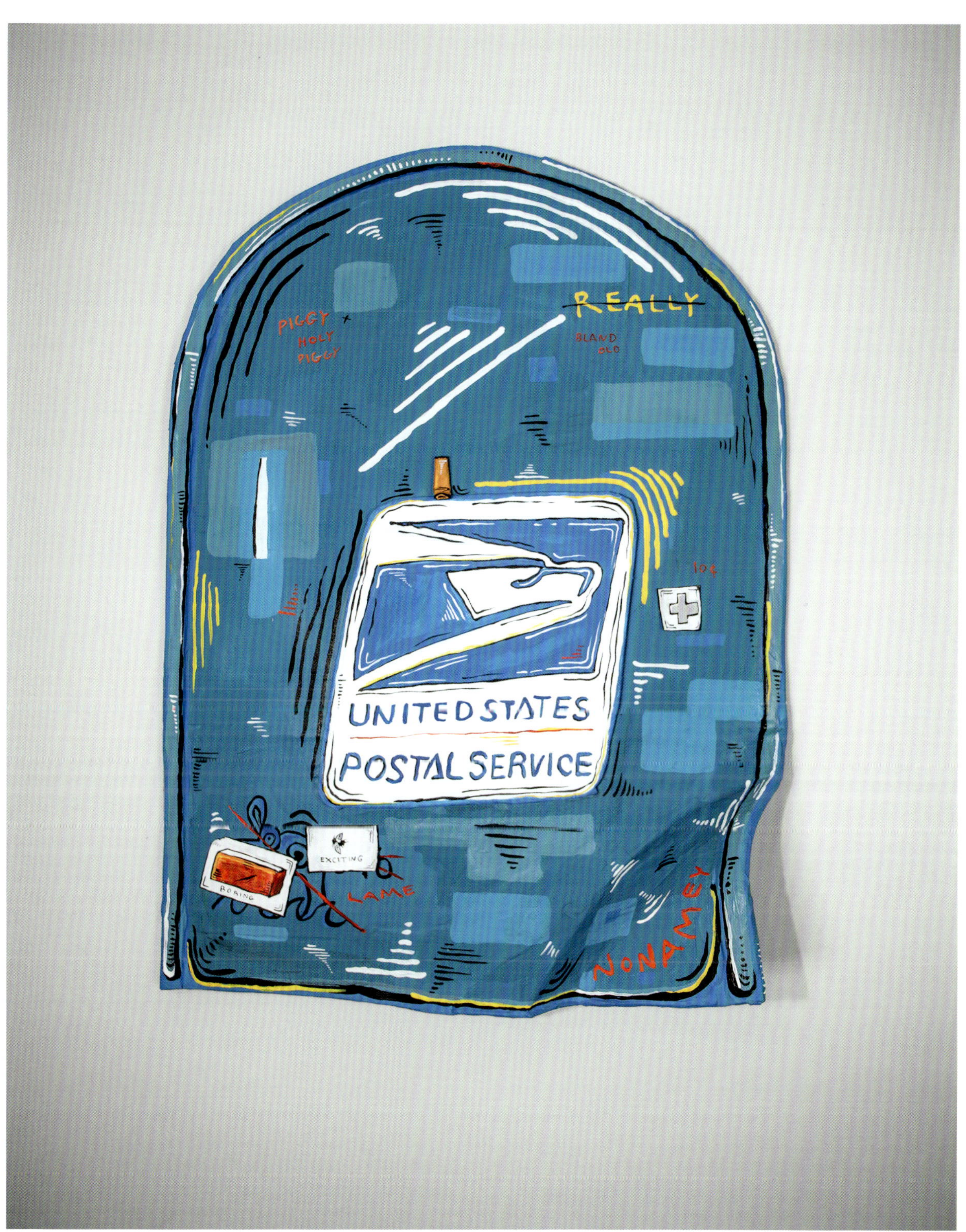

Nonamey (Bad River Band of Lake Superior Chippewa / Mashkiiziibii; b. 1992), *Postal Box,* 2021

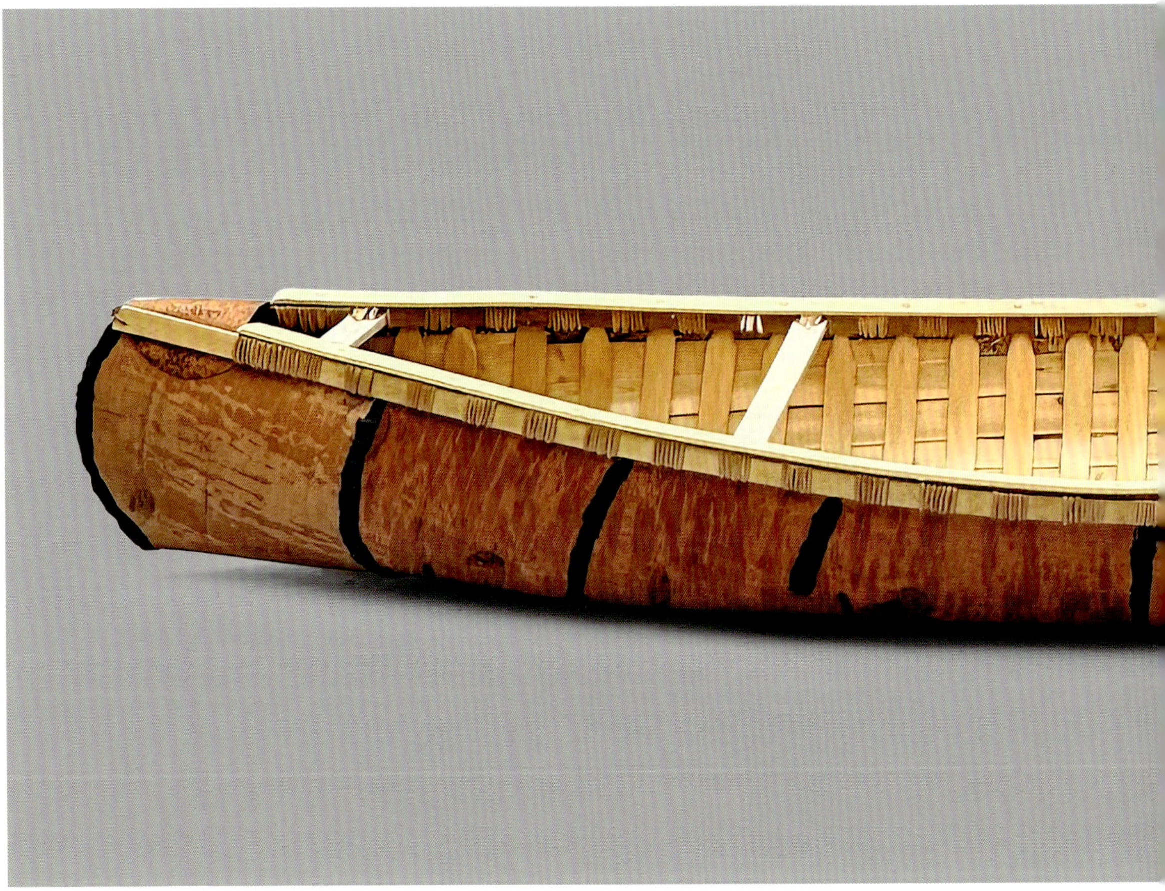

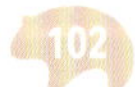

Ronald J. Paquin (Sault Ste. Marie Tribe of Chippewa; b. 1942), *Wiigwaas jiimaan*, 2018

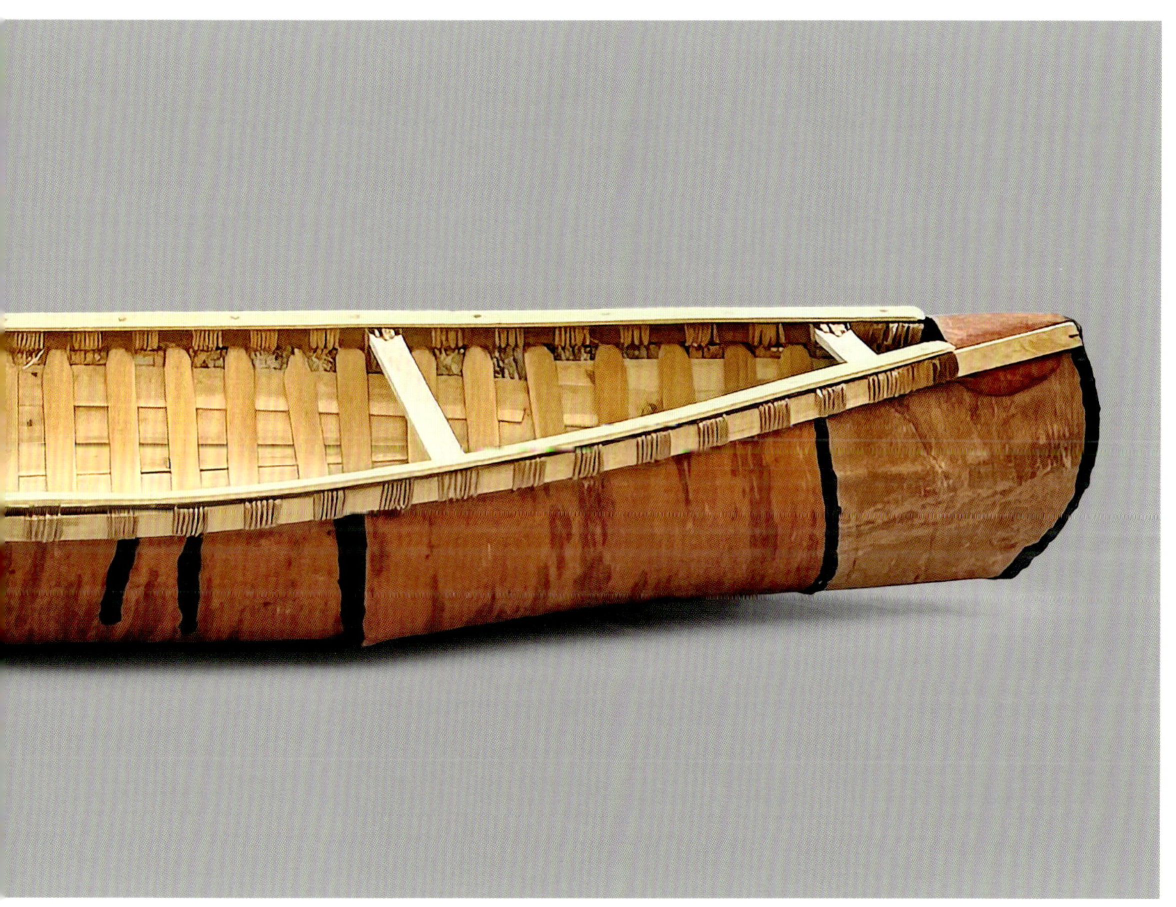

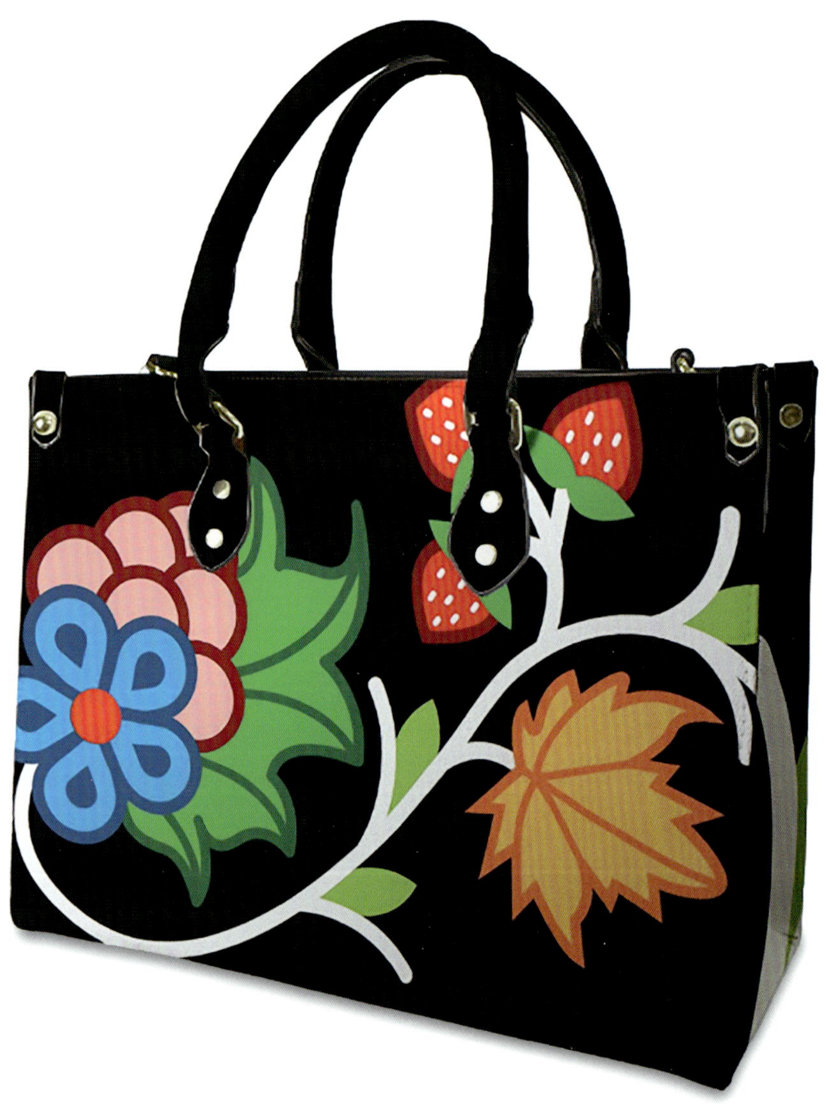

Eva Oldman (Little Traverse Bay Bands of Odawa Indians; Northern Arapaho Tribe of the Wind River Reservation; b. 1981), *Anishinaabe Woodland Strawberry Handbag,* 2024

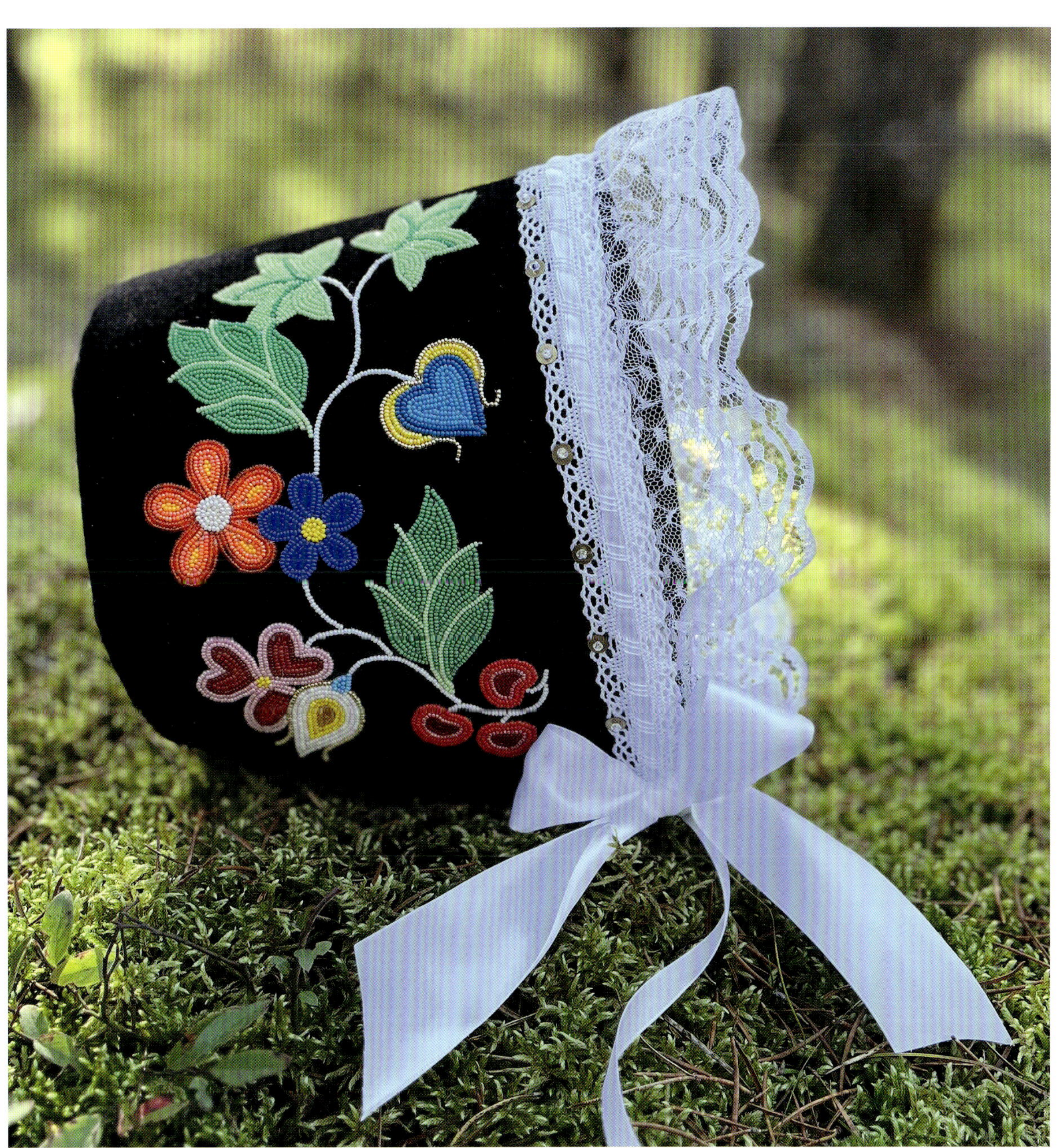

Lisa Passinault (Saginaw Chippewa Indian Tribe; b. 1976), *Woodland Baby Bonnet,* 2023

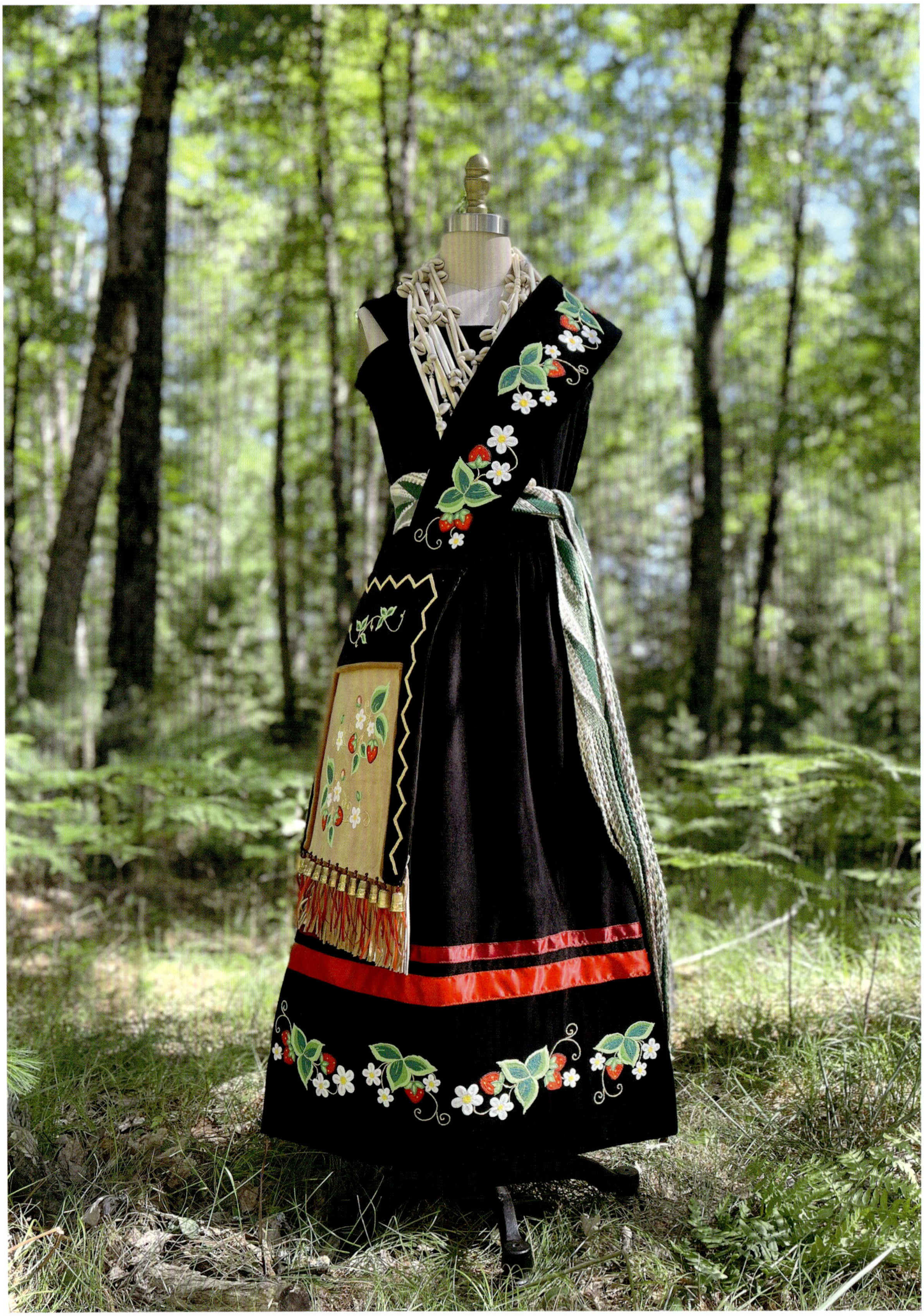

Contemporary Anishinaabe Art: A Continuation

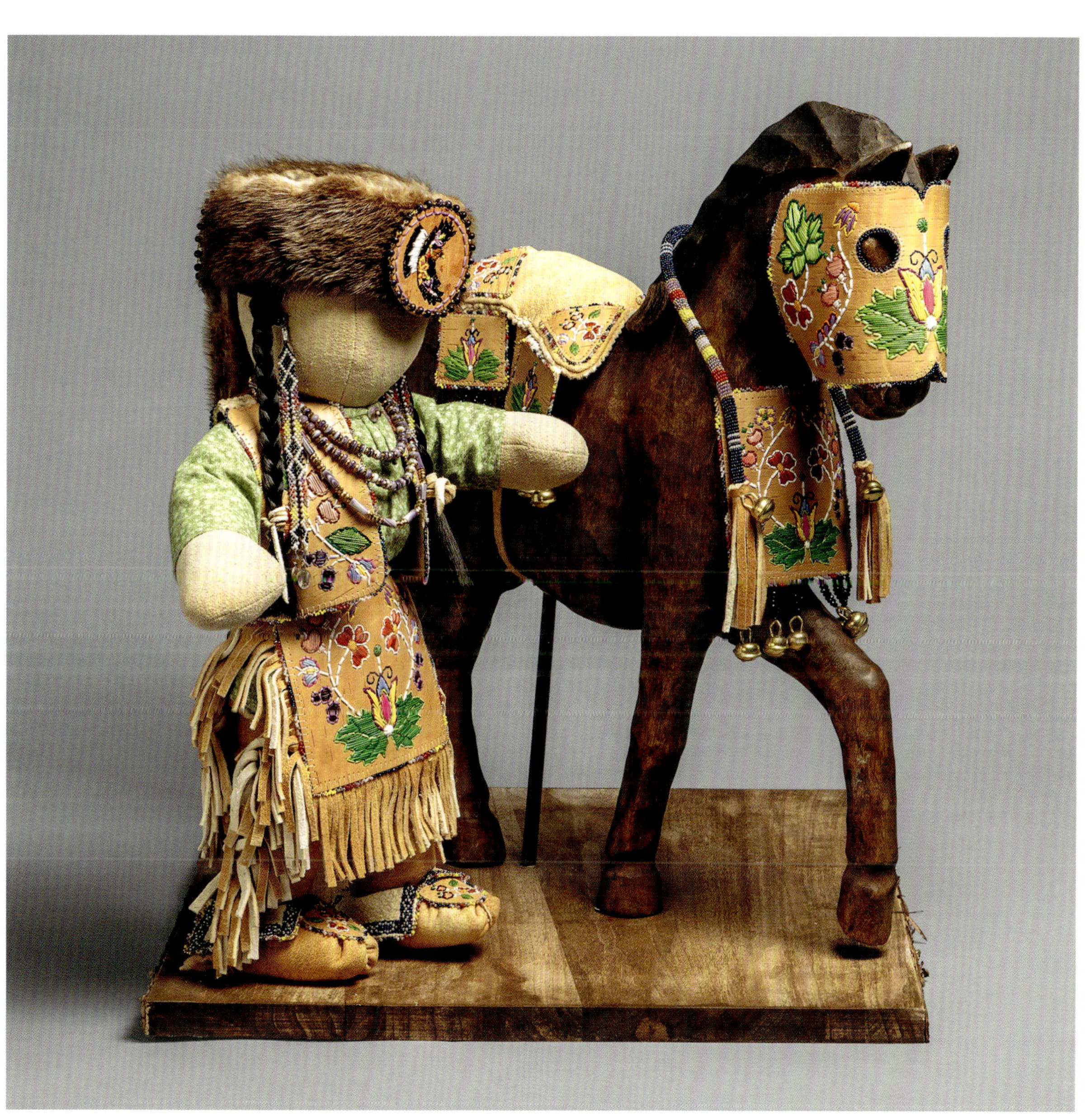

Monica Jo Raphael (Grand Traverse Band of Ottawa and Chippewa Indians; Sičáŋǧu Lakota; b. 1964), *Indede Odayii (My Dad's Horse)*, 2024

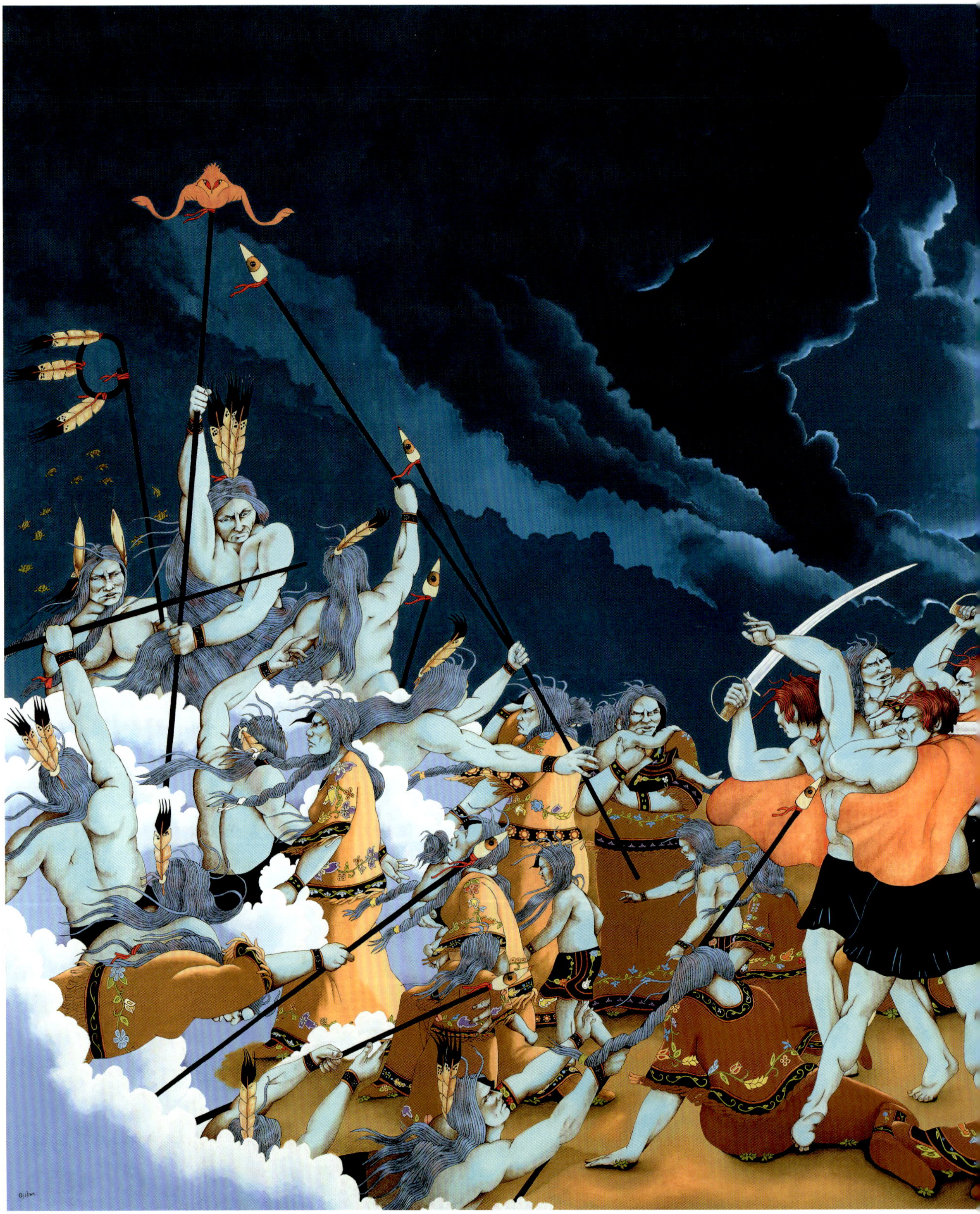

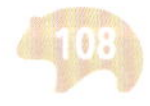

Rabbett before Horses Strickland (Red Cliff Band of Lake Superior Chippewa; b. 1949), *Right to Consciousness*, 2024

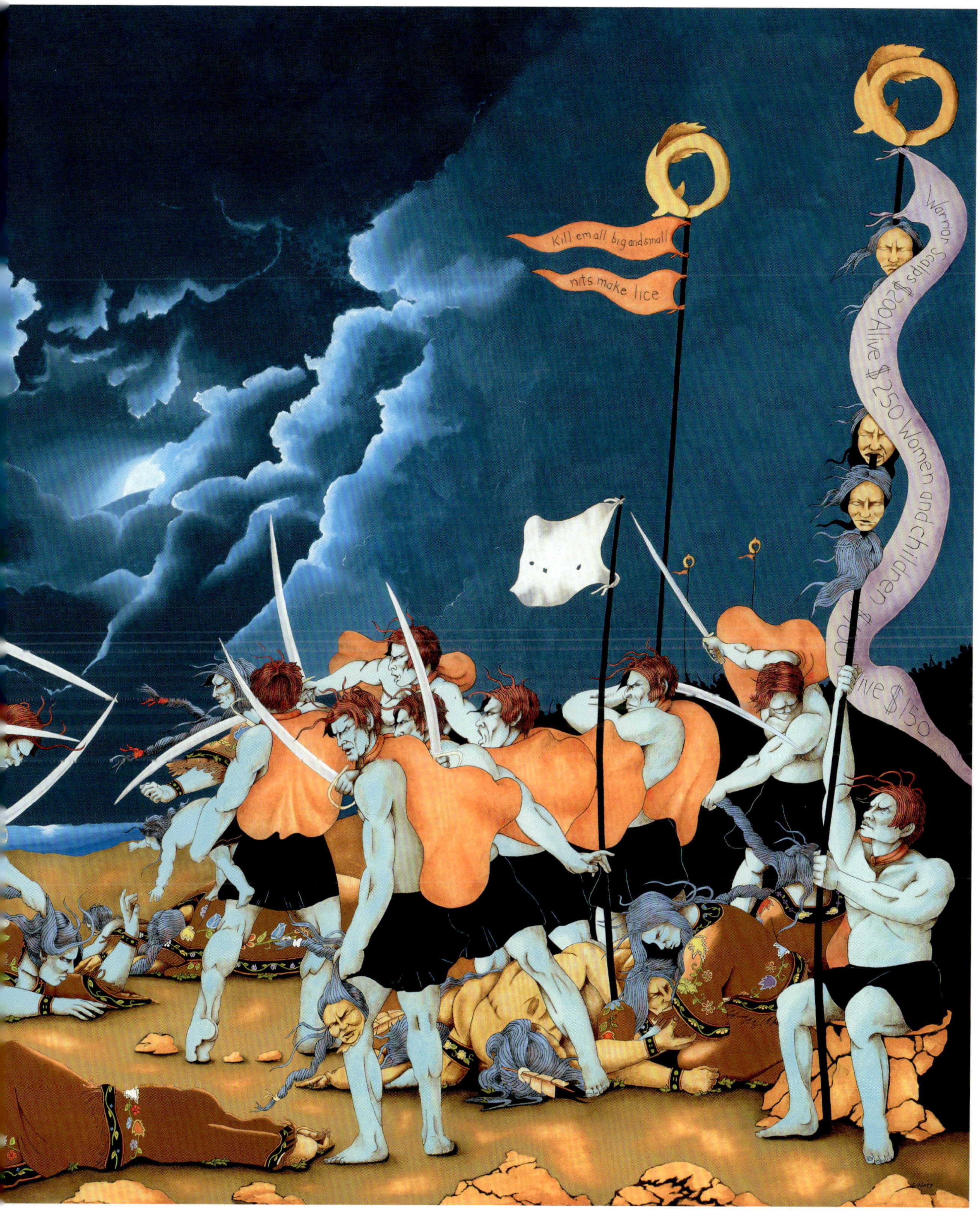

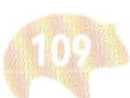

Kill em all big and small
nits make lice
Warrior Scalps $5
$200 Alive $250 Women and children
Alive $150

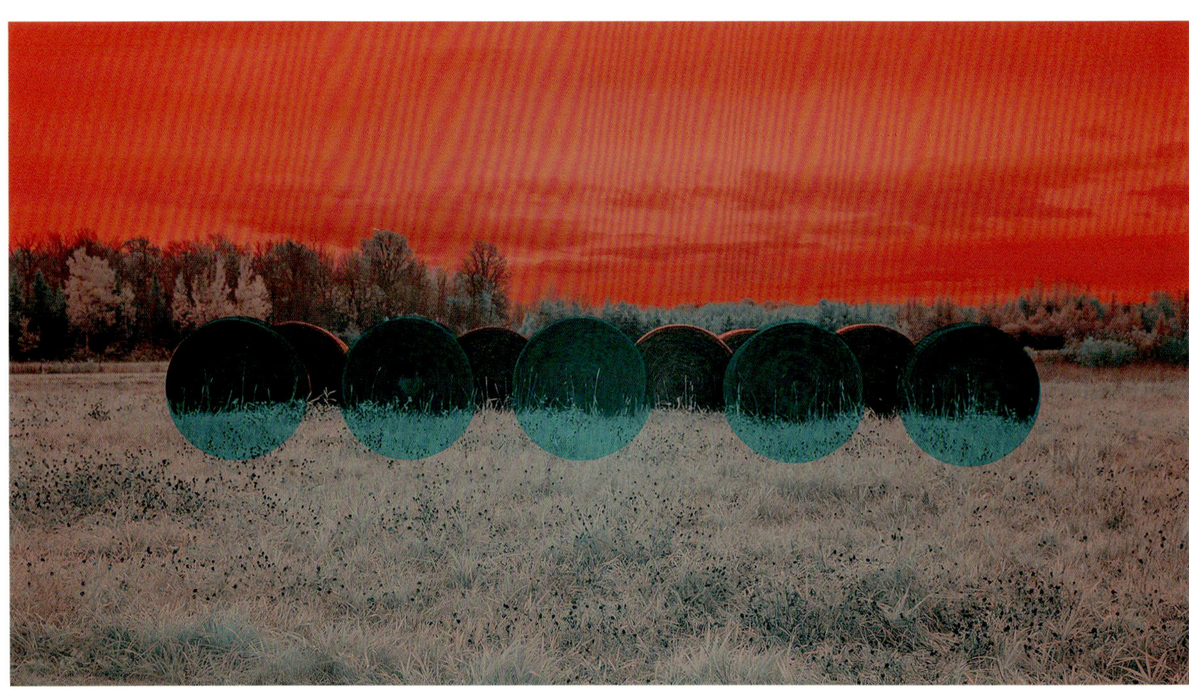

Cressandra Thibodeaux (Sault Ste. Marie Tribe of Chippewa; b. 1966), *Fever Visions I,* 2023

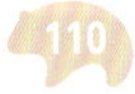

Contemporary Anishinaabe Art: A Continuation

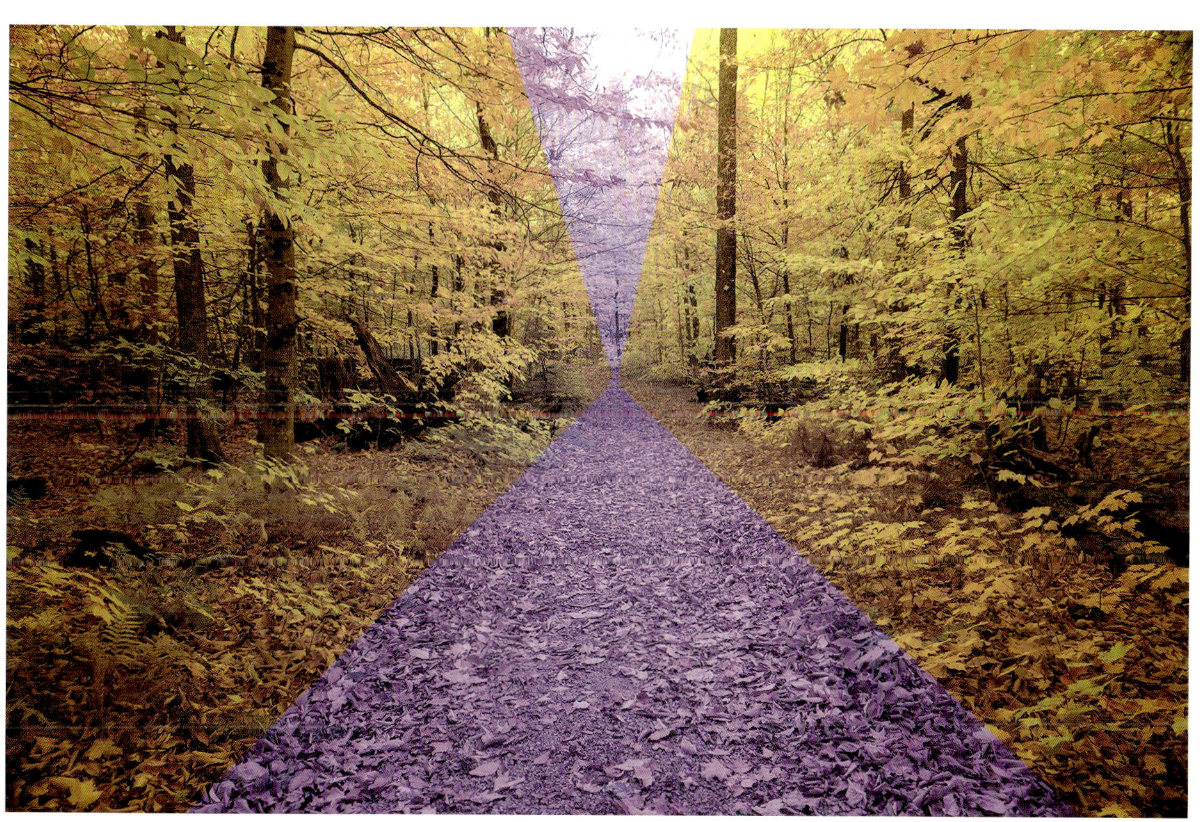

Cressandra Thibodeaux (Sault Ste. Marie Tribe of Chippewa; b. 1966), *Fever Visions II,* 2023

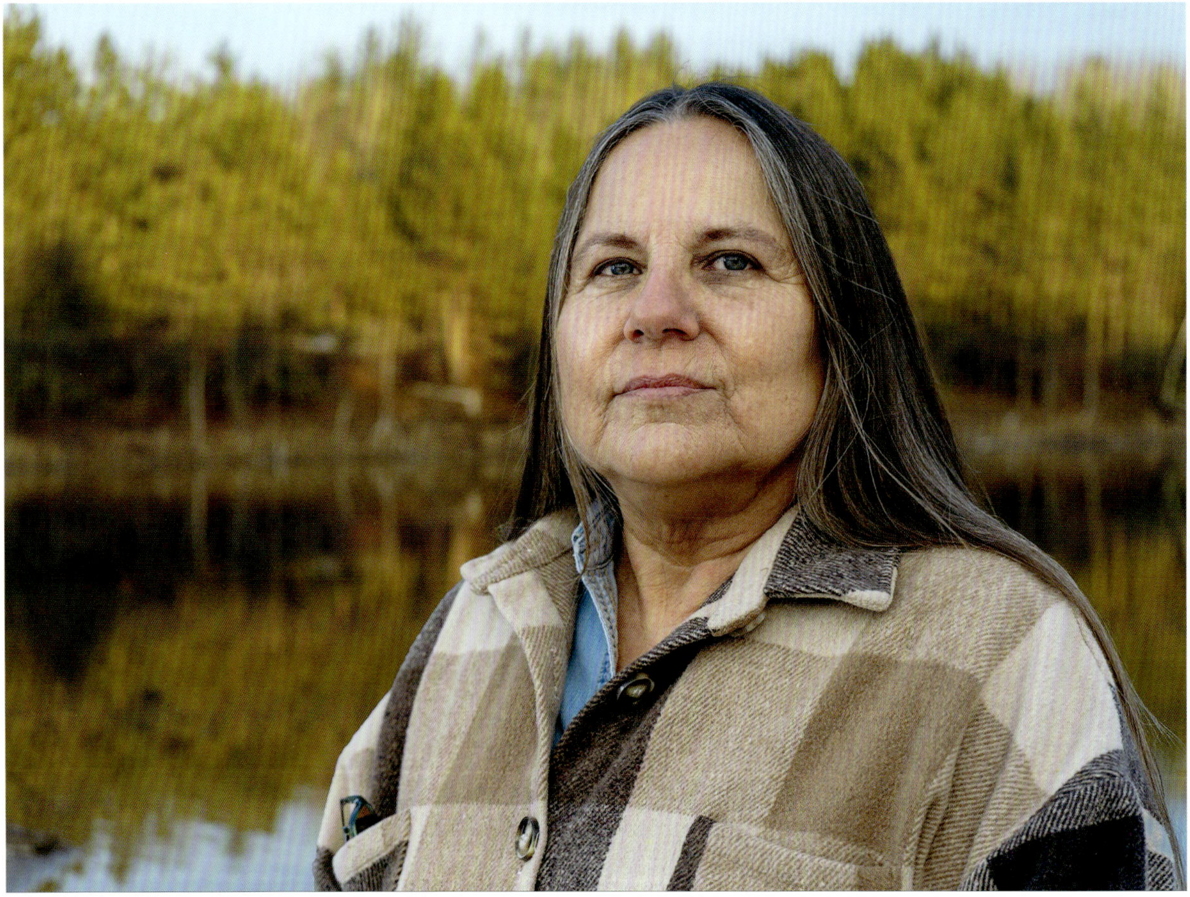

Cressandra Thibodeaux (Sault Ste. Marie Tribe of Chippewa; b. 1966), *Rita Boulley,* 2023

Contemporary Anishinaabe Art: A Continuation

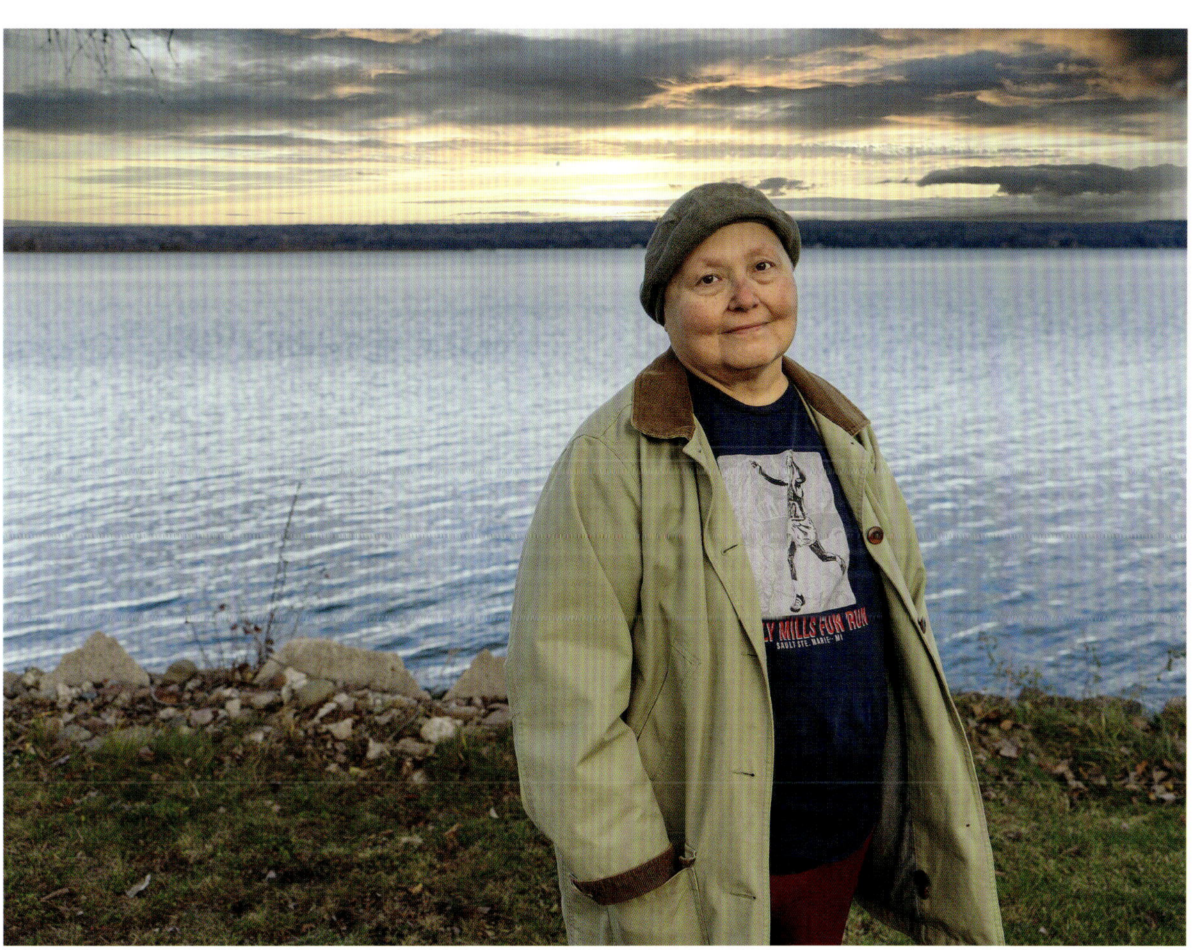

Cressandra Thibodeaux (Sault Ste. Marie Tribe of Chippewa; b. 1966), *Cathy Abramson, 2023*

Maggie Thompson (Fond du Lac Band of Lake Superior Chippewa; b. 1989), *I Get Mad Because I Love You,* 2021–22

Contemporary Anishinaabe Art: A Continuation

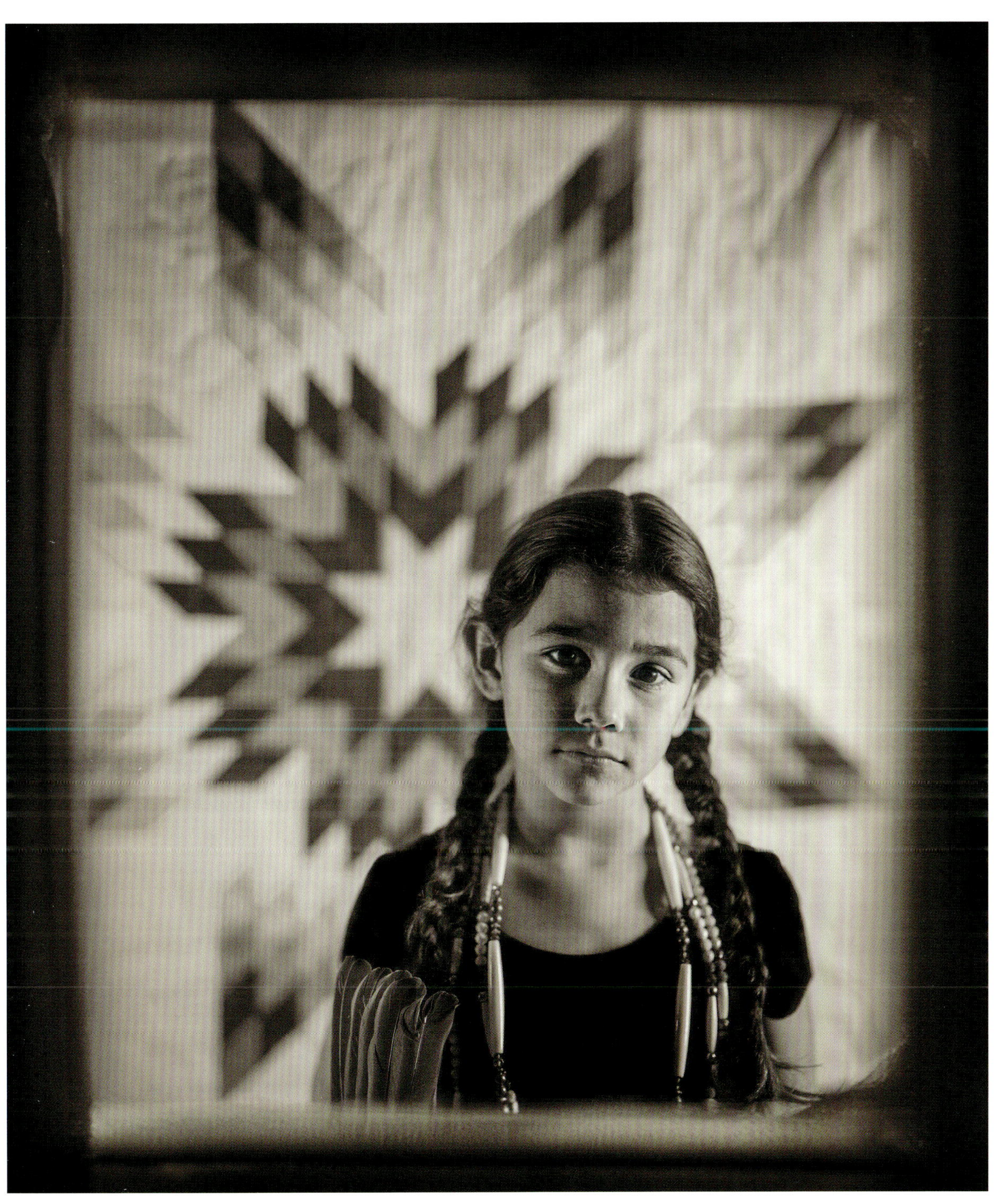

Holly Trevan (Match-E-Be-Nash-She-Wish Band of Pottawatomi; b. 1976), *For Martha,* 2024

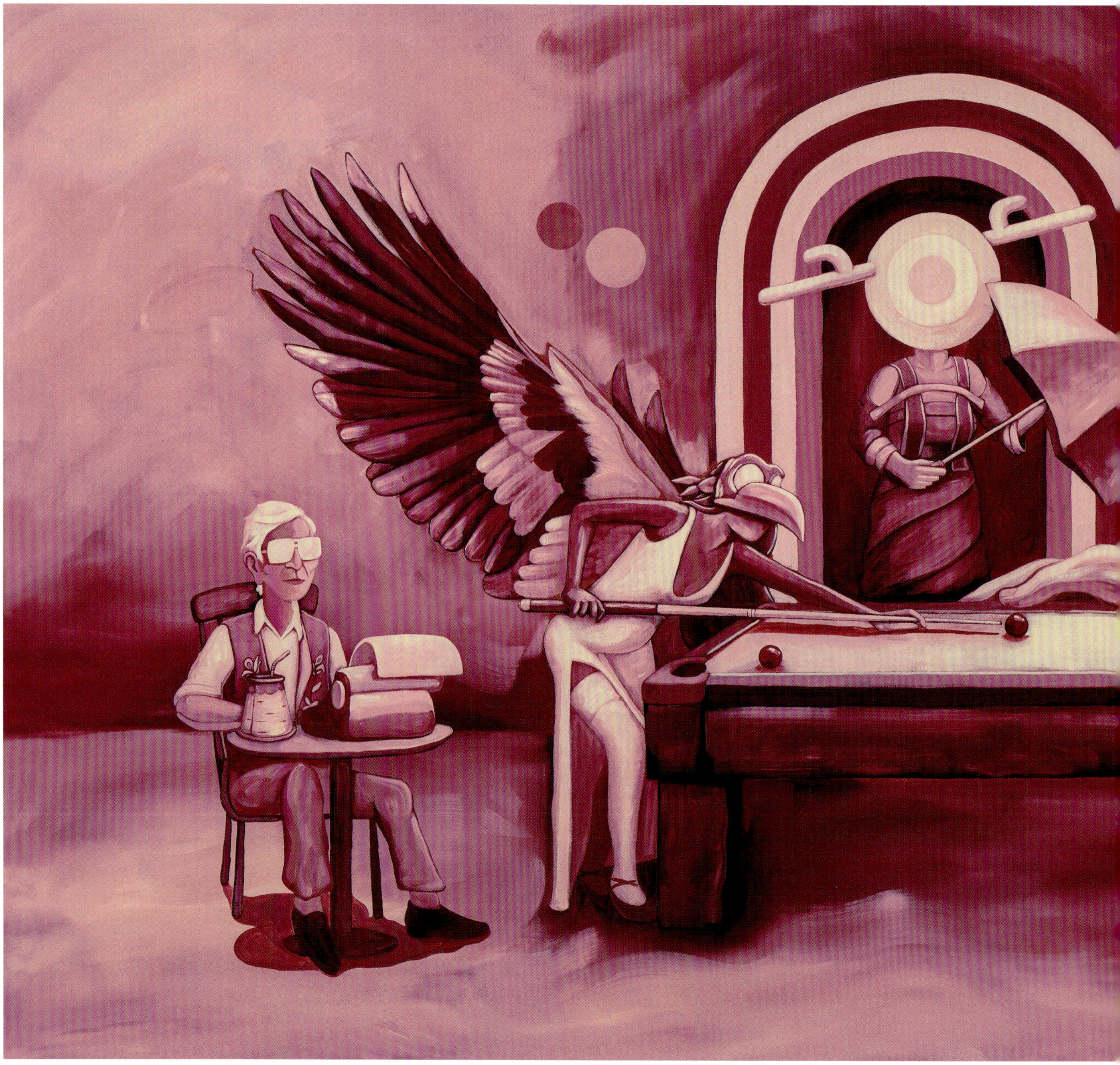

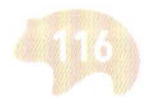

Jonathan Thunder (Red Lake Nation; b. 1977), *Basil's Dream*, 2024

Contemporary Anishinaabe Art: A Continuation

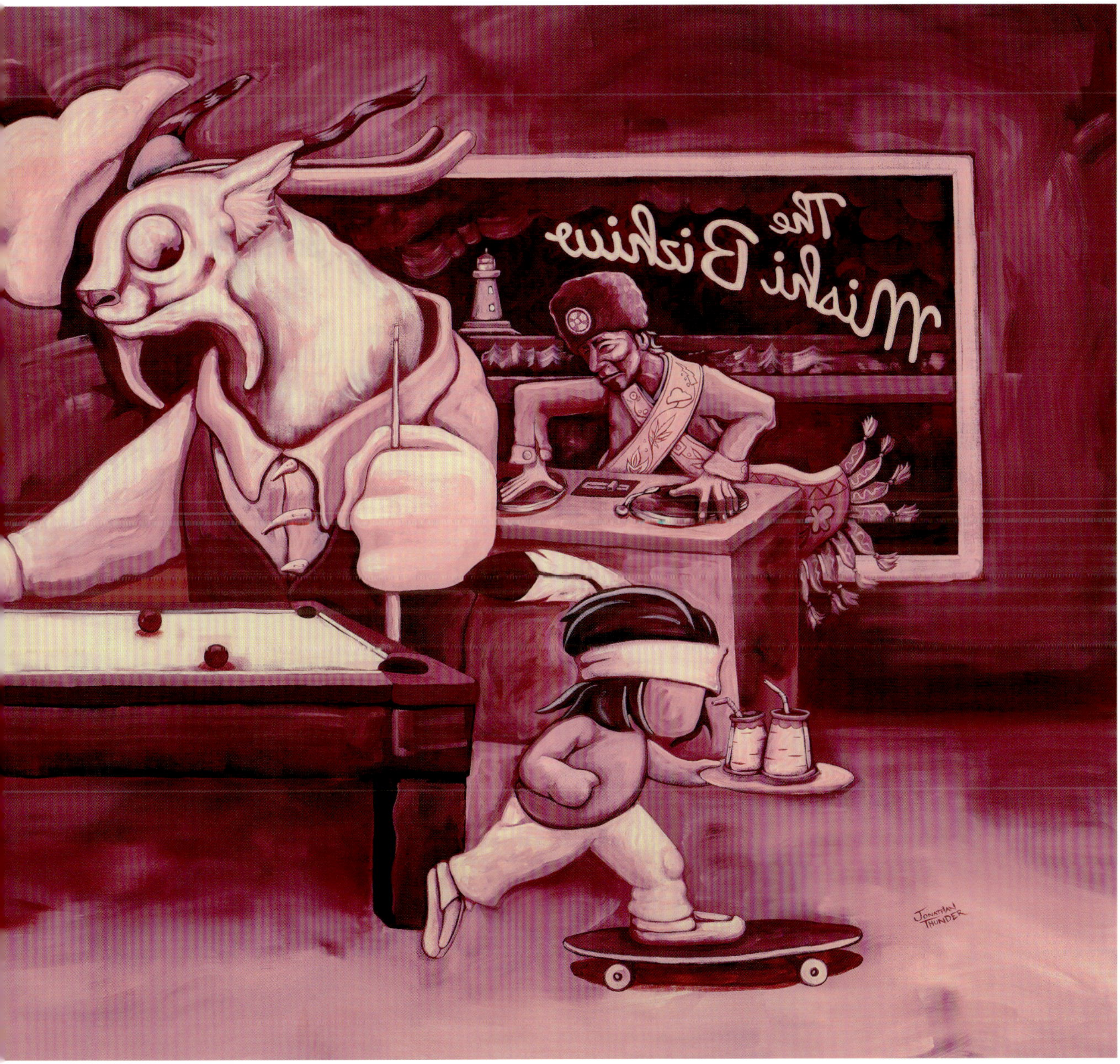

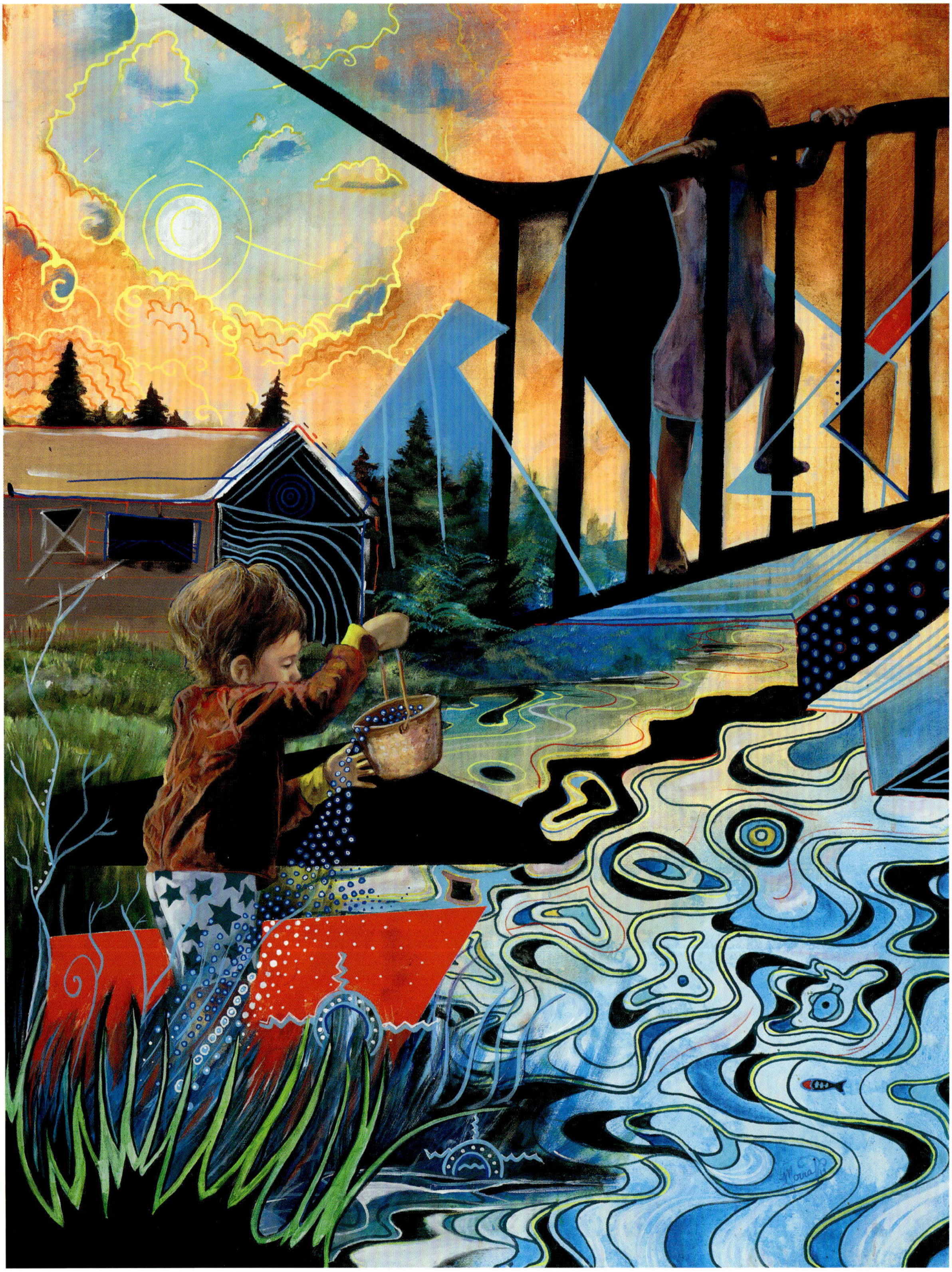

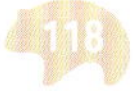

Moira Villiard (Fond du Lac Band of Lake Superior Chippewa; b. 1994), *The Waters of Tomorrow*, 2019

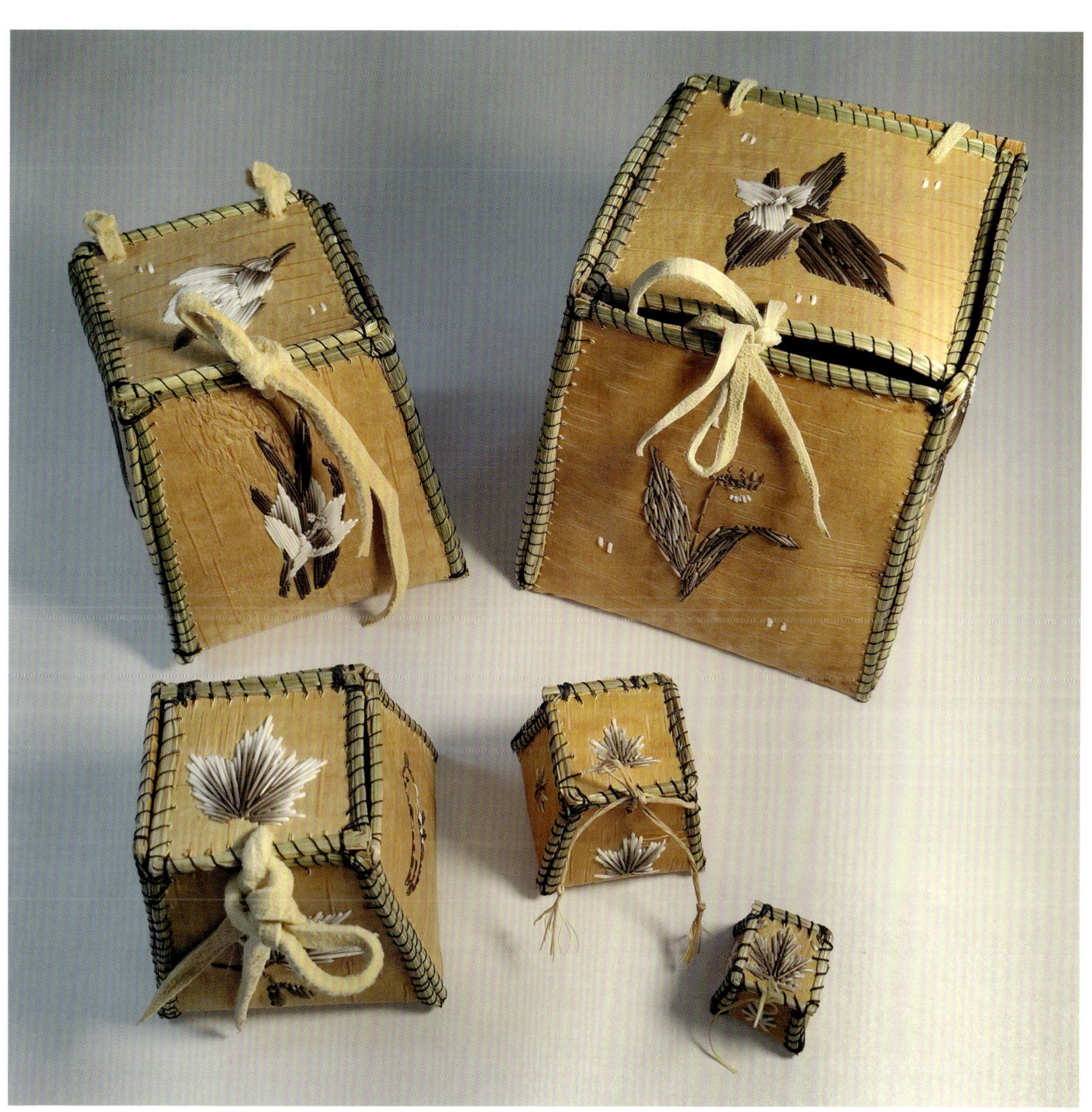

Yvonne M. Walker-Keshick (Little Traverse Bay Bands of Odawa Indians; b. 1946), *Maple Sugar M'kuks,* 2025

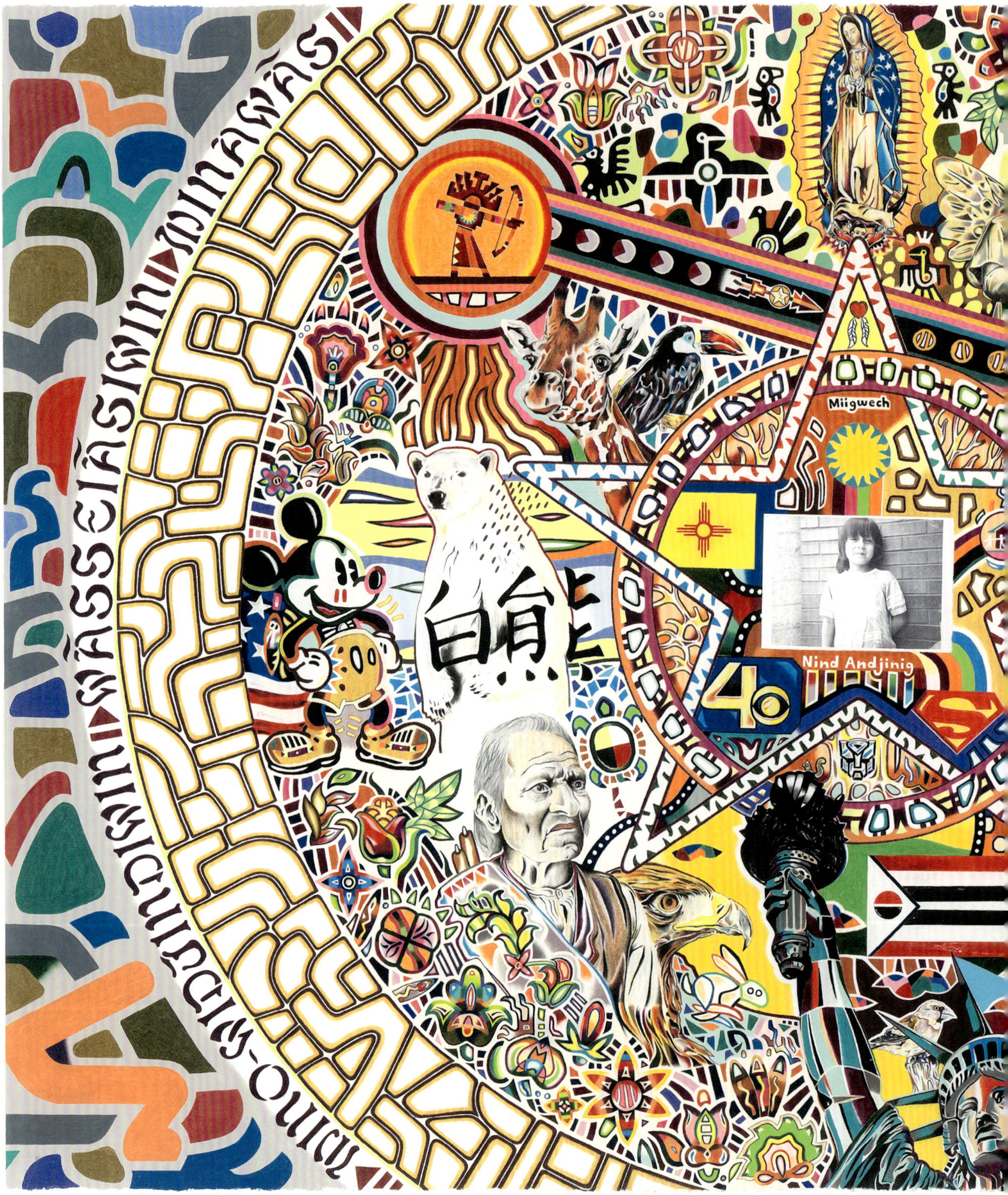

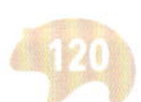

Contemporary Anishinaabe Art: A Continuation

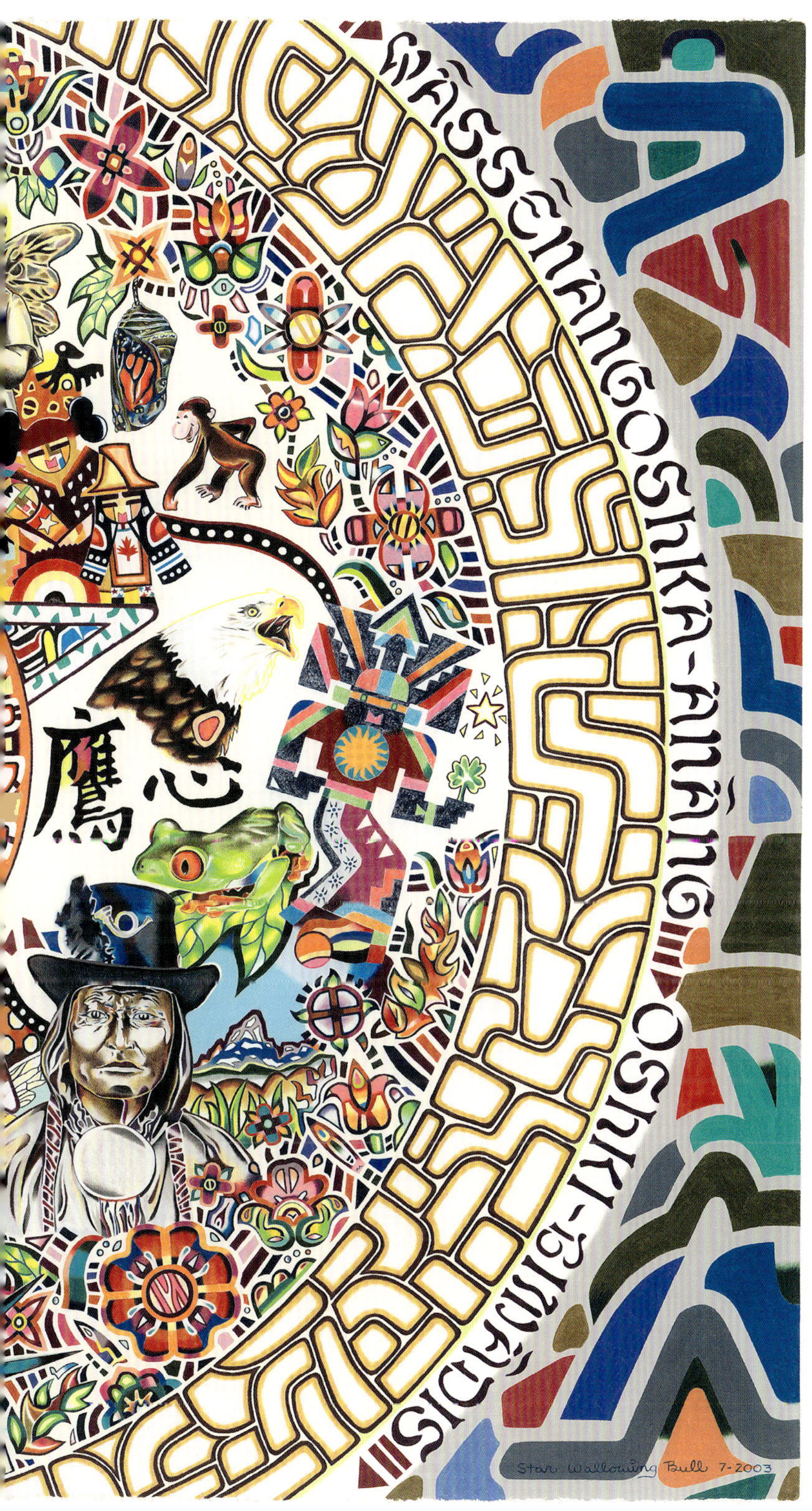

Star WallowingBull (White Earth Band of the Minnesota Chippewa; Northern Arapaho; b. 1973), *Twinkle, Twinkle Little Star Now I Know Who You Really Are,* 2002

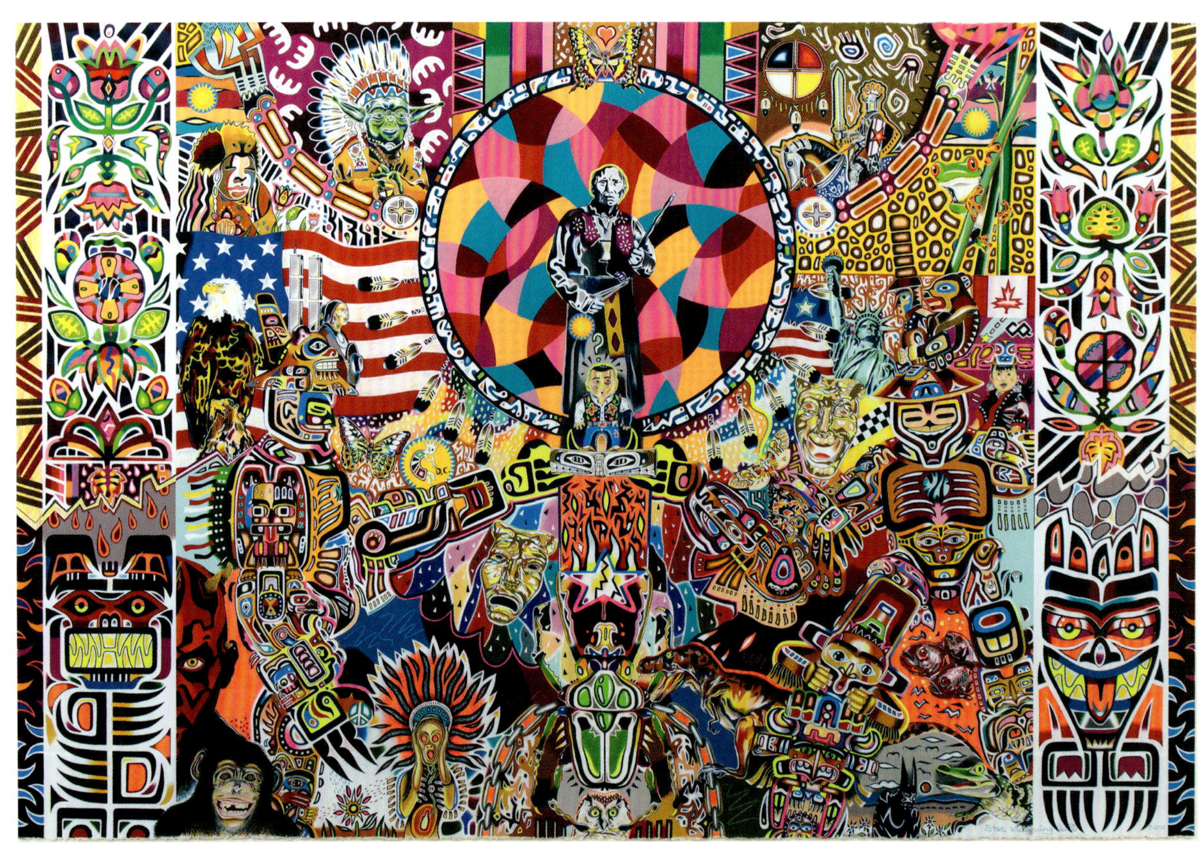

Star WallowingBull (White Earth Band of the Minnesota Chippewa; Northern Arapaho; b. 1973), *Black Elk's Little Sand Man,* 2002

Contemporary Anishinaabe Art: A Continuation

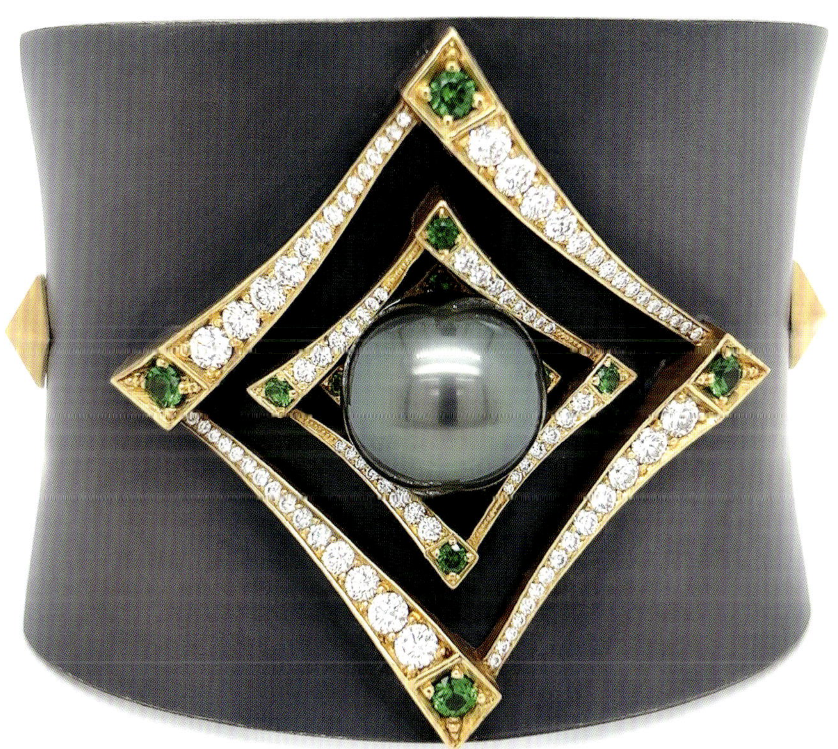

Robin Waynee (Saginaw Chippewa Indian Tribe; b. 1971), *Pearl Cosmos Cuff,* 2023

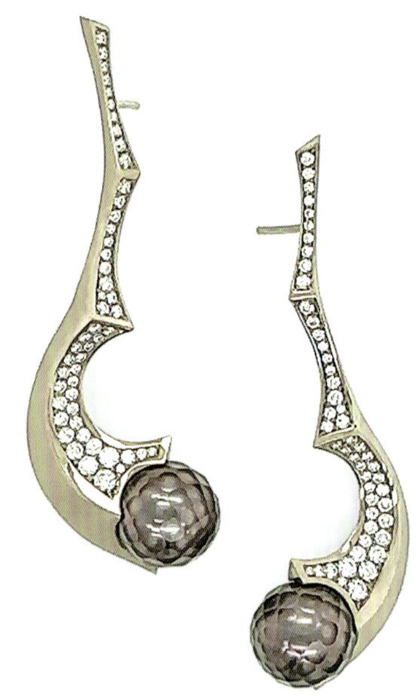

Contemporary Anishinaabe Art: A Continuation

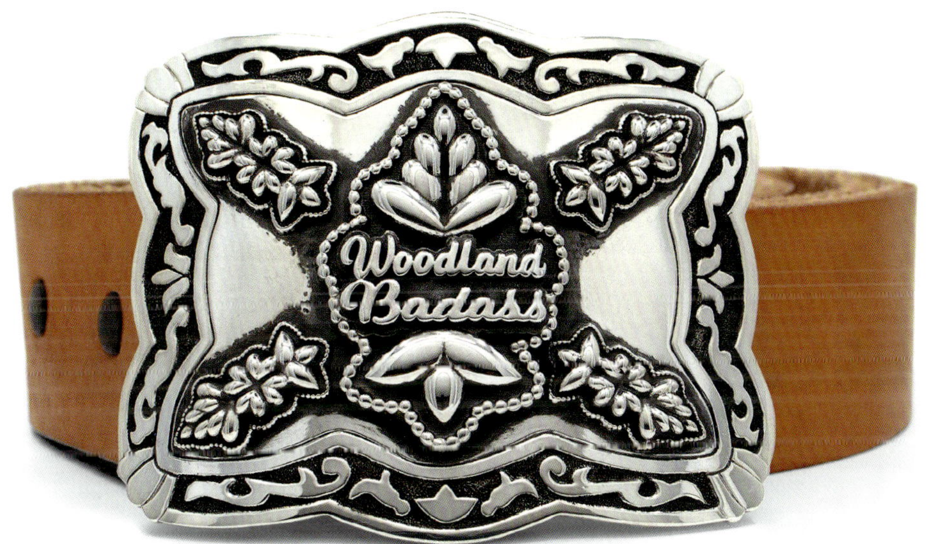

Jodi Webster (Ho-Chunk Nation; Prairie Band Potawatomi Nation; b. 1977), *Woodland Badass Champion Buckle,* 2022

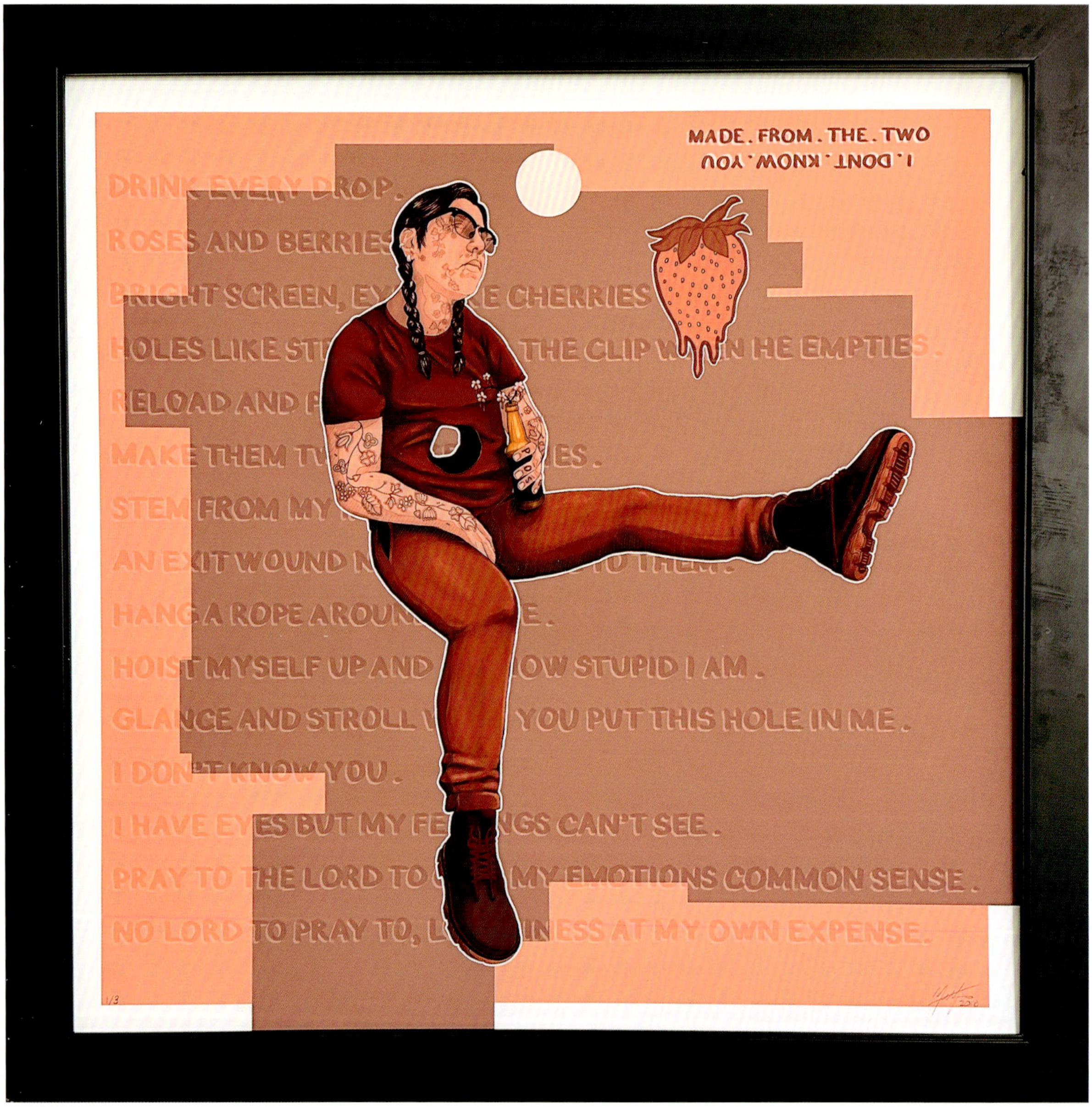

Animkeewa Aankwad White Eagle (Grand Traverse Band of Ottawa and Chippewa Indians; Kiowa; b. 1995), *Made from the Two – I Don't Know You,* 2019

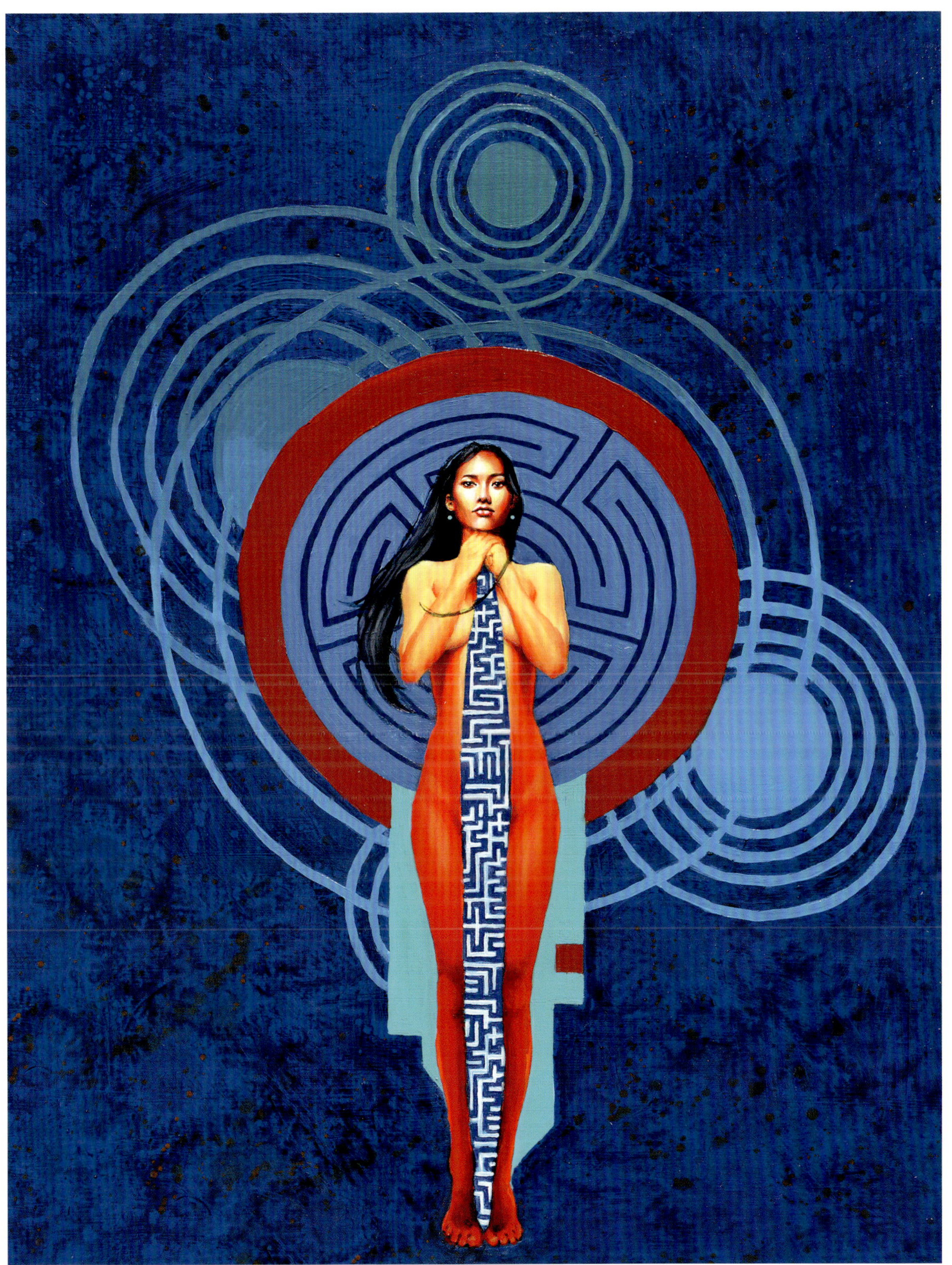

Sarah Wilkinson (Sault Ste. Marie Tribe of Chippewa; b. 1984), *Following the Path Within,* 2024

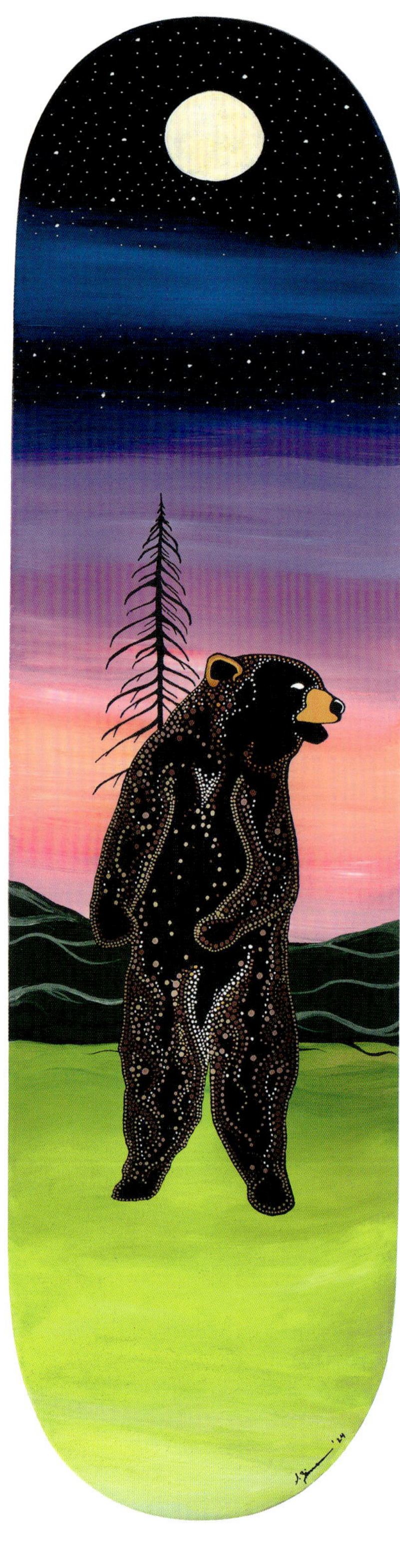

Sam Zimmerman (Grand Portage Band of Lake Superior Chippewa [Direct Descendant]; b. 1978), *Makwa doodem ogichidaa / Bear Clan Warrior*, 2024

  Contemporary Anishinaabe Art: A Continuation

Exhibition Checklist

Adam Avery / Naawikwegiizhig (Swan Creek and and Black River Bands of Chippewa Indians; Saginaw Chippewa Indian Tribe [Direct Lineal Descendant]; b. 1973)

Waabgonii / Blooming Hat, 2020. John Bull top hat, glass seed bead appliqué, 7 1/2 (crown height) × 10 × 12 3/4 in. (19 × 25.4 × 32.4 cm)

Waawaaskone-giizis / Flowering Moon, 2024. Homburg hat, glass seed bead appliqué, 4 1/2 (crown height) × 10 × 12 in. (2 × 25.4 × 30.5 cm)

Adam Avery / Naawikwegiizhig (Swan Creek and Black River Bands of Chippewa Indians; Saginaw Chippewa Indian Tribe [Direct Lineal Descendant]; b. 1973) and **Lisa Kennedy / Waagosh-Kwe** (Saginaw Chippewa Indian Tribe; b. 1973)

Binaakwe-giizis / Falling Leaves Moon Ensemble, 2024–25. Glass seed beads, wool, leather, stretch woven fabric, natural embellishments, top hat: 4 1/2 (crown height) × 10 × 12 (2 × 25.4 × 30.5 cm); jacket: 44 × 30 in. (111.8 × 76.2 cm); skirt: 36 × 34 × 44 in. (91.4 × 86.4 × 111.8 cm); boots: 7 × 3 1/2 × 10 11/16 in. (17.8 × 8.9 × 27.2 cm); clutch: 6 × 10 × 2 1/2 in. (15.2 × 25.4 × 6.4 cm)

Frank Big Bear (White Earth Band of the Minnesota Chippewa; b. 1953)

Anishinaabe Man Trapped in a Trickster's Web, 2023. Color pencil on black illustration board, unframed: 30 × 20 1/8 in. (76.2 × 51.1 cm); framed: 33 1/2 × 23 1/2 × 1 3/4 in. (85 × 59.7 × 4.4 cm). Collection of Bockley Gallery

Three Warriors on Horses (During Climate Change), 2015. Color pencil on paper, 22 1/4 × 30 in. (56.3 × 76.2 cm). Collection of Bockley Gallery

David Bradley (White Earth Band of the Minnesota Chippewa; b. 1954)

Shirley Brauker (Little River Band of Ottawa Indians; 1950–2022)

Bobcat Box, 2018. Stoneware, iron oxide, glass, ledger paper, ink, copper, thread, overall: 14 × 7 3/4 × 7 3/4 in. (35.5 × 19.6 × 19.6 cm). Estate of Shirley Brauker

Earth Mother (venus féminine power), date unknown. Glazed ceramic, overall: 20 1/2 × 8 3/4 in. diameter (52 × 22.2 cm); object: 15 × 8 3/4 in. diameter (38.1 × 22.2 cm); base: 5 1/2 × 7 1/2 × 8 3/4 in. (13.9 × 19 × 22.2 cm). Estate of Shirley Brauker

Red Hands (Missing and Murdered Indian People), 2021. Stoneware, iron oxide, colored slip, overall: 13 7/8 × 5 3/4 in. diameter (35.2 × 14.6 cm). Estate of Shirley Brauker

Andrea Carlson (Grand Portage Band of Lake Superior Chippewa; b. 1979)

Exit, 2018. Screenprint, unframed: 33 1/2 × 47 3/4 in. (85.1 × 121.3 cm); framed: 37 1/2 × 51 1/2 × 2 in. (95.3 × 130.8 × 5.1 cm). Collection of Bockley Gallery

Kelly Church (Match-E-Be-Nash-She-Wish Band of Potawatomi; Grand Traverse Band of Ottawa and Chippewa Indians [Descent]; b. 1967)

Every Picture Tells a Story, 2025. Black ash, copper, sweetgrass, clear transfer paper, 37 × 26 in. diameter (91.4 × 26 cm)

Richard Church (Match-E-Be-Nash-She-Wish Band of Pottawatomi; b. 1947)

Asinaabe (Stone Man), 2017. Inkjet print, unframed: 30 × 45 in. (76.2 × 114.3 cm); framed: 53 × 39 in. (136.8 × 99 cm)

My Cuz, 1978. Inkjet print, unframed: 40 × 30 in. (101.6 × 76.2 cm); framed: 49 × 38 in. (124.4 × 96.5 cm)

Old Fox, 2020. Inkjet print, unframed: 30 × 40 in. (76.2 × 101.6 cm); framed: 50 × 38 in. (127 × 96.5 cm)

Young Shawl Dancer, 2023. Inkjet print, unframed: 30 × 40 (76.2 × 101.6 cm); framed: 54 × 39 in. (137.1 × 99 cm)

Patrick Collins (Saginaw Chippewa Indian Tribe; b. 1973)

Healing Hands, 2024. Oil on canvas, 38 × 48 in. (96.5 × 121.9 cm)

Gordon M. Coons (Lac Courte Oreilles Band of Lake Superior Chippewa; b. 1949)

Washita 1868: Remember Our Relatives, 2022. Annigoni paper, cedar smoke, sheet: 32 × 26 in. (81.3 × 66 cm); framed: 34 × 28 × 2 in. (86.4 × 71.1 × 5.1 cm)

Zoi Crampton (Saginaw Chippewa Indian Tribe; b. 2001)

Exsiccata, 2021. Pressed plants from the Pellston, Michigan, area, including pink smartweed, Queen Anne's lace, and white cedar, glue, unframed: 7 × 11 in. (17.8 × 27.9 cm); framed: 13 × 16 × 3/4 in. (33 × 40.6 × 1.9 cm)

Michelle Defoe (Red Cliff Band of Lake Superior Chippewa; b. 1982)

Ziigwan Binesi – Spring Thunderbird, 2018. Acrylic on canvas, 30 × 20 × 2 in. (76.2 × 50.8 × 5 cm)

Jim Denomie (Lac Courte Oreilles Band of Lake Superior Chippewa; 1955–2022)

Four Days and Four Nites, Ceremony, 2019–20. Oil on canvas, 86 × 120 in. (218.4 × 304.8 cm). Tia Collection

Untitled (Totem Painting), 2016. Oil on canvas, wood, 144 × 16 1/2 × 16 1/2 in. (365.8 cm × 41.9 × 41.9 cm). Tia Collection

Untruthful, 2014. Oil on canvas, unframed: 48 × 48 in. (121.9 × 121.9 cm); framed: 50 1/2 × 50 1/2 × 2 1/2 in. (128.3 × 128.3 × 6.4 cm). Muskegon Museum of Art, Museum Purchase, through the gifts of Robert and Sylvia Kaufman, the Estate of Robert "Paul" and Marjorie McConaughy, Dr. and Mrs. Secundino Veiga, and others, by exchange

Patrick DesJarlait (Red Lake Band of Ojibwe; 1921–1972)

Maple Sugar Time, 1946. Watercolor on paper, sheet, unframed: 15 3/8 × 20 1/4 in. (39.4 × 51.4 cm); framed: 23 × 29 × 1 1/2 in. (58.4 × 73.7 × 3.8 cm). Philbrook Museum of Art, Tulsa, Oklahoma. Museum purchase, 1946.31

David Dominic, Jr. (Little Traverse Bay Bands of Odawa Indians; b. 1970)

Iggy Pop, Ann Arbor 2011, 2011. C-print, sheet: 20 × 20 in. (50.8 × 50.8 cm); framed: 30 × 30 in. (76.2 × 76.2 cm)

Temple of Void, Detroit 2016, 2016. C-print, sheet: 20 × 20 in. (50.8 × 50.8 cm); framed: 30 × 30 in. (76.2 × 76.2 cm)

Dennis Esquivel (Grand Traverse Band of Ottawa and Chippewa Indians; b. 1961)

Our Homeland, 2025. Wood from Northern Michigan, including cherry wood, maple wood, walnut wood, stainless steel, overall: 42 × 20 × 20 in. (anticipated) (106.7 × 50.8 × 50.8 cm)

Out of the Woodlands: Standing Cabinet, 2012. Bird's-eye maple, cherry wood, quilted cherry veneer, stainless steel, overall: 66 × 27 × 13 in. (167.6 × 68.6 × 30.5 cm)

Kent Estey (White Earth Band of the Minnesota Chippewa; b. 1960)

Debwewin – Truth, 2018. Acrylic and acrylic ink on canvas, 30 × 24 × 1 1/2 in. (76.2 × 60.9 × 3.8 cm). Property and on loan from Karen and Jerry Walz

Jessica Leigh Gokey (Lac Courte Oreilles Band of Lake Superior Chippewa; b. 1985)

Companions, 2022. Fabric, 13/0 and 11/0 Czech seed beads, brass sequins, unframed: 26 × 21 in. (66 × 53.3 cm); framed: 30 × 25 in. (76.2 × 63.5 cm). Private collection

She Loves, 2023–24. 13/0 and 11/0 Czech seed beads, upholstery fabric, unframed, overall: 24 × 18 in. (61 × 45.7 cm); framed: 30 × 25 in. (76.2 × 63.5 cm)

Marcella Hadden (Saginaw Chippewa Indian Tribe; b. 1961)

Jingle Dress, 2020. Canvas photograph, unframed: 32 × 20 in. (81.3 × 50.8 cm); framed: 36 × 24 × 1 3/4 in. (91.4 × 61 × 4.4 cm)

MMIW, 2019. Canvas photograph, unframed: 32 × 20 in. (81.3 × 50.8 cm); framed: 36 × 24 × 1 3/4 in. (91.4 × 61 × 4.4 cm)

Terri Hom / Binesikwe (Lac Courte Oreilles Band of Lake Superior Chippewa; b. 1964)

My Brother's Basket, 2020. Birchbark, dyed porcupine quill, sweetgrass, red willow, sinew, 7 1/2 × 12 × 12 in. (19 × 30.4 × 30.4 cm); base: 7 1/2 × 7 1/2 in. (19 × 19 cm)

Heron Hill Designs—Joey Kennedy (First Descendant of Saginaw Chippewa Indian Tribe; b. 1990) and **Daniel Collazos** (b. 1990)

Baakaani-inaadizi: Their Actions Are Different, 2025. Coat: fabric, glass seed beads (11/0 Czech Charlotte cut seed beads, sheen, and vintage); bag: fabric, glass seed beads; hat: wool, velvet, leather, glass seed beads; medallion: birchbark, glass seed beads, paint; boots: leather, glass seed beads; 72 × 36 × 21 in. (anticipated) (182.8 × 91.4 × 53.3 cm); overall: 73 × 24 × 16 in. (185.4 × 61 × 40.6 cm); overall (pants): 34 × 30 in. (86.4 × 76.2 cm); overall (shirt): size large. Courtesy of Joseph Kennedy and Daniel Beck of Heron Hill Designs

Mashkiki Naabikawaaganag, 2025. Birchbark, glass seed beads, paint, brass, horse hair, porcupine quill, each 26 × 13 × 1 in. (66 × 33 × 2.5 cm). Courtesy of Joseph Kennedy and Daniel Beck of Heron Hill Designs

Jacob Keshick (Little Traverse Bay Bands of Odawa Indians; b. 1987)

Open Water, 2025. Birchbark, porcupine quill, sweetgrass, imitation sinew, overall: 4 × 5 in. (10.2 × 12.7 cm)

Pat Kruse (Red Cliff Band of Lake Superior Chippewa; Mille Lacs Band of Ojibwe [Descent]; b. 1971)

Cradle of All Colors, 2019. Birchbark, dyed porcupine quill, imitation sinew, red willow, sweetgrass, birch wood, overall: 41 × 22 × 23 in. (104.1 × 55.9 × 58.4 cm); overall length (cradle, head to foot): 41 in. (104.1 cm); overall height (cradle, at head): 22 in. (55.9 cm); overall width (wood rockers): 23 in. (58.4 cm)

Mary Edmonia Lewis (Mississauga Ojibwe; ca. 1844/45–1907)

Henry Wadsworth Longfellow, 1871. Marble, block: 29 1/4 × 16 1/4 × 13 1/4 in. (74.3 × 41.3 × 33.7 cm); including base: 10 1/2 × 10 1/2 × 29

1/4 in. (26.7 × 26.7 × 74.3 cm). Harvard University Portrait Collection, 1872

Minnehaha, 1868. Marble, overall (by sight): 11 × 6 × 3 1/2 in. (27.9 × 15.2 × 8.9 cm). Detroit Institute of Arts, Museum Purchase, Ernest and Rosemarie Kanzler Foundation Fund

David Martin (Pokagon Band of Potawatomi; b. 1973)

Family Hunt, 2024. Tattooed buffalo hide, sinew, wood frame, unframed: 48 × 48 × 1 1/2 in. (121.9 × 121.9 × 3.8 cm)

ishkwaazhe Shane McSauby (Grand Traverse Band of Ottawa and Chippewa Indians; b. 1990)

Happy Thanksgiving, 2023. .MOV file (H.264 or ProRes), 7 min. 35 sec.

Feather Miigwan (Little Traverse Bay Bands of Odawa Indians; b. 1981)

She Bends the Light to Her Will / Obiskaatebidoon ezhi-dibendang, 2024. Augmented reality displayed via QR code. Courtesy of the artist and Harbor Collective

Wanesia Misquadace (Fond du Lac Band of Lake Superior Chippewa; b. 1967)

Ode to Otter, Hair Comb, 2023. Sterling silver, freshwater pearl, white Tahitian pearl, 5 1/4 × 2 3/4 in. (13.3 × 7.6 cm)

Ode to Otter, Ring, 2023. Sterling silver, fine silver, Sonoran turquoise, 14K gold eye beads, 2 1/2 × 1/2 in. (6.3 × 1.2 cm)

Ode to Otter, Cuff, 2023. Sterling silver, fine silver, Number 8 turquoise, 14K gold eye beads, Kuemboe, pink Tahitian pearl, white sapphire, 2 1/2 × 1/2 in. (6.3 × 1.2 cm)

Water Protector Vessel, 2023. Birchbark, sterling silver, copper, sand and pebbles from Lake Superior, overall: 16 × 3 in. diameter (40.6 × 7.6 cm)

George Morrison (Grand Portage Band of Lake Superior Chippewa; 1919–2000)

Totemic Column, 1995–2024. Stained redwood, granite base, column: 168 × 21 × 21 in. (426.7 ×

53.3 × 53.3 cm); base: 5 × 32 × 32 in. (12.7 × 82.3 × 81.3 cm). On loan from the George Morrison Estate and Bockley Gallery

Untitled, 1962. Oil on canvas, 36 × 72 in. (91.4 × 182.9 cm). Tia Collection

Norval Morrisseau (Bingwi Neyaashi Anishinaabek First Nation; 1932–2007)

Bear, Fish, Bird – Interdependence, ca. 1990. Oil on canvas, wood, overall: 51 1/2 × 64 in. (130.8 × 162.6 cm). Private collection

Elder Teaching the Next Generation to Communicate in Harmony with All Living Beings, 1991–92. Acrylic on canvas, overall (left panel): 30 × 48 in. (76.2 × 121.9 cm); overall (middle panel): 48 × 48 in. (121.9 × 121.9 cm); overall (right panel): 30 × 48 in. (76.2 × 121.9 cm). The Estate of Norval Morrisseau

Punk Rockers Nancy and Andy, 1989. Acrylic on canvas, unframed: 48 × 36 in. (121.9 × 91.4 cm). The Estate of Norval Morrisseau

Nonamey (Bad River Band of Lake Superior Chippewa / Mashkiiziibii; b. 1992)

Dress for Nookomis, 2023. Acrylic on reclaimed fabric, 48 × 36 × 1 in. (121.9 × 91.4 × 2.5 cm)

Postal Box, 2021. Acrylic on sculpted cardboard, 28 × 20 × 5 1/2 in. (71.1 × 50.8 × 13.9 cm)

Eva Oldman (Little Traverse Bay Bands of Odawa Indians; Northern Arapaho Tribe of the Wind River Reservation; b. 1981)

Anishinaabe Woodland Strawberry Handbag, 2024. Waterproof fabric, microfiber leather, brass hardware, 15 × 5 × 16 in. (38.1 × 12.7 × 40.6 cm)

Ronald J. Paquin (Sault Ste. Marie Tribe of Chippewa; b. 1942)

Wiigwaas jiimaan, 2018. Birchbark, cedar wood, spruce roots, bear grease, pine pitch, ashes, overall: 24 × 144 × 36 in. (60.9 × 365.7 × 91.4 cm). Private collection

Cherish Parrish (Match-E-Be-Nash-She-Wish Band of Pottawatomi; b. 1989)

Jingle Dress Dancer #2: The Last Roses, 2025.

Black ash, birchbark, copper, waxed thread, adhesive, porcupine quill, 18 × 6 × 5 in. (43.1 × 15.2 × 12.7 cm)

Lisa Passinault (Saginaw Chippewa Indian Tribe; b. 1976)

Woodland Baby Bonnet, 2023. Black cotton velveteen, 13/0 Czech Charlotte cut seed beads, lace, ribbon, 9 × 6 1/2 × 9 in. (22.8 × 16.5 × 22.8 cm)

Woodland Strap Dress and Bandolier Bag, 2020. Dress: black cotton velveteen, 13/0 Czech Charlotte cut seed beads, ribbon; bandolier bag: black cotton velveteen, 13/0 Czech Charlotte cut seed beads, brain tanned leather, 24K gold beads, brass thimbles, overall: 62 × 22 × 22 in. (157.4 × 55.8 × 55.8 cm); bandolier bag: 40 × 14 1/2 in. (101.6 × 36.8 cm)

Konstance Patton / Ke-nee-go-keshek (Little River Band of Ottawa Indians; b. 1983)

G-Ma's Sharp Objekts, 2011. Resin, gold, needles, wood, overall: 8 × 2 × 2 1/2 in. (20.3 × 5 × 6.3 cm); base: 7 × 7 in. (17.7 × 17.7 cm)

Jason Quigno (Saginaw Chippewa Indian Tribe; b. 1975)

Maawandoonan (Bring Them Together), 2025. Black granite, sculpture: 84 × 55 × 13 in. (213.3 × 139.7 × 33 cm); base: 13 × 55 × 30 in. (33 × 139.7 × 76.2 cm); overall: 96 × 55 × 30 in. (243.8 × 139.7 × 76.2 cm)

Monica Jo Raphael (Grand Traverse Band of Ottawa and Chippewa Indians; Sičáŋǧu Lakota; b. 1964)

Indede Odayii (My Dad's Horse), 2024. Hide, birchbark, dyed porcupine quill, glass beads, wampum, brass bells, thread, wood, found object (horse), overall (including attached based): 18 1/8 × 20 1/2 × 17 1/2 in. (46 × 52 × 44.4 cm); mount (wood base): 3/8 × 19 × 15 3/4 in. (0.9 × 48.2 × 40 cm). Loan from the Eiteljorg Museum of American Indians and Western Art, Indianapolis, Indiana

Monica Rickert-Bolter (Prairie Band Potawatomi Nation; b. 1986)

Bojkwansi Nipton / Dragonfly Weave, 2023. Mixed-media composition printed on aluminum, unframed: 36 × 24 in. (91.4 × 61 cm); framed: 37 ×

25 × 1 1/4 in. (94 × 63.5 × 3.2 cm)

Mish Amo Ndobmadzen / Bee Trying to Stay Alive, 2024. Mixed-media composition printed on aluminum, unframed: 24 × 60 in. (61 × 152.4 cm); framed: 24 × 60 × 3/4 in. (61 × 152.4 × 1.9 cm)

Rabbett before Horses Strickland (Red Cliff Band of Lake Superior Chippewa; b. 1949)

Right to Consciousness, 2024. Oil on canvas, 84 × 156 in. (213.4 × 396.2 cm)

Cressandra Thibodeaux (Sault Ste. Marie Tribe of Chippewa; b. 1966)

Cathy Abramson, 2023. Photographic print on archival paper, 16 × 20 in. (40.6 × 50.8 cm)

Fever Visions I, 2023. Photographic print on archival paper, 13 × 19 in. (33 × 48.2 cm)

Fever Visions II, 2023. Photographic print on archival paper, 15 × 24 in. (38.1 × 61 cm)

Rita Boulley, 2023. Photographic print on archival paper, 16 × 20 in. (40.6 × 50.8 cm)

Maggie Thompson (Fond du Lac Band of Lake Superior Chippewa; b. 1989)

I Get Mad Because I Love You, 2021–22. Beads, filament, jingles, overall: 48 × 72 × 1 in. (121.9 × 182.9 × 2.5 cm). Tia Collection

On Loving, 2022–23. Vinyl, beads, threads, zippers, overall: 10 × 126 in. (25.4 cm × 320 cm); each: 10 × 42 × 90 in. (25.4 × 106.7 × 228.6 cm). Tia Collection

Jonathan Thunder (Red Lake Nation; b. 1977)

Basil's Dream, 2024. Acrylic on canvas, 84 × 180 in. (213.4 × 457.2 cm)

Holly Trevan (Match-E-Be-Nash-She-Wish Band of Pottawatomi; b. 1976)

For Martha, 2024. Encaustic on Van Dyke brown print, 16 × 20 in. (40.6 × 50.8 cm)

Wayne Valliere (Lac du Flambeau Band of Lake Superior Chippewa; b. 1964)

Ojibwe Hunter's Birchbark Canoe. Birchbark, cedar wood, spruce root, pine pitch, 24 × 192 ×

36 in. (60.9 × 487.6 × 91.4 cm)

Moira Villiard (Fond du Lac Band of Lake Superior Chippewa; b. 1994)

The Waters of Tomorrow, 2019. Acrylics and water-soluble oil on canvas, unframed: 48 × 36 × 1 1/2 in. (121.9 × 91.4 × 3.8 cm)

Dawn Nichols Walden (Mackinac Band of Chippewa and Ottawa Indians; Ojibway; b. 1949)

Random Order XIII, 2006. Cedar bark, cedar roots, bear grasses, 23 3/4 × 14 1/2 in. (60.3 × 36.8 cm). Smithsonian American Art Museum, Gift of Robert and Sharon Buchanan

Arnold Shawanoo Walker (Little Traverse Bay Bands of Odawa Indians; Shawnee [Descent]; b. 1966)

Wolf Walking Alone, 2025. Birchbark, porcupine quill, overall (height × diameter): 4 3/4 × 3 in. (12 × 7.6 cm). Courtesy of Kelly Church

Yvonne M. Walker-Keshick (Little Traverse Bay Bands of Odawa Indians; b. 1946)

Maple Sugar M'kuks, 2025. Birchbark, porcupine quill:
1) 1 × 1 in. (2.5 × 2.5 cm);
2) 2 × 2 in. (5 × 5 cm);
3) 3 × 3 in. (7.6 × 7.6 cm);
4) 4 × 4 in. (10.1 × 10.1 cm);
5) 5 × 5 in. (12.7 × 12.7 cm)

Odeimin Gèsis Walker-Keshick (Little Traverse Bay Bands of Odawa Indians; b. 1982)

Turtle Island, 2024. White birch, porcupine quill, sweetgrass, cedar bark, 7 × 5 × 7 in. (17.7 × 12.7 × 17.7 cm)

Star WallowingBull (White Earth Band of the Minnesota Chippewa; Northern Arapaho; b. 1973)

Black Elk's Little Sand Man, 2002. Color pencil on paper, unframed: 36 × 50 in. (91.4 × 127 cm); framed: 42 1/2 × 56 in. (108 × 142.2 cm). Plains Art Museum, Museum Purchase

Twinkle, Twinkle Little Star Now I Know Who You Really Are, 2002. Color pencil on paper, 30 1/4 × 44 in. (30.2 × 111.7 cm). Collection of Bockley Gallery

Jillian Waterman (Saginaw Chippewa Indian Tribe; b. 1985)

In Case of Emergency Bury Me and Watch Me Grow, 2024. Upcycled fabric, Bear Island flint corn

Robin Waynee (Saginaw Chippewa Indian Tribe; b. 1971)

Pearl Cosmos Cuff, 2023. Sterling silver, 18K yellow gold, 13.3 mm Tahitian pearl, tsavorite garnet (.60 mm), VS1 diamond (1.48 ctw), 2 1/2 × 5 in. (6.2 × 12.7 cm)

Warclubs, 2023. 18K palladium white gold, faceted Tahitian pearl, VS1 diamond (.93 ctw), 2 × 3/4 × 1/4 in. (7.6 × 1.9 × .63 cm)

Jodi Webster (Ho-Chunk Nation; Prairie Band Potawatomi Nation; b. 1977)

Faculty of Sight II, 2019. Brass, copper, currency, enamel, powder coating, images printed on aluminum, unframed: 25 × 31 × 6 1/2 in. (63.5 × 78.7 × 16.5 cm)

Woodland Badass Champion Buckle, 2022. Sterling silver, overall: 2 1/2 × 3 × 7/10 in. (6.3 × 7.6 × 1.7 cm)

Jason Wesaw (Pokagon Band of Potawatomi; b. 1974)

Teaching Blanket, 2025. Dyed muslin, duck cloth, canvas, flannel, ornamented with found objects, 40 × 60 in. (101.6 × 152.4 cm)

Delina White (Leech Lake Band of Ojibwe; b. 1964)

Woodland Elegance, 2019. Top: embroidered silk, sequin, ribbon; skirt: embroidered silk, sequin, ribbon; shawl: embroidered taffeta, sequin, satin floral appliqué; underskirt: lace, 70 × 25 × 25 in. (177.8 × 63.5 × 63.5 cm)

Gerald White (Leech Lake Band of Ojibwe; b. 1957)

Biikwakadoo-bagaamaganan: Anishinaabeg, 2025. Wood, brass, 25 3/4 × 3 1/2 in. (64.4 × 8.9 cm); 25 × 3 in. (63.5 × 7.6 cm); 24 1/2 × 3 1/4 in. (62.2 × 8.3 cm); 23 × 3 1/4 in. (58.4 × 8.3 cm); 22 3/4 × 2 3/4 in. (57.8 × 7 cm); 22 × 3 in. (55.9 × 7.6 cm)

Animkeewa Aankwad White Eagle (Grand Traverse Band of Ottawa and Chippewa Indians; Kiowa; b. 1995)

Made from the Two – I Don't Know You, 2019. Giclée print, 30 × 30 in. (76.2 × 76.2 cm). Private collection

Sarah Wilkinson (Sault Ste. Marie Tribe of Chippewa; b. 1984)

Following the Path Within, 2024. Giclée print, unframed: 12 × 18 in. (30.4 × 45.7 cm); framed: 26 × 20 in. (66 × 50.8 cm)

Summer Yahbay (Saginaw Chippewa Indian Tribe; b. 1977)

Nmamiikwendis: I Am Proud of Myself, 2024. Rabbit fur, deer hide, Czech and India seed beads, 58 × 16 × 1 in. (174.3 × 40.6 × 2.5 cm)

Sam Zimmerman (Grand Portage Band of Lake Superior Chippewa [Direct Descendant]; b. 1978)

Makwa doodem ogichidaa / Bear Clan Warrior, 2024. Acrylic and ink on skateboard deck, unframed: 32 × 8 in. (81.3 × 20.3 cm); framed: 35 × 12 × 3 in. (88.9 × 30.5 × 7.6 cm)

List of Lenders

All works have been loaned by the artists or their estates unless otherwise noted.

We are grateful to the following institutions and individuals for the gracious loans provided:

Bockley Gallery

Kelly Church

Eiteljorg Museum of American Indians and Western Art

Megan Frawley

Harvard University Portrait Collection, 1872

Harbor Collective

Muskegon Museum of Art

Philbrook Museum of Art

Plains Art Museum

Smithsonian American Art Museum

Tia Collection

Karen and Jerry Walz

Private collections

Acknowledgments

This exhibition would never have come to fruition without the insights, patience, thoughts and kindness of so many people. I am grateful to all of them. Salvador Salort-Pons, PhD, the Mary Anne and Eugene A. Gargaro, Jr. Director, President, and CEO, has been instrumental in supporting the exhibition from its inception. He understood and echoed the desire that the first large exhibition of Native American art in over thirty years feature the Anishinaabe.

I am also immensely grateful to the team of Anishinaabe advisors: to Kelly Church and Jason Quigno for approaching the institution with the idea for this exhibition, and to them and the rest of the advisors, Monica Rickert-Bolter, Jonathan Thunder, and Jodi Webster, for their instrumental guidance. To all of the talented artists who submitted their artwork to the exhibition and worked with us on their labels, thank you for agreeing to show your work at the Detroit Institute of Arts (DIA).

My colleagues at the DIA were also crucial in making the exhibition come to life. Megan DiRienzo, the interpretative planner, kept her eyes on the end goal of providing the best experience for all visitors.

I am grateful to my administrative assistant, Rachel Higinbotham, for her hard work and scheduling assistance with the exhibition. I am ever so thankful to my research assistant

Caitlyn Webster. Her commitment to the checklist and to the artists and making sure the team remained in communication with them as she completed her other research tasks for the exhibition and Native American Collection is commendable.

The visions of the exhibition designer, Theodora Doulamis, and graphic designer, Eva Oldman (Little Traverse Bay Band of Odawa Indians; Northern Arapaho Tribe of the Wind River Reservation), were profound. The color schemes and designs allowed for the artworks to take center stage in a powerful and engaging way.

The internal team was equally helpful: Deputy Director, Art, Education, and Programs, Judith Dolkart, and Vice President, Exhibition and Collection Strategies, Jennifer Paoletti; the Exhibition team of Elena Berry and Paul Talpos; the Registrar team of Terry Segal, Amy Dunn, and Miranda Malec; and the Conservation team of Elizabeth Homberger, Ellen Hanspach-Bernal, James Storm, and Howard Sutcliffe. Thoughtful insights and suggestions came from Caitlin Grames and stellar assistance from Terry Birkett, James Johnson, and Tracey Morton and the rest of Collections Management. Maria Ketcham, thank you for all of the interlibrary loans and your patience with my returns. Many thanks to Nina Sapp and her dedicated Development team: Kasia Bielak-Hoops and Laticia Nelson for supporting the grant process, and Rosemarie Gleason, Edward Maki-Schramm, Jessica Trombley, Laura Orme, and Carly Britton for their help with fundraising and event planning. Aaron Bogart, PhD, editor, thank you for organizing and executing the production of the catalogue, and to the talented, energetic Neebinnaukzhik Southall (Chippewas of Rama First Nation) for their designs and suggestions. Thank you to the writers who spent time thoughtfully thinking and writing about Anishinaabe art and what it means to the art world as a whole: Matthew L. M. Fletcher, JD (Grand Traverse Band of Ottawa and Chippewa Indians), Kendra Greendeer, PhD (Ho-Chunk Nation; Red Cliff Band of Lake Superior Chippewa [Descendant]), Christopher T. Greene, PhD, and Shawnya Harris, PhD.

Thank you to all of the DIA team members for supporting this exhibition.

I am very grateful to all of the exhibition lenders, especially Cory Dingle, of the Norval Morrisseau Estate: your dedication to the artist, your friend, is evident in the way you protect and defend his artwork and memory. Also, thank you for your encouragement, kindness, and support. Laura Smith and your team at the Tia Collection, thank you for your patience and adeptness in accepting the multiple loan requests. Todd Bockley, your knowledge is vast, your

suggestions generous, and your support and representation of Great Lakes artists have been foundational for an exhibition such as this.

Thank you to the Ford Foundation for your generous support. Thank you to the Teiger Foundation for your support of this contemporary art exhibition. Thank you to the Luce Foundation for your continuous support of the Native American Art Collection at the DIA. Thank you to the Mellon Foundation for providing research support for the exhibition.

Finally, thank you to the individuals both inside and outside of the DIA for their support of this project. Eloise De Quintal, Lucia Cantero, Heath Fogg-Davis, Euphemia Sue Franklin (Sault Ste. Marie Tribe), Christina Gibbs, Alesha L. Hamilton, Monique Harding, Paulla Dove Jennings (Narragansett), Jessica Herczeg-Konecny, Katherine Kasdorf, Linda Knight, Paula Lee, Shaine Mathieu, Emma Notus, Dr. Theodore Young, Toni-Ellen Weeden Wright (Pequot descent), the Bronx Family, and the Griffith Family.

Denene De Quintal, PhD, Assistant Curator, Native American Art, Detroit Institute of Arts

Photo Credits

All images courtesy of the artist unless otherwise noted.

PP. 59, 60–61 © Frank Big Bear. Courtesy of the artist and Bockley Gallery

P. 74 © Jim Denomie Estate. Tia Collection. Photo: James Hart Photography

P. 75 © Jim Denomie Estate. Tia Collection. Courtesy of the Jim Denomie Estate and Bockley Gallery, Minneapolis

P. 76 © Muskegon Museum of Art

P. 90, Photo © President and Fellows of Harvard College

P. 93 © George Morrison Estate and Bockley Gallery. Photo: Adam Reich

PP. 94–95 © George Morrison Estate. Tia Collection. Courtesy of George Morrison Estate and Bockley Gallery

PP. 96, 98–99 © Estate of Norval Morrisseau

PP. 120–21 © Star WallowingBull. Courtesy of the artist and Bockley Gallery

This catalogue is published in conjunction with the exhibition
Contemporary Anishinaabe Art: A Continuation, September 28, 2025–April 5, 2026

The exhibition was organized by the Detroit Institute of Arts

Editor: Denene De Quintal, PhD
Editor, Exhibitions: Aaron Bogart, PhD
Project Management: Elena Berry
Designer: Neebinnaukzhik Southall (Chippewas of Rama First Nation)
Color Separations: Professional Graphics
Printing: Brilliant Graphics

ISBN: 978-0-300-28412-6

Library of Congress Control Number: 202594406

10 9 8 7 6 5 4 3 2 1

Published by:
Detroit Institute of Arts
5200 Woodward Avenue
Detroit, MI 48202
www.dia.org

Distributed by:
Yale University Press
302 Temple Street
PO Box 209040
New Haven, CT 06520
www.yalebooks.com/art

Authorized Representative in the EU:
Easy Access System Europe
Mustamäe tee 50, 10621 Tallinn, Estonia
gpsr.requests@easproject.com